CW00796478

Minding the Markets

Minding the Markets

An Emotional Finance View of Financial Instability

David Tuckett

© David Tuckett 2011

All rights reserved. No reproduction, copy or transmission of this publication may be made without written permission.

No portion of this publication may be reproduced, copied or transmitted save with written permission or in accordance with the provisions of the Copyright, Designs and Patents Act 1988, or under the terms of any licence permitting limited copying issued by the Copyright Licensing Agency, Saffron House, 6-10 Kirby Street, London EC1N 8TS.

Any person who does any unauthorized act in relation to this publication may be liable to criminal prosecution and civil claims for damages.

The author has asserted his right to be identified as the author of this work in accordance with the Copyright, Designs and Patents Act 1988.

First published 2011 by
PALGRAVE MACMILLAN

Palgrave Macmillan in the UK is an imprint of Macmillan Publishers Limited, registered in England, company number 785998, of Houndmills, Basingstoke, Hampshire RG21 6XS.

Palgrave Macmillan in the US is a division of St Martin's Press LLC, 175 Fifth Avenue, New York, NY 10010.

Palgrave Macmillan is the global academic imprint of the above companies and has companies and representatives throughout the world.

Palgrave® and Macmillan® are registered trademarks in the United States, the United Kingdom, Europe and other countries.

ISBN: 978–0–230–29985–6 hardback

This book is printed on paper suitable for recycling and made from fully managed and sustained forest sources. Logging, pulping and manufacturing processes are expected to conform to the environmental regulations of the country of origin.

A catalogue record for this book is available from the British Library.

A catalog record for this book is available from the Library of Congress.

10 9 8 7 6 5 4 3 2 1
20 19 18 17 16 15 14 13 12 11

Printed and bound in Great Britain by
CPI Antony Rowe, Chippenham and Eastbourne

For Francesca, Anna, Chiara and Miranda

Contents

Acknowledgements

The work on which this text is based has spanned the last ten years, beginning with an invitation from Peter Fonagy in 1997 to join the Psychoanalysis Unit at UCL and then lengthy conversations with Richard Taffler, now at the University of Warwick Business School. Both Peter and Richard have been enormously helpful throughout and I am indebted to them for frequent support and intellectual stimulation. It was Richard who provided the term 'emotional finance' and who has pioneered its use. Peter is a constant source of inspiration and example. I would also like to thank the Research Board of the International Psychoanalytic Association for a small but morale-boosting grant at the beginning of the work.

Mervyn King was kind enough to read my first efforts to understand asset price bubbles and has been enormously informative, supportive and encouraging throughout this work's development, despite his many other commitments. In 2003 he directed me to John Kay's work and so to a programme of updating and re-learning my very rusty economics. At this stage John Kay, Alan Budd and Gabriel de Palma were among the economists kind enough to help me critique and refine my thesis and to help me identify a series of problems I needed to address. In the UCL Economics department Mark Armstrong, Steffen Huck and Antonio Guarino were also generous enough to talk with me and offer advice and literature to read so that I was eventually able to feel confident enough to create a proposal to apply for and gain a 2006 Leverhulme Research Fellowship. This provided me with the necessary time and support to undertake the research interviewing that provided the data for this book. Susan Budd, John Goldthorpe, Alex Preda and Neil Smelser (all sociologists) have also been very generous and helpful in assisting me with the formulation of some key ideas and research theses from a sociological viewpoint. Rudi Vermote helped me to understand neuroscience and its relation to psychoanalysis. I am grateful to Adair Turner for inviting me to talk with him and a colleague at the FSA very early in 2009 about regulatory policy and to George Soros who was kind enough to spend a morning later in 2009 talking over his ideas and experience. Rob Johnson, the Executive Director of the Institute of New Economic Thinking (INET), provided me with a very interesting viewpoint on politics and economic policy in the US and made possible my attendance at INET's inaugural conference. This was an invaluable opportunity to meet and talk with people and to learn the current state of economics.

George Akerlof (who as well as being very encouraging also introduced me to Bewley's important work using interviews), Sheila Dow, Victoria Chick, Mervyn King, David Shanks (who put me in touch with relevant psychology literature), Dennis Snower, Richard Taffler and Liz Allison have all been kind enough to read and comment on various parts of the manuscript as it developed. They can in no way be blamed for any of its remaining blemishes.

In conducting the research itself I should like to acknowledge the generosity of all those I interviewed both in the main study and the pilot that preceded it. Everyone I spoke to was very conscientious, serious and thoughtful about the questions asked and gave generously of their time. They must remain anonymous. Donald Bryden, Arno Kitts, Geoff Lindy, Arnold Wood, Paul Woolley and especially Richard Taffler were crucial in providing the many contacts necessary to generate a sample. Nicola Harding in the Psychoanalysis Unit was then both creative and persevering in successfully making contacts and fixing appointments on three continents.

Arman Eshraghi, Robert Burton and Andrew Sanchez assisted with various analyses of the interview data, thus allowing me to test whether two pairs of eyes saw the same things. Ed Dew assisted me with information about recent changes in US financial regulation.

I am grateful to my agents, first the late Paul Marsh and then Steph Ebdon, for tireless efforts to promote these ideas and to find me the right publisher and so to Lisa von Fircks at Palgrave Macmillan for enthusiastically taking on the project. I also want to mention the extraordinarily creative help I have had from Richard Baggaley, who was kind enough to read several early drafts of the manuscript and to make all kinds of suggestions that led to its complete restructuring and rewriting as well as to its current title.

Finally, I would like to acknowledge all the help I have received from my family and especially my wife, Paola Mariotti. Fieldwork and book writing on top of an existing job are a considerable labour and would be impossible without a lot of support, tolerance and love.

Preface

The ruinous financial crisis of 2008 has provoked many words, but not enough change, in the way financial markets are organised, in the way we understand them in economics, and in the way they are regulated. Greed, corruption, trade imbalances, regulatory laxity, and panic, all frequently cited as causes, do not create behaviour on their own. At the heart of the crisis was a failure to understand and organise markets in a way that adequately controls the human behaviour which financial trading unleashes. What happened in 2008 and the period before required judgements made by many human beings subject to human psychology. It is these judgements in the institutional context in which they are made and how they combine to produce crisis that this book aims to understand.

I spent much of 2007, just before the crisis, conducting a series of detailed research interviews with senior financiers in Boston, Edinburgh, London, Paris, New York, and Singapore. It is what they told me about the context of their decision-making and the judgements they had to make which I present in this book. Their responses suggest that traditional economic approaches, including the recent development of behavioural economics, do not capture the essence of what happens in financial markets and why they produce crises.

Taking the uncertainty my respondents described as the major experience in financial markets, I offer an alternative way of understanding the markets, which prioritises the role of narrative and emotion and the way they influence judgement in social context. Based on my observations, I find that financial markets necessarily create dangerously exciting stories, problematic mental states, and strange group processes in which realistic thinking is fundamentally disturbed. From this position I will argue that, as currently organised, financial markets are inherently unstable. I will also suggest we can make them safer only if we understand how and why financial assets unleash powerful emotions and stimulate narrative beliefs which disturb human judgement.

Unfortunately, despite the catastrophic nature of the crisis and its ongoing effects currently felt in nervous sovereign bond markets and massive government cutbacks, there are strong signs of a tendency not to learn from what has happened and to return to business and even understanding as usual as quickly as possible. To put an end to understanding as usual, and to suggest ways forward, is the main aim of this book. In the final chapter I will suggest that those who work in key positions in the financial network and those who regulate financial markets need to try to work together to conduct a nonpunitive enquiry into what happened leading up to 2008 along the lines of what was done in South Africa post-apartheid. To make financial markets and the behaviour within them safe there is a need to learn from experience and to see that a very different kind of regulation and self-regulation than what we have had is necessary.

Core concepts

There has been a growing recognition in economics as in many other sciences that emotion matters much more than has previously been thought. But the way it has been included in economic thinking so far does not do justice to the phenomenon. The theoretical innovation offered in this book is to set out the role of varying mental states and their impact on thinking processes to show how they can systematically modify preferences, expected outcomes, and decision-making in a dynamic and path-dependent but nonlinear way.

The core concepts I have developed to use in this book cannot be defined and expressed in the precise and elegant way used in mathematics. They are complex and need to be lived with and internalised. They will be elaborated (particularly in Chapter 3 pp62–65 and 65–70) so that their full meaning is much clearer by the end of the book. But meanwhile here are some simplified working definitions:

Uncertainty: *Used only in the sense described by Knight (1921) and Keynes (1936), recognising that ultimately we cannot know what will happen in the future.*

Unconscious Phantasies: *The stories (saturated with emotion) we tell ourselves in our minds about what we are doing with other people (and "objects") and what they are doing with us, of which we have only partial awareness.*

Object Relationship: *The affective relationships of attachment and attraction we establish in our minds with "objects" – that is, people, ideas, or things, of which we are only partially aware.*

Phantastic Object: *Subjectively very attractive "objects" (people, ideas, or things) which we find highly exciting and idealise, imagining (feeling rather than thinking) they can satisfy our deepest desires, the meaning of which we are only partially aware.*

Ambivalent Object Relationship: *A relationship in our minds with an object to which we are quite strongly attracted by opposed feelings, typically of love and hate, of which we are only partially aware.*

Divided State: *An alternating incoherent state of mind marked by the possession of incompatible but strongly held beliefs and ideas; this inevitably influences our perception of reality so that at any one time a significant part of our relation to an object is not properly known (felt) by us. The aspects which are known and unknown can reverse but the momentarily unknown aspect is actively avoided and systematically ignored by our consciousness.*

Integrated State: *A state of mind marked by a sense of coherence, which influences our perception of reality, so that we are more or less aware of our opposed ambivalent and uncertain thought and felt relations to objects.*

Groupfeel: *A state of affairs where a group of people (which can be a virtual group) orient their thoughts and actions to each other based on a powerful and not fully conscious wish not to be different and to feel the same as the rest of the group.*

I propose that when investors buy, sell, or hold all classes of financial assets they are understood as establishing ongoing and unconscious *ambivalent object relations*. In their simplest form, object relations are stories told in the mind. They are representations of the imagined emotional relationship between subject and object which produce good and bad feelings – for example, I love him, he likes me, I hate her, they make me anxious. Most object relations are somewhat ambivalent because emotional relationships are often conflicted – I love *and* hate him, I want to be part of that group and away from it, and so forth. Sometimes the conflicts are so powerful they are too unpleasant to know. In the state of mind that I will elaborate later and which I call *divided,* conflicting representations of relationships to an object are present in the mind but not consciously experienced and so not available for thinking – the relationships are not all conscious. One moment the relationship may be consciously felt as only loving and the next only hating, although it is actually both. The theoretical potential of a *divided state* is that it highlights the potential for what economists might consider as preference reversals. In a divided state, a relationship may unpredictably move from all loving to all hating or all hating to all loving. This is observed frequently in personal and work relations and in the relations professional investors have with assets in financial markets. A *divided state* contrasts with an *integrated state* in which conflicts are more or less known along with the uncomfortable feelings they create and so can be thought about. *Integrated* states are therefore not only more realistic and stable but also more emotionally challenging. *Divided* states are adopted partly because emotional conflicts can be intolerably frightening or frustrating.

As far as I am aware the potential importance of *ambivalence* and its effect on economic life was first noted by Neil Smelser in his presidential address to the American Sociological Association (Smelser 1998). He took the idea from Freud just as the general idea of object relationships derives from Freud's earliest psychoanalytic formulations (Freud 1900). Although Freud's thinking has been pronounced dead by many who have never read him, there is now substantial cross-disciplinary research, particularly in the field of attachment (Mikulincer and Shaver 2007), which backs his insight that relationships to people and things are represented in the mind consciously and unconsciously on an ongoing basis, are invested with desires and feelings, and have a major impact on attention and thinking. Evidence will be discussed in Chapter 3 (pp59–62) that an almost continuous interchange is observable between those parts of the brain concerned with primitive affects (like trust, anger, and sexual attraction) and those with "higher" cognitive functions. This interaction forms the substrate for all thinking and decision-making. There is also little observable difference between the observable brain events which accompany real and imaginary scenarios (Damasio 2004).

The core concepts I have mentioned above have their origin in a time when I became interested once more in economics and in what happens to human judgement in financial markets after a very surprising and in fact disturbing afternoon in March 1999, around the height of the dotcom bubble.

I was then editor of the *International Journal of Psychoanalysis* and an honorary director of a small US electronic publishing company. As a charitable scholarly venture we had recently archived many of the key works in psychoanalysis and distributed them modestly successfully to colleagues worldwide on a CD. I was, therefore, very surprised to find myself invited to sit down that afternoon with two rather excited people who wanted to pay several million dollars to purchase the business from the U.K. and U.S. charitable institutes who had financed it and also to offer my colleagues and me ongoing and significant sums as advisers. Their idea was to help to develop the company and then offer its shares to the public as what they thought could be a very successful "dotcom". One of the two men was a very experienced and successful venture capitalist working for one of the most prestigious London investment banks. Although he and his colleague knew very little about psychoanalysis or electronic publishing they thought our business model, expertise, and search technology could transplant to other disciplines. In fact over several weeks and some fascinating and exciting meetings, we eventually worked out that our venture did not need to take on any debt and could fund its development from its own revenue streams. We, therefore, said no – to the significant sums and to the excitement. The company survives and prospers today as a U.S. not-for-profit. The incident left me curious.

As well as being a psychoanalyst, I had undergraduate and graduate training in economics and sociology. The question for me was how such very able and experienced people could have been so excitedly convinced they "had" to own a dotcom, and then expected to make a great deal of money by floating it off – bearing in mind they knew little about psychoanalysis, publishing, or the new Internet method of product delivery. As the bubble shortly collapsed and most of these new enterprises became worthless I came to realise something it seems had hitherto been known, but, in fact, ignored. Whatever else goes on in an asset price boom and bust, it looks primarily like an emotional sequence. From a clinical psychoanalytic viewpoint it is a well-known and path-dependent emotional sequence of *divided* states – in which unrealistic manic excitement takes over thinking, caution is split off, and there is huge and even violent resistance to consciousness of many signs of reality. Because reality is unconsciously divided off from experience, the state can persist for a long time but will inevitably collapse into panic and paranoia before blame becomes dominant. At this final stage learning is unlikely unless the whole experience can be integrated and loss worked through.

Looked at more closely through the lens of the detailed descriptions available (Mackay 1848; Galbraith 1993; Kindleberger 2000; Shiller 2000), it seemed to me that asset price bubbles occur because a story gets told about an innovative object of apparent desire (such as a dotcom share, a tulip bulb, or a complex financial derivative) which becomes capable of generating excitement in a situation where outcomes are inherently uncertain. The story ushers in *divided* state–object relationships to the underlying reality and thinking processes about that reality become dominated by what I will call *groupfeel*[1].

In discussion with Richard Taffler, I coined the term *phantastic object* to cover the situation (Tuckett and Taffler 2003, 2008). The term conjoins "phantasy" as in unconscious phantasy and "object" as in representation and is elaborated in a later chapter. The phantasy stimulated is about much more than just a story of getting rich. Rather it is a story about participation in an imagined object relationship in which the possessor of the desired object plays with the omnipotent phantasy of having permanent and exclusive access to it and all good things. Tom Wolfe describes the story in *Bonfire of the Vanities* and Michael Lewis in *Liar's Poker*. Aladdin had a lamp and the Emperor his new clothes. Taffler and I went on to suggest that this concept could have wide applications and form the basis of what Taffler christened Emotional Finance (Taffler and Tuckett 2007).

After using my interview material to describe the way my respondents set about the task of buying, selling, and holding assets in the everyday situation of uncertainty they experienced, I will suggest financial markets always have the potential to embrace stories about *phantastic objects* and to be overtaken by *divided states* and *groupfeel*. In the years leading to the 2008 crash it was financial derivatives which became experienced as *phantastic objects,* and, after leading to *divided* emotional states and *groupfeel,* produced a catastrophe.

The central point, it seemed to me when I looked at asset price bubbles, was that in every case once the "story" that there is a *phantastic object* gets about and gains some acceptance, there is *groupfeel*. Uncertainty then disappears, thinking is disturbed, and the intense excitement being generated compromises judgement. The lack of uncertainty begs the question where it has gone, which was why the concept of a *divided* mental state seemed useful. It captures the emotional relationship to reality that has become dominant and helps to explain how an infected group feel free from doubt – how those in it become able to conduct a compelling love affair with the idea that the phantastic object has changed the reality of the world. Understanding this as *groupfeel* within a *divided* emotional state also helped to explain why normal caution about risk-taking is always so confidently "split off" (not thought) and alternative views so dismissively lampooned as out of date. It also made sense of the ease with which behavioural rules (such as prudential ones about bank capital requirements or bond-rating assessments) were always altered without too much fussy thinking so that what will later be recognised as excessive risk-taking and excitability become normal. It also seemed to explain why the significant sceptics who doubt or criticise what is happening gain no traction and are invariably dismissed, ignored, greeted with derision, or even threatened. Warren Buffet, for example, warned that financial derivatives are "financial weapons of mass destruction" (Buffett 2003 p14).

Narratives and mental states

Research can be topic oriented or discipline oriented (Gigerenzer 2008 pv). The aim of my research is topic oriented: to understand how and why financial markets become unstable using whatever we know. By contrast and particularly for the past 60 years, economics has tended to be a normative discipline pursuing a specific analytical paradigm using a relatively narrow range of methods. To a considerable extent these norms have been powerfully enforced, to the extent that when major new insights have been incorporated – such as Simon's ideas about the limits to rationality or more recent ideas about the role of cognitive and emotional processes – this has happened within very strict limits (Gigerenzer 2008 p85 et seq). Behavioural economists have actually gone so far as to emphasise rather apologetically that their aim is to improve the field of economics "on its own terms" modifying "one or two assumptions" that are "not central" (Camerer, Loewenstein et al. 2004 p4). This has gained them only some acceptance.

Change for its own sake has little point. But if economics is to reach an adequate understanding of financial instability and its important consequences for human welfare, my findings suggest a much more significant engagement with other social disciplines is required as well as a significant shift both in methods and analytical frameworks (see also Akerlof and Shiller 2009; Akerlof and Kranton 2010).

The core concepts I have just introduced come from standardised interviews in the field with seasoned professionals, not laboratory experiments with psychology or economics students and not questionnaires administered to samples from whole populations. In Chapter 9, I will explore how my concepts have implications for the core theory of motivation used in standard economics in which individuals "make choices so as to maximise a utility function, using the information available, and processing this information appropriately" (della Vigna 2009 p315). At the same time I will stress that unless altered beyond recognition I think they cannot be captured by introducing one or two modifications into the conventional utility function.

The main reason for insisting on difference is because, when I interviewed them, the situation I found my respondents describing was fundamentally uncertain. Typically modern economists carefully define what I have in mind as Knightian uncertainty (Knight 1921), and distinguish it from risk. They then spend a lot of time discussing risk (known unknowns) and seem to ignore uncertainty. But Knightian uncertainty (unknown unknowns) makes all the difference. In that context, for instance, logico-deductive-based thinking and prediction of the kind enshrined in probability theories (and then modelled by economists as rational decision-making and optimisation under constraints) may be worth using but may also be of limited value and perhaps not even rational at all. Trying to work out what to do when the relationship of past and present to future is uncertain is not the same as dice-throwing or playing roulette.

My respondents were not trying to predict runs of dice or wheels and balls. These are the wrong analogies for what almost anyone interviewed in a financial market is trying to do. Rather, what my financiers described to me was trying to decide what they thought were the various uncertain futures that might unfold for the future price of various financial assets. To do this they looked at (made guesses about) what they thought would happen and its likelihood, what others thought, what others were doing, and what everyone would do in future. They used every method they could to think of to determine what to buy, sell, or hold and they also thought about the responses in the social-institutional situation in which they found themselves – what others would think if they did this and that happened, or, if not, what would be the particular outcomes and what would everyone feel about them?

Interviews quickly revealed the decision context just mentioned and so a significant consequence of a suppressed premise in economic thinking – namely the practice of treating all kinds of markets for all kinds of objects as essentially the same. As I mention in Chapter 2 (p27), even in the first pilot interview Richard Taffler and I did of a senior asset manager in 2006, I was forced to realise very rapidly that financial assets were not like other goods and services and to treat them as such was likely to be in error.

In the first chapter (p19), I will describe the three crucial and inherent characteristics of financial assets I found influencing the judgements of those I interviewed. First, they were volatile, meaning that they could easily create excitement at quick reward or anxiety about rapid loss. Second, they were abstract, meaning that they are not concrete items that can be consumed but are symbols that have no use in and for themselves, so that their value today is entirely dependent on their possible future value and that value is fundamentally uncertain and dependent on the reflexive (Soros

1987) expectations of traders. Third, that when trading them rigorous evaluation of which aspects of performance are skill and which are luck is not really possible. These three facts and the uncertainties they introduce meant that it was far from rational to value financial assets (and financial performance) only by calculating risk and probabilistic returns in the way economics and finance textbooks suggest. Rather, to make decisions in the context they inhabited, my respondents had to organise the ambiguous and incomplete information they had into imagined stories with which, if they believed them and were excited enough by them, they then entered into an actual relationship which had to last through time.

Understanding the function of narrative in human minds and how it works in everyday life will be reviewed from the viewpoint of psychology, psychoanalysis, and cognitive neuroscience in Chapter 3. Its importance has begun to interest economists (Akerlof and Shiller 2009). Narrative is one of the important devices humans use to give meaning to life's activities, to sense truth, and to create the commitment to act. Although its procedural logic is different from that in logico-deductive reasoning, it is not necessarily inferior to it – particularly in contexts where data is incomplete and outcomes are uncertain (Bruner 1991).

The fact that their value can go up and down a lot means that financial assets instantly provoke the most powerful human desires and feelings – excitement and greed around possible gains, and doubt, envy, persecuted anxiety, and depression about potential loss. Such feelings are not just dispositions in a utility function. They influence managers' daily work in an ongoing dynamic way and also affect the responses to them of their clients and superiors. In particular, holding an asset takes place through time and creates experience which can disrupt or confirm a story. News, therefore, creates emotion and so particularly do price changes. Price in a financial market functions as a signal. As new information which might threaten the future of the "story" emerges, the holder of a financial asset has to be able to tolerate his worries as he watches his cherished investment fall in price and wonder why. She/he knows there may really be good reason to rethink and sell but does not know for sure. This characteristic of financial assets means that in effect the original decision to buy has to be made again and again and again for as long as one holds the stock – a point, missed by current economic theory, which, as discussed in Chapter 1 (p20), is strangely static in its treatment of time.

Such facts about financial assets are the reality context. They place severe limits on even the most ingenious actor's capacity to make decisions. They make it unlikely that all reasonable agents will draw the same conclusions even if they have the same data. Because my financial actors were not able to see the future with certainty, their thinking about the value of securities was saturated with the experience of time, the memory of past experience, experiences of excitement and anxiety and of group life, as well as the stories they told themselves about it all. From this perspective, rather than describe financial markets as trading in probabilistically derived estimates of fundamental values, as in the standard text books, I will suggest they are best viewed as markets in competing and shifting emotional stories about what those fundamentals might be – but with one version or another of the story and its emotional consequences getting the upper hand at any particular time and for some of the time.

The Organisation of this book

Chapter 1 is devoted to a brief review of what we know about what happens in financial crises (including the last one) and how economists explain it as well as to an elaboration of the special characteristics of financial assets. The next chapter introduces my study method by describing what four of the asset managers told me and shows how, by using interviews, my main hypotheses about uncertainty, *ambivalent object relations*, telling stories, *groupfeel,* and mental states emerged from the data. In Chapter 3 I look at what modern cognitive, biological, and social science has established about narrative, groups, and emotional mental states. The next five chapters describe the main findings and elaborate on the concepts discussed above. Chapter 9 then sets out the core elements of emotional finance as a new theoretical approach to the economics of financial markets, showing how and why normal markets are at risk to turn into financial crises at any time. Finally, Chapter 10 looks at what we can do to make markets safer.

1
The Special Characteristics of Financial Assets

The catastrophic economic and social events unleashed by the financial crisis of 2008 appeared to many people to make clear what theories about financial markets had come to ignore. Emotions really matter. As central bankers have known for a very long time, financial markets depend on credit and this in turn depends on trust and confidence (Bagehot 1873; Pixley 2004; King 2010). When they disappeared, as they did in October 2008, the fear that obligations would not be met became too great an obstacle for agents to wait for each other to pay and trading stopped. The system froze dramatically and economic activity halted.

Doubt, trust, and confidence are subjective mental states which intertwine with the stories we tell ourselves about what is going on. Economic life involves human relationships of exchange of longer or shorter duration. Such relationships are accompanied by the stories we tell ourselves about what is happening to them and the mental states that are stimulated. At their simplest, human relationships of exchange involve a story being told to create a belief that continued attachment to the relationship will be excitingly rewarding or a source of danger and disadvantage. The word 'credit' is actually based on the Latin verb 'to believe'.

In a Chapter 3. I will be reviewing how modern cognitive neuroscientists and psychologists have built up knowledge about the way emotions and decision-making are linked. A core of the somatic marker theory from neuro-biology is that decision-makers encode the consequences of alternative choices affectively (Reimann and Bechara 2010) and it is now commonplace to consider that emotions ('gut' feelings, Gigerenzer 2007) are essential and valuable human capacities which make effective judgement and commitment to action possible. From this viewpoint it might seem obvious to a complete outsider that emotions would play a major part in theories about financial markets. But they do not. I will discuss below how and why standard economics and finance theories ignores them and how even the new field of behavioural economics, which makes use of what we know from laboratory experiments in cognitive psychology, limits their role greatly. Nearly all economic approaches before 2008 focused on how well markets worked. They also took little account of the frequently observed fact that financial markets are full of dynamically varying moods and emotions (like exuberance and panic).

The financial agents of economic theory are modelled to show how a market might work. They have a 'utility function' which determines their preferences when making any decision and can be rational or irrational. If they are rational they are constrained as to how they make their choices. They must select preferences consistently, always maximise their returns, and have calculating abilities based on the correct probabilistic application of the likelihood their decision will prove fruitful so that they always know the best thing to do. If they do not then they are irrational and in error and will not survive long and so do not matter. Rational financial agents, therefore, are not the real people of everyday experience: people who dream about what they want to achieve and think as hard as they can, but are uncertain between several best courses they can imagine, or people who manifestly and frequently change their minds and their expectations of reward or loss. Neither are they people who tell stories to make sense of an uncertain world about which they have incomplete and ambiguous information. Rather, they are the more or less passive recipients of unambiguous information.

The manifest consequence of focusing on how markets might work and discounting how they might not has been that economic theories have had very little inclination to say much about financial crises and very little useful to suggest about preventing them. Before 2008, insofar as explanations were offered at all, they were that financial crises are either an error or a mirage. In this view the failure of real financial markets is caused by the failure of regulators and politicians to make them work like the markets economists model (Dow 2010), or, if not, they are the result of unavoidable external events (shocks) which introduce inevitable uncertainty into calculation and to which the market actually adapts as well as can be expected (Brunnermeier 2001; Pástor, Veronesi et al. 2004).

To support my argument about accepted theories and then to open up an alternative way of thinking in which belief and emotion are placed at the heart of the matter, the remainder of this chapter will overview the main lines of current economic theory as it applies to financial markets. I will go on to explore explanations being offered for the 2008 banking crisis and then place them in the context of earlier asset price bubbles. I will suggest that understanding the role of subjective mental states in thinking in social groups is a missing element in current theories which we can identify as potentially valuable for understanding the causes of financial crises and doing something about them. For example, by looking at some specific characteristics of financial assets (as compared to other goods and services) I will show we can quite quickly see that it is likely that any theory of trading in financial markets which leaves out uncertainty, memory, the subjective experience of time, the subjective experience of excitement and anxiety, and the subjective experience of group life, will be unlikely to explain how people trade or why this leads to crises. Some details of the interview study I conducted to explore such experience and its methodology will follow in the next chapter. In later chapters I will then try to build up an argument about the normal functioning of the everyday financial markets and eventually reach conclusions as to how and why financial crises (especially the crisis of 2008) actually happen before setting out the requirements for a substantially new framework for understanding financial markets set within contemporary social, psychological, and biological understanding of the human decision-making processes.

Standard economic theories

For most purposes standard economic theories start with the fact that over 50 years ago Arrow and Debreu (1954) demonstrated that a competitive market economy with what is called a fully complete set of markets can, if certain further assumptions are made about them, have a uniquely efficient outcome. In macroeconomics economists like Robert Lucas (1972) went on formally to demonstrate that if human beings are not only rational in their preferences and choices but also in their expectations, then the macroeconomy will have a similar strong tendency towards a best-state equilibrium, with sustained involuntary unemployment a 'non-problem'.

These works set out a formal mathematical basis for the operation of Adam Smith's 'Invisible Hand' but to do so relied on assumptions which 'only need to be stated to be seen as very dodgy' (Solow 2010). In other words, no taxes, no elements of monopoly, a complete range of markets for present and future goods and services, all buyers and sellers having the same information, and a lot of them able to process it and act on it 'rationally'. Having the same information means understanding all information the same. Rationally means always maximising utility and optimising profits and being able to do that so that faced with the same information a second time they make the same decision. This 'economic man', in other words, lives in a static, well-ordered world 'that presents a fixed repertory of goods, processes and actions' where all decision-makers 'have accurate knowledge' and 'each decision maker assumes that all the others have the same knowledge and beliefs based on it' (Simon 1997 pp121–6). Given such assumptions there is never more than one optimal decision outcome, both for individuals and for the market as a whole. Although individuals are free to innovate and decide what they like, there is always a behavioural path which if not taken will not lead to survival. Divergence is terminal. In this way, so long as the required conditions obtain in all imaginable markets, any current organisation of markets and what happens in them results in the best of all possible worlds.

In finance theory this approach translates into a theory of asset pricing comprising modern portfolio theory, the capital asset pricing model, and the efficient market hypothesis (EMH) (Fama 1970; Fama and Miller 1972). EMH is the standard neoclassical theory of economics applied to financial markets. It is a theory of 'market efficiency' with a very narrow technical meaning. Markets are efficient because they assimilate new information bearing on the risk and reward from holding assets in such a way that prices always reflect the true cost of capital. Two highly significant assumptions are made here. The first assumption is that before any new information arises all existing information about the future risks and rewards from holding an asset is 'in the price'. As no one has any better information than anyone else, prices should then follow a random walk. In other words, each change in price is caused by a new 'independent' event with no relation (path dependence) to the last. This means that price can play no role as a signal of value and the next move could go in any direction at any time. The second assumption is that expected price changes are contained within the bell curve of a normal distribution. Financial economists recognise that we cannot know what will happen tomorrow (uncertainty). But they take the view that because no one can guess better than anyone else what will happen the only rational thing to do is treat future events as random and apply standard probability theory. This decision allows them to model what might otherwise be entirely uncertain outcomes as predictably contained within a known distribution. The model suggests financial intermediaries have no role except in creating a diversified portfolio implying grounds for a highly sceptical view of many classes of money-making experts (Kay 2003), such as those I interviewed. The evidence is that, on average, investment managers do not outperform a random choice of stocks and past performance of such managers is a poor guide to their future success (Kay 2003; Rhodes 2000). But this finding invites a sceptical view of the theory: given the huge number of people employed to provide and analyse information and to manage money in the financial markets, why are there so many financial intermediaries and why are they able to be paid so highly?

Modifying the information assumptions of standard theory

Standard economic approaches are sometimes misconstrued through oversimplification. Although such economic theories start from the parsimonious and apparently oversimplified paradigm just outlined, in fact much of the most admired work completed in the last half century has been devoted quite explicitly to using this method of analysis to specify why the information assumptions in the standard models mean that there are many conditions under which markets don't work in the idealised EMH way. The cofounder of the Arrow-Debreu thesis, Kenneth Arrow himself, spent much of his career exploring situations where one partner in an economic exchange might know less than another and the implications of such a condition. In various ways he showed how such information asymmetries made his illustration of a Pareto efficient equilibrium inapplicable in the real world where this would often be true, as in the world of insurance (for example, Arrow 1963). His work gave rise to what came to be known as informational economics. It examines what happens to the usual results if participants to an economic transaction have different information.

George Akerlof (1970) gave economics one of the most admired stories in the information economics tradition. It deals with what he called 'quality uncertainty' and the implications for EMH if one party to a transaction has more knowledge than another – a situation fundamental to the trading of financial assets. Akerlof supposed that in the secondhand car market well-informed sellers face ignorant buyers and that there were two kinds of car – reliable cars and lemons. The seller knows which he thinks he has but it is difficult for the buyer to tell. His formal analysis showed how the price of used cars will be discounted to reflect the incidence of lemons in the population. It will be an average of the values of good cars and lemons. But that average is a good price for the owner of a lemon, but a disappointing price for the seller of a reliable car. So owners of lemons will want to sell and owners of reliable cars will not. As buyers discover this, that knowledge will pull down the price of secondhand cars. And things will get worse. The lower the average price, the more reluctant the owners of more reliable cars will be to sell and the more suspicious buyers will get, driving things down further. The end result will be that secondhand cars will be of poor quality and many secondhand cars will be bad buys even at low prices.

Akerlof's paper is a paradigm example of what is possible through formal economic analysis. Its conclusions went well beyond secondhand cars to any situation where there are differences in information between buyer and seller even to contexts relevant to the trading of financial assets; that is, to situations 'in which the choice context of "trust" was important' (Akerlof 1970 p500). Trust mattered because 'the difficulty of distinguishing good quality from bad is inherent in the business world'. It may explain 'many economic institutions' and be 'one of the more important aspects of uncertainty'.

The framework for property relations described by the Latin term 'caveat emptor' (buyer beware!) is in widespread use in discussion of financial assets. If financial markets are like those for secondhand cars (and with rational actors), this framework could mean there will be no market at all. Since we have markets, the conclusion highlights how building trust must be a crucial element in the way financial markets work and demonstrates how parsimonious abstract modelling can very efficiently and rigorously get to the heart of a matter. Buyers can only be persuaded to trust sellers and so come into the market if the underlying situation of information asymmetry is somehow modified. One way is for sellers to try to frame the information context in which decisions are made to make the buyer more confident in the seller – for example, by advertising 'one owner' or 'lady driver', by offering to show service records or a report from an independent agency, or by taking explicit measures to share the risk of things going wrong in future, such as a guarantee from a reputable source. Some of these devices are discussed in Akerlof's original paper. They all act on the buyer's information and might give grounds for a rational person to engage in an exchange they otherwise would not. It is interesting to me that formally Akerlof is restricting his analysis to rational actors and information. But I have always found a strong hint in the paper that what is at stake is not just information but confidence which is an emotional state. More information and various kinds of guarantees might be said to provide reasons to trust sellers. If so, already in 1970 Akerlof was anticipating his much more recent interest in how social and psychological factors might function alongside reason and calculation. However, in general the other classic analyses in information economics, which similarly showed how markets could settle far from an efficient equilibrium, and that equilibria can be multiple and fragile (for example, Mirrlees, 1997; Stiglitz, 1974; Grossman and Stiglitz, 1980), all stay within a rational decision-making framework.

Information economics is much admired and most economic textbooks and the standard work on financial markets have included many examples of information failure. They can be added to other problems identified when there are limits to perfect competition (Robinson 1948) or incomplete markets due to 'spillover' situations where the side effects of an activity, for instance a factory polluting a local environment, are not paid for by the polluter (Bator 1958). Therefore, 'as every modern economist knows' (Allen and Gale 2001) ordinary standard economic theory fails to take into account that the 'real' world is more complex than the world of neoclassical economics. The problems identified include: the incentive problems that arise between employers and employees, managers and shareholders, financial institutions and their customers; the difficulties that arise when information is asymmetrically distributed; the transaction costs and moral hazard that prevent the existence of more than a small fraction of the number of markets envisaged in the general equilibrium model; and the lack of perfect competition that results from long-term financial relationships or the existence of powerful institutions. There are also the problems that come from anticipating what competitive others will do, which may sometimes lead to everyone taking a less than optimal solution, as in the Prisoner's Dilemma game, where, under rational behavioural assumptions, because two prisoners cannot communicate they will choose to betray each other rather than stay silent and escape punishment (Dresher, Shapley et al. 1964).

The list of established reasons for thinking markets will not be efficient is a long one. And many of the factors from information economics, such as agency and incentive issues as well as quality uncertainty are particularly applicable to financial markets. One response to it all has, nonetheless, been to develop arguments about how things *could* still work out and produce the desired EMH equilibrium. Agency problems, for example, can be overcome if incentive problems are dealt with. Or spillover effects can be mitigated by creating markets in futures, as with carbon emission trading. However, what is both noticeable and curious is that these new theories developed over the last 30 years, which suggest regulatory engineering is required to make markets work properly, have coincided with an apparently opposite development in the main financial centres. There we have witnessed a headlong rush to deregulation of financial markets. While information-modified theories have ruled academic economics, therefore, unmodified EMH theories seem to have ruled finance and financial policy.

The crisis of 2008 and two questions not answered

The crisis of 2008 has already received considerable attention. There are narrative accounts detailing what happened in some investment banks (Tett 2009; Lewis 2010) and academic treatments concerning the developments in US housing markets (for example, Bar-Gill 2008; Gorton 2008; Shiller 2009). But to evaluate any claim to explain the crisis we first have to decide what are the main elements to be explained.

What immediately stands out is that the seriousness of the crisis was the result of faulty risk-taking in banks and the shadow (not regulated) banking system. But it was more than that. Bondholders had been eager to participate in the new products banks had created because they believed them to offer higher returns for ordinary rates of risk. Equity holders were more than delighted to invest heavily in the financial sector engaging in this activity. For several years it had appeared to outperform. In short there was widespread but ultimately misinformed agreement that innovative financial derivatives had increased returns and both spread and lowered risk – a belief that allowed banks to go on and on increasing the amount of debt they issued. The major element in the crisis, therefore, was an 'inappropriate' pricing of risk. The price mechanism in competitive financial markets was not working as standard theories had generally presumed it to do (Dow 2010).

Eventually banks and financial intermediaries realised that their risk positions were not what they thought and then there was a liquidity crisis based on the fear of default. Banks became totally unwilling to trust each other and lend to each other even overnight. Any kind of banking loan or stock then collapsed in value and credit markets also seized up. Uncertainty had made trust impossible and economic relations of exchange infinitely anxiety provoking. As a result, in the second half of 2007, for most of 2008, and even into 2009, the main financial institutions were loath to risk lending to each other or anyone else at *any* price. This failure of markets to function and the fall in bank shares caused a collapse in asset values, a loss of liquidity on an unparalleled scale, and the failure of several leading financial institutions. These events in the financial market then had huge effects on world trade and the real economy and these in turn created further collapses as investors anticipated reduced asset values due to recession. The loans governments then had to make to get the banking system going again threatened sovereign debt and precipitated further crises and expenditure cuts.

About the immediate cause of these troubles there is no doubt. Loan default in US housing markets became much more common than expected and then escalated to drive prices down and defaults up. Property prices in the United States had risen to unstable levels in an escalating Ponzi process which for a long time not many people thought could end. In fact, property booms are regular and repetitive (Shiller 2009) and this type of situation had been predicted (Minsky 1982). The crucial question is how and why mortgage debt and all kinds of derivative bets based on it became so important to the heart of the global financial market that such a predictable and repetitive event as a fall in property prices should threaten to bring down much of the banking industry.

One set of explanations for what happened can be constructed from the economic theories we have just been discussing. Pricing in credit markets eventually failed because they did not live up to the standards of the perfect markets of EMH. They failed because they were too 'imperfect'. The main argument here is along the lines that the relative opaqueness associated with innovative over-the-counter credit trades created by new financial products and the consequent lack of publicly available information about risk created such intense quality uncertainty that it eventually became difficult for market agents to form a rational view of their value. When value was questioned the market then stopped. According to this set of ideas, then, the seizure was caused by failures to regulate and certify new products, perhaps accentuated by the incentive systems governing the relationships between innovators and rating agencies. When it became clear that the agencies were wrong, trust evaporated.

A second set of explanations that can be constructed might focus on how the behaviour of financial intermediaries is dependent on the specification of their contractual relations. Stiglitz (2010) provides an incisive analytical account of just this showing how the propositions he and others developed in information economics proved correct. Misaligned incentives (such as financial firms being organised as quoted companies rather than partnerships and the development of the bonus culture) enabled some agents to increase their potential rewards from risk-taking without facing the potential losses. They then took too many risks. If the contracts between agents had been properly regulated, written and transparent enough to be checked, then perhaps each agent within the market would have been correctly motivated (incentivised) and so forced to take risk appropriately. But Simon (1997 p21) had already questioned the faith many economists had put in the potential for contract specification based on financial incentives actually to determine human behaviour without unintended consequences. Allen and Gorton (1993) had also constructed a model in which agency problems between investors and portfolio managers would produce asset price bubbles even though all participants are rational. Similarly, formal modelling of bank lending under conditions of easy credit, or when there has been financial liberalisation, demonstrated that 'agency problems' could lead to risk slippage and distort asset prices (Allen and Gale 2003 pp298–310).

Explanations of this second kind seem to be favoured by most mainstream economists and policymakers when combined with macroeconomic triggers and 'externalities'. The latter are widely held to explain the markets' failure in 2008 as a 'systemic' one, meaning that although each individual market participant reacted at each point in time in a perfectly rational way to existing market conditions (according to standard theory and as far as observable), the pricing of risk did not take into account the way in which counterparty risk can spill over from one institution to another without this being realised in the price. A combination of circumstances then conspired so that what had seemed to each of the individual agents making decisions quite rational spilled over into a 'bad equilibrium', akin to a classical bank run.

In this explanation, individual actions were pursued as beneficial because of certain underlying conditions. One was the incentive structure in place in many financial institutions (agency problems and bonus systems creating moral hazard) and another was pressure on yields due to the cheap and easy availability of credit (arising from financial liberalisation and trade and currency imbalances primarily between the United States and China). It encouraged excessive leverage across the market. These features together are offered to explain both the credit boom and then, once things went sour, the ensuing credit crunch (See, for example, FSA 2009).

Such explanations provide rationales. But are they adequate? There are reasons to suggest that they are not.

First, while it is easy to follow the line of reasoning that suggests cheap credit removes some obstacles to borrowing, it is not so immediately obvious why this should cause lenders or borrowers to forget about potential liquidity issues and to lose the power to make prudential assessments about default risk. Nor is it clear why sophisticated institutions and those who invested in them should 'forget' what had nearly happened to US banks during the Latin American debt crisis or US housing loans only a few years before during the savings and loan crisis. Even more significantly, it is not obvious why in many cases banks exchanged risks between different departments within their own institutions without adequate enquiry. Nor is it clear why many professional investors both scrambled after opportunities to own the new derivatives or simply to 'trust' rating agencies actually known to receive fees from the institutions creating the new financial instruments they were rating.

What the various mainstream explanations overlook is the most important issue. No one had to join in. Not every institution did so or did so as enthusiastically as others (Tett 2009; Lipsky 2010).

Why not? What is it that makes some firms and individuals able to abstain while others abandon prudential behaviour? The question is not asked in standard approaches because ambiguity and uncertainty is ruled out. To ask it at all highlights the fact people in markets have to make decisions in ambiguous situations. The simplistic causal relations assumed in standard explanations between increased flows of liquidity from trade imbalances and massively increased leverage at financial institutions hide a suppressed premise. If situations are uncertain and ambiguous there could be potentially intervening variables (such as states of mind) influencing the freedom economic agents have to say 'no'.

Leading up to 2008, the questions are: what factors might have influenced the abandonment of fairly prudent assessment of loans, and, beyond that, what happened to the corporate governance of major banks and financial institutions? Current explanations of financial crises lack any theory to explain the excited shift in risk-reward calculation that always takes place in them.

Behavioural economics and finance

The relatively new discipline of behavioural economics has its origins in the acclaimed efforts by Amos Tversky and Daniel Kahneman (1971; 1974) to introduce knowledge of psychology into the understanding of economic decision-making. The assumptions standard economics relies on about the reality of rationality and optimisation under constraints had long seemed doubtful. Even in modified form they depend not just on modelling the behaviour of human social actors as consistent and rational in a means-end sense, but also on the idea that information is unambiguous and that it can be used to predict the future by using the laws of probability. The questionable assumptions are that there is no uncertainty about the meaning of information, that past information is available and useful to predict the future, and that it can be used to make decisions by calculating 'demons' (Gigerenzer, Todd et al. 1999).

Tversky and Kahneman (1971) pointed out that if rational behaviour is defined by adherence to known principles of statistical inference, then most people are not compliant. They provided evidence suggesting that when people assess the chances of different things happening like the outcome of an election, the guilt of a defendant, or the future value of a currency, they draw on simple heuristic principles which reduce the complex task of assessing probabilities and predicting values to 'simpler judgemental operations'. They then showed how much the behaviour of ordinary human agents in the laboratory was significantly biased, insofar as the standard for unbiased judgement was defined using the insights of Bayesian statistical inference to assess optimal decisions based on beliefs 'expressed in numerical form as odds or subjective probabilities' (Tversky and Kahneman 1974 p1124). How most people think, to judge by many laboratory experiments and some field situations, was shown to differ from how they 'should' think if they were applying basic statistical reasoning. Normal judgements can be described as full of sources of error such as representativeness bias (including base rate bias),[1] the availability bias, and various kinds of framing. In sum, laboratory and field studies show how various heuristics short-circuit optimisation and probabilistic risk calculation. Modelling economic problems with real people of this kind inevitably produces large deviations from rational behaviour (for example, Tversky and Kahneman 1974; Camerer, Loewenstein et al. 2004) and, therefore, a long way from EMH theorems.

Kahneman and Tversky (and behavioural economists who have followed their lead) also became interested in the role of emotion in decision-making. Kahneman himself went so far as to state that the introduction of the 'affect' heuristic (Finucane, Alhakami et al. 2000) was probably one of the most important developments in the study of judgement heuristics in the past few decades (Kahneman 2003). In simple terms, the affect heuristic captures the idea that when offered many stimuli, people almost immediately respond in terms of good or bad. Moreover, when they feel good they feel they are taking less risk than when they feel bad.

Kahneman argued there was compelling evidence that every stimulus evokes an affective evaluation, which is not always conscious (Zajonc 1980; Bargh 1997; Zajonc 1998) and that automatic affective valuation – which would be the emotional core of all attitudes – is the main determinant of many judgements and behaviours (Kahneman and Ritov 1994; Kahneman, Ritov et al. 1999; Kahneman 2003). Supporting this position, Kahneman, Schkade, and Sunstein (1998) interpreted jurors' assessments of when to award punitive punishments as a mapping of outrage onto a dollar scale of punishments, and Loewenstein et al. (2001) in the article, 'Risk as Feelings', analysed how emotional responses, such as the intensity of fear experienced, govern diverse judgements, such as the probability of a disaster. Such findings led Kahneman (2003) to state in his

Nobel lecture that 'the natural assessment of affect' should join representativeness and availability in the list of general-purpose heuristic attributes, and then to add that 'the failure to identify the affect heuristic much earlier' and its subsequent enthusiastic acceptance in recent years 'reflect significant changes in the general climate of psychological opinion' (Kahneman 2003 p710).

Building on these insights and undertaking both field and laboratory studies, behavioural economics has complied an impressive array of findings, particularly over the last 15 years, and become almost a mainstream element in economics and finance (Shefrin 2002; Camerer, Loewenstein et al. 2004; della Vigna 2009). In its finance application it is widely used by professional investors to spot instances where by being 'calm' and 'rational' they can exploit behaviourally created anomalies. But it is still far from clear exactly what behavioural economics can really contribute, either to understanding financial markets or to any really significant shift in standard economic thinking.

For instance, Gul and Pensendorfer (2008) question whether psychology or any other theory of motivation and human functioning is of any relevance to standard economics. They make the point that behavioural economics either extends standard choice theory by including new variables which allow models to specify a richer set of preferences over the same economic choices or necessitate novel descriptions of the relevant economic outcomes. They then argue, first, that the subsequent analysis is very similar to 'what can be found in a standard graduate textbook' and, second, that since in the standard approach 'the term utility maximization and choice are synonymous', the relevant data are always revealed preference data'. In other words, it doesn't matter why people choose what they do because the data about whatever they do choose reveals what they want and that is all that matters. From my point of view this argument need not detain us. It is actually not so far from some behavioural economists' own statements to the effect that they want to improve the field of economics 'on its own terms', modifying 'one or two assumptions' that are 'not central' (Camerer, Loewenstein et al. 2004 p4), and it takes psychology to imply no need for any real change. This can only be so if economists wish to model economics much as they have been doing and without uncertainty. A purpose of this book is to show that once uncertainty is properly included just about everything changes.

A further reason why behavioural economics has done less to change standard economics than might be imagined is that standard modelling demonstrates that markets can work perfectly well according to EMH principles even if not all agents are 'fully rational' (Bunday 1996; Kay 2003). The result allows economists *both* to accept that behavioural economists may have an interesting set of points about how the world works that allow the discipline to be more realistic while changing little. In financial markets it can even be imagined that this creates a role for professional investors. They supply the behavioural rationality that might be missing from others and discipline the market. The result is no great need to change standard theory very much. In fact, what may have been the main impact of behavioural economics so far has been its ability to develop a set of policy recommendations to try to nudge behaviour in markets to be more like the behaviour economists usually model and so, by implication, make results more Pareto-optimal (Hilton 2003; Thaler and Sunstein 2008).

Behavioural economists have developed an impressive tool box of terms to cover the various cognitive and affective biases and heuristics that Kahneman, Tversky, and others unearthed. They have fed them into existing models by modifying one or two aspects of the main utility function of standard economics and so adjusted preferences, tastes, and the responses to and uses of information accordingly. Nonetheless, there is a major theoretical limitation. Behavioural economists do not take anything from real life psychology and neurobiology that is relevant to the task of considering the impact on human agents, working in social groups, making decisions under uncertainty. Review articles such as those by Camerer et al. (2004) and della Vigna (2009) mention emotions but they miss the real point: emotion exists to help economic human actors when reason alone is insufficient. Their use of emotion and behavioural heuristics, therefore, fits too easily into the tendency to frame economic discussions in the context of rational versus irrational action. As Berezin (2005) has pointed out, the problem with rational choice is its assumption that individuals 'experience social life as a series of either/or or zero-sum choices in a series of atemporal and ahistorical contexts.' In fact, choices under uncertainty are not like that. Agents can only be rational in those limited instances where the choice context is stable. The utility of rationality, therefore, clearly recedes before empirical reality. Given the reality of the uncertain and ambiguous situations in which economic agents find themselves in financial markets, it is often not so sure what a fully rational action might be. If outcomes are uncertain and information open to ambiguous interpretation, would two agents faced with the same information make the same choice? Would the same agent with the same information necessarily make the same choice a second time?

Behavioural economists have missed the point about heuristics in much the same way that economists more generally miss the point about bounded rationality, by losing its essence (Gigerenzer 2008). Effective methods of decision-making depend on ecological context. Rationality is bounded or short-circuited when the situation in which decisions are to be made is governed by uncertainty or the absence of useful data limits probabilistic reasoning. Simple decision rules, emotions, and 'gut' feelings may then very quickly and efficiently facilitate good decision-making in uncertain but urgent situations (Gigerenzer 2007). Probabilistic reasoning, in fact, offers a rational approach only if one is able to ignore uncertainty, has reliable data to make forward extrapolations, ample time and opportunity to make the calculations, and grounds for believing that the past is a good guide to the future (see Rebonato 2007). On many occasions simple 'one-' or 'two-reason' heuristics may produce better predictions (Gigerenzer, Todd et al. 1999). Moreover, while emotion may create states of mind that lead to error, using it and intuition may be either the only or the best way to produce effective, fast, and adapted decision-making (Gigerenzer, Todd et al. 1999), an argument increasingly supported by cognitive neuroscience (for example, Damasio 2004).

The point is that if we are seeking to understand judgement under uncertainty the behavioural approach, opposing supposedly rational and non-rational agents, shares all the significant disadvantages of standard theory. Moreover, because behavioural economics has largely been a matter of contesting whether or not economic agents are rational, I have not seen it offer a significant explanation for financial crises beyond the general idea that humans are limited and crises follow from error. It leads to the policy conclusion that either crises are inevitable or that actions can be taken to help economic agents to behave more as they 'should' (Hilton 2003).

Keynes, Minsky, and animal spirits

Working over 70 years ago, well into the Great Depression and at a time when as now it seemed counterintuitive to suppose financial markets necessarily produce the best of all possible outcomes, Keynes (1936; 1937) elaborated on his earlier work (Keynes 1930) to provide economics with a theory of behaviour under uncertainty. He pointed out that it would not be rational (in the strict mainstream sense) to make any positive decision to invest under uncertainty. While to be rational we can draw on theory and evidence based on past experience as far as possible, this cannot be sufficient to guide action with respect to an uncertain future. His *General Theory* (Keynes 1936) differed, therefore, from then classical economics by stressing the crucial role of entrepreneurial psychology (animal or animating spirits) within market institutions and providing technical reasons to suppose that classical economic theory was wrong to treat markets as self-correcting.

Keynes's analysis was later elaborated by Minsky, an economist with direct experience of banking, who argued that useful economic theory should be institution-specific (Minsky 1982). His work emphasised that our economy operates within a modern capitalist system with a big government sector, with long-lived and privately owned capital, and with exceedingly complex financial arrangements (Papadimitriou and Wray 1998). Minsky's (1982) 'financial instability hypothesis' specifically predicted the Ponzi finance experienced leading up to 2008 and its consequences, considering its occurrence inevitable in unregulated markets.

Keynes's and Minsky's ideas focus attention on changes in market senti-ment, trust, and conventional judgement. Akerlof, mentioned earlier, together with Robert Shiller, has recently argued it is time for neoclassical economics to recover such Keynesian thinking. They suggest the paradigm of economic analysis should shift towards greater interdisciplinary engagement – particu-larly with psychology and social science. In their analysis of the financial crisis, Akerlof and Shiller identify beliefs, captured in economic stories about what is happening, confidence, and trust, as key variables because, following Keynes, they emphasise the vital role animal spirits (mental states underpinning beliefs and action) play in economic decision-making. They also stress the importance of institutions for setting ground rules. Drawing on Shiller's (2000; 2009) analy-sis of the dotcom and subprime asset inflations, they emphasise the importance of a kind of confidence inflation and deflation based around and supported by widely shared stories about what is happening in an economy. Fluctuations in confidence create fluctuations in trust and credulity (and so increasingly cor-rupt practices in a boom together with increased suspicion in a recession) and so underpin and accelerate macroeconomic fluctuation (Akerlof and Shiller 2009).

One story told in the new book picks up from Akerlof's (1970) paper. The starting assumption is that competitive capitalism causes products to be offered for profit. The insight introduced into analysis is that how to make profits from consumers is open to 'interpretive action' (as a sociologist would put it). While the laws of supply and demand do make it necessary for firms to sell at a profit, what matters to them is that they can offer whatever it is people *think* they want, or perhaps can be persuaded to want, which is not necessarily what they *really* and truly want. Akerlof and Shiller tell how in the nineteenth century 'Dr' William Rockefeller successfully sold snake oil to credible consumers in the Midwest while in the twentieth century his son, John D, sold them oil. They argue one was 'deception' and the other 'more constructive', but they both made their sellers rich. The example leads them to the question of how to regulate issues of quality uncertainty and to discuss the need for consumer protection (as with the licensing of physicians or pharmaceutical products) and the special difficulty of providing it in the case of financial securities about which 'there is something inherently unknowable' about their 'worth'. In financial markets the willingness to sell and buy snake oil may vary with the prevailing state of optimism and so may be especially likely eventually to lead to 'excesses and to bankruptcies that cause failures in the economy more generally' (Akerlof and Shiller 2009).

Crises in history

Another way of trying to understand and explain financial crises is to con-sider them historically. Reinhart and Rogoff (2009) made a careful quantitative analysis of what is known about financial crises in 66 countries over 'eight centuries of financial folly'. They show that again and again they have the same features: 'Countries, banks, individuals and firms take on excessive debt in good times without enough awareness of the risks that will follow when the inevitable recession hits' (pxxxiii).

They stress that the most commonly repeated and most expensive investment advice ever given in the boom just before a financial crisis stems from the belief that 'this time is different' – meaning that reality has somehow changed and that 'old' rules of valuation and procedures no longer apply.

In a financial bubble what happens, at its simplest, is that asset prices rise and rise aided by increased liquidity, and then, after a period of high volatility, fall back dramatically. The particular steps are persistently described in accounts dating back to the South Sea bubble and the Dutch tulip bulb crisis (see for example, Mackay 1848; Galbraith 1993; Kindleberger 2000; Shiller 2000, 2009; Tett 2004, 2009). Kindleberger proposed a sequence of eight steps:

Displacement→New opportunities→Boom→Euphoria→ Dismissal→Unease →Panic→Revulsion

All these authors agree that an expansion of credit is always present in asset inflation whether this is understood as initially caused by overenthusiasm for a class of new investments, 'loose' monetary or regulatory policies the consequences of which were not fully appreciated at the time, 'unexpected' consequences of financial deregulation, or trade imbalances due to currency disequilibria. What matters is that bank borrowing allows those who want to purchase the exciting asset to do so more aggressively (by increasing leverage). This in turn drives up prices, increasing the value of collateral, and so allowing further rounds of borrowing and buying which then have to unwind.

Kindleberger (2000), however, mentions something else. 'In my talks about financial crisis over the last decades', he writes, 'I have published one line that always gets a nervous laugh: There is nothing so disturbing to one's well being and judgment as to see a friend get rich' (p15). This comment suggests that financial bubbles are more than just technical events. He draws attention to the involvement of crude emotions such as greed, envy, and fear. In fact, in reading Mackay, Kindleberger, Galbraith, Shiller, and the others, it is evident that as prices go first up and then down, six fairly distinct factors can be distinguished, each providing significant emotional challenge.

First, there is always some new and potentially exciting but not well understood innovative development. This becomes the focus of market attention and assets potentially benefitting from it are purchased. The feedback mechanisms then kick in: price increase, increased enthusiasm, increased demand, increased prices, more enthusiasm, and so on. This is an emotional as well as technical inflation. 'Segments of the population that are normally aloof from such ventures' (Kindleberger 2000 p15) join in.

Second, as Smelser (1962) recognised many years ago, new developments, like the Internet or securitised mortgages described by Shiller (2000, 2009), become associated with a narrative rhetoric that in some exciting way the world has changed.

Third, as Galbraith (1993) emphasised, the inventors of the innovations (which always have some underlying merit) are always charismatically portrayed as exceptionally and mysteriously clever.

Fourth, also as described by Galbraith (1993), as a euphoric stage is eventually reached the pressure to join in becomes almost irresistible and those who doubt or criticise what is happening are dismissed, ignored, greeted with derision, or even threatened. It becomes adaptive to join in, and warning signs are ignored.

Fifth, the emotional and technical inflation may continue for quite a while but eventually a phase of unease sets in; 'uneasiness, apprehension, tension, stringency, pressure, uncertainty, ominous conditions, fragility,' wrote Kindleberger (2000 p95).

Sixth, there is panic and the crash, followed finally by an aftermath. Kindleberger calls this final phase 'revulsion'. Looked at in detail it contains a marked tendency to blame or even criminalise those who are held responsible, but it is striking that there is often no real attempt to explore how everyone came to believe them, to have become convinced 'this time is different'.

An emotional trajectory

From the perspective of clinical psychoanalysis the six stages identified are a rather well known and path-dependent *emotional* sequence in which the way people seemed to be thinking about the balance between risk and reward relationships was being influenced by several severe but linked modifications in their state of mind (Tuckett and Taffler 2003; 2008).

Excitement→Mania→Manic defence (unease)→Panic→ Shame, Blame or Mourning

Based on this observation Richard Taffler and I set out a theory of *phantastic objects* to offer a possible new way of understanding the sequence of events in an asset price bubble. I will clarify this new term more extensively in Chapter 5 (p86 et seq) but a *phantastic object* is a mental representation of something (or someone) which in an imagined scene fulfils the protagonist's deepest desires to have exactly what she wants exactly when she wants it. The specific possibilities vary but they all allow individuals to feel omnipotent like Aladdin (who owned a lamp which could call a genie), or like the fictional bond trader, Sherman McCoy, who felt himself a Master of the Universe (Wolfe 1987). In psychoanalytic thinking beliefs in the existence of such 'phantastic objects' have their origins in the earliest periods of human mental development and are never entirely extinguished (Tuckett and Taffler 2008).

We can postulate that what happens in the case of financial bubbles is that beliefs about what is risky, what is desirable, what is possible, and what is likely, all shift in an expansive or excited direction under the influence of the kind of generalised belief or covering explanatory story common in all mass movements (Smelser 1962; 1998). Crucially, the idea is that something innovative and exceptional was changing the world – a 'phantastic object' was at work. Think of the 'South Sea', Tulip Bulbs, Joint-Stock Companies, the Japanese 'Miracle', the East Asian 'Miracle', Junk Bonds, WorldCom, Enron, Dotcoms and China. To these we can now add Collaterised Debt Obligations, Credit Default Swaps, Broad Index Secured Trust Offerings, and Structured Investment Vehicles. Such innovations occur and will keep occurring. Some of them get picked up and increasingly publicised and then many people get drawn into the belief that they are phantastic.

The point is that *phantastic objects* create and are created by states of mind. After the initial phase, once some euphoric momentum is reached, the emotional development underlying the belief tends to indicate only a one-way path. There are two reasons. There is the excitement propelling the move forward and the pain that would have to be undergone if it were to be reversed. The latter would entail loss of the euphoric dream and giving up expectations. Sceptics are felt as spoilers and it is to stave off frustration that they are especially maligned during this phase. The doubts they raise about the new story need to be refuted and so are mocked and maligned through dismissal. *Groupthink* (Janis 1982), in which everyone in a group thinks the same because they want to feel the same, is at work. It usually seems that the in-group has the grail and the out-group are trying to spoil things. While this continues there is an additional sense of triumph over rivals and asset price values continue to get unrealistically high. The period of unease and jitteriness mentioned by Kindleberger can then last some time.

To a psychoanalyst, unease and psychosomatic manifestations like back pain or upset stomach signify unconscious anxiety and doubt, but not the availability of conscious reflective questioning. However, eventually a tipping point is reached and doubt spills over into thought and action. Prices collapse catastrophically. At this point the covering story, which was good enough to make many feel well when things were going well, gets more studied attention. It is found to be wanting, like the Emperor's new clothes.

The emotional finance approach (Taffler and Tuckett 2007; 2010) to financial instability is based on a theory of mind and a theory of thinking based on mental states. It draws attention to the different ways ambiguous information about an uncertain future can be processed depending on an individual's state of mind. Change the state of mind and the conclusions reached about the same information at a later time period may differ. Both euphoria and unease can persist for significantly long periods of time, even many months. The final tipping point, when the meaning of information to hand changes dramatically, is unpredictable and it is not necessarily accompanied by any really new information or certainty. This was the case during both the dotcom affair and also the financial derivatives mania preceding the 2008 crash. Before that crash news of trouble about subprime mortgages and instruments based on them was in the market for 18 months or more. But during it sales of new financial instruments and subprime derivatives were often escalating and stock market prices for bank and other shares hit several all-time highs (Tett 2009).[2]

The concept of the *phantastic object* and the emphasis on states of mind and *groupfeel* are together designed to capture the fact that whether they involve houses, dotcoms, or tulips, periods of asset price inflation and the increasingly leveraged loans that accompany it require educated investors and bankers to join in what is (with hindsight) a scarcely credible process. Assumed valuations require implicit assumptions that long-term historical records are obsolete. Extreme beliefs about long-run rates of change are implicit, although these have never previously persisted for longer than very short periods or for very rare companies. But now they are extrapolated for the foreseeable future (Meltzer 2003).

How do such processes emerge from 'everyday' markets? In other words, why do phantastic objects get established? In the chapters that follow, I will use the material from interviews I conducted with asset managers in 2007 to describe the world that financial actors actually seem to inhabit and why I think individual thinking can regularly become disturbed in financial markets. Although each investor may be attempting to make careful, independent decisions based on factual premises, I will show how the situations they face in their world are such that it is easy to see that they are invariably likely to get caught up in group behaviour, implicitly looking over their shoulders and making decisions by *groupfeel*; caught up in 'homogenous behaviour...to the detriment of the diversity that is indispensable for the smooth functioning' of neoclassical markets (Trichet 2003).

Economists tend to make little distinction as to the characteristics of the different items the markets they study trade. In my argument this is a mistake. The valuation of financial assets cannot be undertaken without recognising the role of uncertainty. The experience of buying, holding, or selling financial assets is different from that of trading other goods and services because they have different characteristics. In the interviews I found three linked and essential characteristics of financial assets created a decision-making environment that is completely different from that in other markets. It was an environment in which there is both inherent uncertainty and inherent emotional conflict linked with specific states of mind and particular institutional arrangements.

Three characteristics of financial assets

Once reflected on from an emotional stance it is rather easy to see that the three fundamental characteristics of financial assets I will mention might rather inevitably create complex states of emotional experience which alter dynamically as time goes by. Understood in this way the focus of theoretical analysis must shift from understanding time as a mathematical variable (as in physics and current economic modelling) towards understanding it as something which stimulates sequences of experience and states of mind. What comes to matter is not mechanical time but 'inside time' or 'subjective time' as the forgotten economist, George Shackle, put it (Ford 1993 p690). As soon as I began pilot interviews and had to select the questions to ask I saw that for my respondents there was an experience of time before making a decision to buy an asset, another experience of time when the decision was made, and many more moments in time while the asset was held before it was finally sold, if at all. There was even time after it was sold when it could be bought again or the decision regretted. The point is that from this viewpoint decisions are not made once. They are made again and again and again. Uncertainty about the future value of assets creates inherent and irresolvable conflicts for the human actors trading or holding them at the first decision moment but also at ongoing dynamic ones. The experience of conflict through time, therefore, is at the heart of the financial system.

First among the three characteristics I want to highlight is that financial asserts tend to be *volatile*. Their value can go up and down a lot in short or long periods of time. They can even come to be worth nothing. This characteristic (a focus of finance theory from Bachalier (1900) to Black and Scholes (1973) and beyond) has considerable power to generate primitive impulses and emotions and to do so through time – on the one hand impatient, greedy excitement about potential future reward and on the other panicky anxiety about future potential loss. Think of a gold rush. Waiting to find out what one has got evokes both impatience and doubt; maybe it will just be fool's gold. The point is that as time passes, economic actors, like Antonio in Shakespeare's *Merchant of Venice*, have a significant set of experiences. They wait for news about prospects. Will the ships come in? The assets people do or do not own (or which they imagine they may come to own or watch others obtain) generate the most powerful human feelings; principally triumph, elation, and omnipotence or hate, guilt, sorrow, and envy. Such feelings are not a sign of irrationality. As I will elaborate in Chapter 3, they are an essential part of our human adaptive capacity and are even essential for good decision-making. Feelings and their biological correlates motivate us, help us to think and make life meaningful.

Thus, while any investor may try more or less to the best of his or her ability independently to calculate the future on the basis of factual premises, the future is inherently uncertain. Future values can only be calculated by making assumptions that we have arrived at through imagination and anticipation. Inevitably those involved have feelings about what they anticipate and imagine, as well as feelings about their observations of others. In fact, as we will see in the next chapter and thereafter, thinking about future rewards and risks of loss means telling oneself stories and imagining relationships and outcomes. Such activity is not to be shrugged off as epiphenomenal. Imagined experience and real experience tend towards equal significance, in the demonstrable sense that in experimental situations involving functional Magnetic Resonance Imaging (fMRI), imagining subjects are observed to produce electrical and chemical activity in their brains that is pretty much the same as those they produce when actually living them out (Bechara and Damasio 2005).

A second and related characteristic of financial assets is that they are *abstract* in the sense they cannot be enjoyed for themselves. They have no value other than what they can be exchanged for. This well-known[3] feature has a huge implication for the subjective experience of owning them. Purchasing a financial asset is not experientially like purchasing a consumer good such as a television.

In purchasing a television, a 'rational' consumer can consult a range of information about price and quality and on that basis make a decision. After taking his television home he can then sit down and enjoy it, thinking little more about it. He uses it. Afterwards the price may go up or down or new, superior models may arrive. If he even notices them such events may cause regret in the coming weeks and months, but the television is there to be used and if the purchaser is really upset he can sell it in the secondhand market, take a loss, and buy the newest model.

With financial assets the situation is very different as they have no intrinsic value but one determined by ambiguous information and varying expectations about an uncertain future that plays out in time. The owners of financial assets necessarily continue, start, or end a dependent relationship on them, which can result in reward or loss at any time. The relationship, therefore, will evoke not just fantasies about the future but also consequent emotions. It is a conflictual relationship based entirely on an intrinsically uncertain view of the asset's expected value in the future. The exchange value of financial securities is represented by symbols on paper or by an impermanent flow of numbers on a screen, the movement of which can cause joy or despair. Both feelings are inevitable. Prices can and regularly do go down, promoting fear of loss, as well as up, promoting triumph and excitement. In fact, assets which go up over 12 months are very likely to have been going down for half the available days during that time. Therefore, the result of the 'relationship' may be that the asset will produce an exciting reward. Alternatively, it may not only disappoint but also create despair by seriously losing value or even coming to be worth nothing.

A significant consequence of this abstract characteristic is that decisions to form and maintain a relationship with such objects will depend on an individual's ability to maintain conviction about their future expectations under pressure. I will elaborate more thoroughly in Chapter 3 how neurobiological findings show that this is made more difficult by the fact that anxiety engages the oldest parts of the brain in the amygdala and nucleus accumbens and so tends to bypass more ordinary thinking in the prefrontal cortex (Charuvastra and Marder 2009). Sustaining conviction under pressure and the mechanisms through which this is done are bound to be important for financial market actors. It is a fact that trading frequently (nervously changing one's mind) is expensive and is likely to destroy any gains. So when new information about better or worse opportunities emerges, the holder of a financial asset who wants to see a long-term thesis play out will have to be able to tolerate worry as s/he watches the cherished investment struggle, all the time also knowing that there may really be good reason to rethink and sell. In a sense this characteristic of financial assets means that they are never really bought or sold. The original decision to buy has to be made again and again and again for as long as one holds the stock. This creates an experience through time with which individuals must cope. Correspondingly, a decision to sell may shortly create regret and a wish to reverse it.

The third important characteristic of financial assets is a consequence of the two earlier features and also gives rise to further inherent emotional conflict. The feedback given to investors is 'noisy', in the sense that it is extremely difficult to determine cause and effect and so to draw any secure conclusions about whether an investor's efforts in buying, holding and selling them is a result of skill or luck (for example, della Vigna 2009). This is a fact with consequences. How can performance be evaluated? Which investment professionals are to be trusted? And how do you monitor them? The range of variables and time periods involved make assessment and feedback, whether about one's own performance or that of others, unreliable. Good performance in one period is rarely a good guide to that in another and in financial markets it is extremely difficult to distinguish reliably between the operation of luck and good judgement.

Moreover, as in gambling, short-term experiences of apparent success or failure and the resulting excitement or anxiety may be quite misleading. Such factors pose major problems when a professional investor or his or her clients try to assess whether he or she has really done well, particularly if the costs of professional management are taken into account (Kay 2009). Such facts are also particularly significant because human evolution based on natural selection has given us the psychological capacity to split excitement and anxiety or risk and reward with profound consequences for unconscious learning.

Donizetti's opera, *L'elisir d'amore,* can be used to extend the point Akerlof and Shiller made with their story about the two Rockerfellers. In it Nemorino is a poor peasant in love with Adina, a beautiful landowner, who torments him with her indifference. When Nemorino hears Adina reading to her workers the story of Tristan and Isolde, he is convinced that a magic potion will gain Adina's love for him. But he is afraid she loves the self-important Sergeant Belcore who appears with his regiment and immediately proposes marriage to Adina in front of everyone. Dulcamara (the self-proclaimed Dr Encyclopaedia) arrives, selling his bottled cure-all to the townspeople. Nemorino innocently asks Dulcamara if he has anything like Isolde's love potion. Dulcamara says he does, selling it to Nemorino at a price matching the contents of Nemorino's pockets. The bottle contains only wine, but at the end of a long story, after much gaming and many complications, Nemorino does marry Adina and, as they bid a fond farewell to the 'doctor', all agree that the elixir has done its job.

The story shows how the distinction between snake oil and 'real' medicine is not so clear. What people wanted from Dr Encyclopaedia was something they could not reliably expect to get in a concrete way. Nonetheless, they were still prepared to purchase and were satisfied with the outcome, which is one reason why market provision of consumer goods and services (which leaves it up to consumers to decide what they want) has proved very superior to efforts to plan economic production centrally. The point of products of the elixir variety is to fulfil dreams which human social actors may be willing to regard as fulfilled even when this is not credible in the framework of 'external reality'. There is a question of quality uncertainty, to use Akerlof's original term, but the underlying issue is still deeper.

Models in any discipline necessarily simplify down to parsimonious essentials and then seek to generalise. In doing so, standard economic theories (in which for reasons given earlier I include much of behavioural economics) have opted to leave out ambiguity, uncertainty, human memory, the experience of time, experiences of excitement and anxiety, and the experience of group life. The fact that future stock market prices are mostly unpredictable (follow a random walk), and the reasonable conclusion that few if any investors will 'beat' the market except by chance, has been taken to mean that what individuals decide and so what experiences they have is of no importance to the final outcome. Narrative history doesn't matter. Moreover, neither do dreams of the future. Whereas ordinary experience lets us know that what will happen next is inherently uncertain (and so a cause of ineradicable anxiety and doubt), economic models leave uncertainty to one side. By modelling risk within a normal distribution the future appears to become predictably probable and calculable. Economic agents, therefore, have no subjective experience of time, no imaginative dreams about the future, and, above all, no useful memories.

A significant unintended consequence of this standard perspective infuses the points I made earlier about the main explanations that economists and the government agencies that relied on them have offered for the events leading up to the 2008 crash. They have argued that trade imbalances (and perhaps lax central bank credit policies to deal with them) created cheap credit and so excess leverage. Or they thought that lack of transparency around the credit derivatives made it hard to value them. But how would such ideas work at the level of an individual financial actor making decisions? I suggested earlier there was a suppressed assumption, which is that actors are denied the possibility to think and to say 'no'.

Like economists, sociologists do not seek to explain what interests them through individual behaviour. But following Weber and Schutz (Parsons 1937; Schutz 1967; Weber, Roth et al. 1968) they do consider it necessary for theories to make sense at the level of the actor's subjective perspective. This creates scope to create rules to guide the interpretation of data in a given situation prior to action, for instance, status, role, generation, or gender differences might be modelled to influence differential responses to the same data. The suppressed assumptions economics make are highly significant. Everyone makes the same interpretation. Standard economic agents are modelled with access to a great deal of past data to which to fit regression lines and make predictions, but not, for example, with interpretive skills based on institutional position to sense repeating historical narratives. It is the latter that might warn them about the present possibility to repeat history. But because economic models posit people who, when offered the chance to make more and more large loans, can't remember the last bubble (or don't believe they happen) and apparently have no choice, the implicit implication is they will all automatically have lost their capacity to judge the risk of loans defaulting. In this way economists exclude a whole level of analysis and human action. The economist's world is one without ambiguity, uncertainty, emotional memory, and the experience of anxiety. Agents project the future with calculations but not with feelings. It is not the world anyone lives in but one populated by mindless automatons. If we really thought bankers or political leaders made decisions in such a world it might make us feel distinctly uneasy.

The interview findings I will shortly present will show that the valuation of financial assets while buying, holding, or selling them takes place in a world of ambiguous information about uncertain futures and is inextricably linked with the stories people tell about their futures, the stories they tell about new information that comes in when they hold them, the stories they tell about what others in the market are doing, and the stories they tell about what their clients or employers will be thinking when they see what they have been doing. In telling stories respondents exercised imagination. They even dreamed. Quality assessment in the situations of uncertain information they faced was not only difficult, but context and mood-related. They frequently felt both anxious and excited. Perception and evaluation is dominated by mood (Damasio 2004) and context (Berns, Laibson et al. 2007; Vlaev, Kusev et al. 2010). As time passes and prospects vary, therefore, it is likely to be in the nature of the ups and downs of financial asset valuations and the stories about them that will produce conflicting desires and emotions as well as conflicting options. The stories on which asset values depend are efforts to know future outcomes which are unknown and ultimately unknowable in advance. Consequently the conflicts in holding assets and evaluating those who hold them for clients are also inherently irresolvable in any final way.

The problem of uncertainty and quality multiplies in financial markets due to the nature of financial assets. Everyone in financial markets has to deal with this psychic 'reality'. There is, therefore, greater uncertainty and more inherent conflict when we try to evaluate the claims of two Rockefellers selling shares in their two enterprises. Although a rational actor will make some checks, how to separate the quality offered by financial salesmen has no obvious solution. The problem also surfaces insofar as the usual solutions to build confidence are not easy to apply. Real guarantees can be offered for secondhand cars but not for financial products (as indeed for most medical treatments). So while ratings agencies used 'fancy' statistics to provide what looked like guarantees (creating an attractive feeling) they did not offer 'money back'. Triple A ratings offer a fast and frugal stamp of reputability like the various risk measures and protections offered by asset managers or, indeed, the solid architecture traditionally associated with banks. But actually they are 'covering stories' with little substantial meaning, whose capacity to provide security may disappear instantly when there is a change in mood.

Summary

Financial markets appear to be the quintessential example of a market which depends nearly entirely on human imagination and emotion. A satisfactory understanding of them seems to require a theoretical framework able to include those aspects of psychology that can recognize the role of emotional conflicts and emotional states that are the consequence.

2
Four Fund Managers

Whether they run retail funds, closed funds, or manage money on behalf of large corporations, sovereign states, 'high net worth' private clients, or pension funds, asset managers are the group of financial professionals charged with managing the world's money. During the first eight months of 2007 I interviewed 52 such people working in major centres in the United States, the United Kingdom, France, and Asia. As luck would have it, this timing was opportune, allowing me to talk to some of them about the quite large falls in world equity markets in May 2006 and February 2007, the first signs of subprime difficulties causing hedge fund bankruptcies in April 2007 and the beginning of the credit crunch in August 2007.

Those I spoke to (who included hedge fund managers) had been at least ten years in their roles and personally controlled at least one billion dollars. They instructed brokers and traders to buy and sell assets of many kinds as well as asset-backed and other derivatives. Some worked in small boutique partnerships but must most were part of the asset management arms of very large financial service institutions. Their institutions, which have been called giant funds (Turner, Haldane et al. 2010), are at the apex of the financial system. They collect huge sums of money from clients all over the world and in doing so set the tone for what those clients can expect from their investments. With all that money, and perhaps with additional borrowed moneys to allocate, they decide what assets to buy, sell, and hold based on the strategies they advertise and the information they obtain from brokers, analysts, and all kinds of information services. The managers I interviewed mostly dealt in equities but some also bought, held, and sold bonds and derivatives. They used a combination of active and quantitatively based techniques and invested in every major world market. They had to make decisions about what was happening in every currency and together controlled over $500 billion dollars held in stocks or bonds in most of the world's economies and a very wide range of industries. Thirty-nine were essentially 'stock pickers', one traded only in bonds, another

26

was a very experienced investment analyst, and nine used highly quantitative techniques in which they made few decisions about individual assets but pro-grammed computers to make their day-to-day choices. Two used a particularly complex and thorough combination of stock-picking and quant techniques. Each interview was tape-recorded and transcribed and so produced qualitative data capable of systematic analysis.[1]

This chapter aims to give the reader a sense of the reality of the experi-ence of asset managers and to demonstrate how field interviews, because they offer direct contact with actual decision-makers, may have more use as a data source than economists have usually thought. I mentioned in my preface that the overlooked significance of the characteristics of financial assets and of the uncertainty facing asset managers became evident rather quickly. As I spent the first half hour of the first pilot interview trying to work out what questions to ask, to test whether the respondent was behaving in the manner expected by standard theory, it already became apparent that focus was not very useful. The respondent was the highly successful head of a major desk. He had a lot of research and computer resources on which to draw. He tried to use them rationally, but, as he volunteered with some embarrassment, ultimately it was 'touchy-feely' guesswork. In this chapter I aim to show in detail why that was so by looking at my interviews with four of the managers from the main study sample.[2]

Fred Bingham

Fred Bingham had been in the finance industry for over 20 years when I met him in March 2007. He had a university background in economics, history, and politics and had passed subsequent professional exams. He was responsible for a range of private client portfolios, family trusts, charity and pension funds with mandates to invest in the United Kingdom and valued at just over half a billion dollars. The team he belongs to manages about $6 billion.

Managing information

Talking to Bingham, one is immediately aware of just how much information he is subjected to at any point of his day – information which might impact assets he does own, those he is thinking of buying, and those he has owned before. Many companies issue shares and bonds which one might invest in all over the world and there are also many other types of assets. The companies and the potential impact on them of a wide range of political, social, techni-cal, meteorological, economic, and other factors are the object of comment, rumour, reports, and analysis 24 hours a day. It is quite impossible for him to be fully informed. So one of the first decisions he has had to make has been to frame his search behaviour and to limit his universe. His mandate is some help. Formally, it restricts his attention to the United Kingdom. Even so, just in that market there are already a lot of companies he could hold – over 350 – and because many of them operate in a global environment, where to judge their success it is relevant to know about the competition, he cannot be too myopic. He needs to keep in mind a range of international macroeconomic, social, and political issues which might impact his companies in any of the markets where they do business and to be aware of the competition and legislative threats from a far larger number of companies domiciled all over the world.

To assess all this Bingham relied on information and analysis coming from others – a range of brokers to whom he related – allowing him to keep an eye on a hundred or so companies. 'We deal with a range of brokers from the biggest to the smallest. We do a lot with regional brokers. ... I'm guessing, but 100 companies', that's how many 'we're pretty interested in'.

Once Bingham starts to look at individual companies for himself (rather than just relying on brokers and analysts who will be advising other people as well), he has pages of detailed company reports, expert analyses, newspaper and other generated gossip, public and private statements by company managers, and impressions gained from seeing them at factory visits or by talking to their competitors in similar industries. He can also look and see who else is buying and selling their shares. To make sense of a particular company's prospects it may be necessary to find out about and to develop expertise on an almost limitless range of topics – Bingham has had to learn about such things as the difference between sucrose sprinkled on cereal and sucrose in fizzy drinks and the intricacies of European motor industry regulation and so on and on and on.

Many of the others I interviewed initially narrowed their large universes of data by buying 'feeds' from information companies whose computer programmes then helped them by ranking companies according to their level of potential interest using simple metrics like price to book. But this is not for Bingham. 'We're very much nonquantitative. It's very much the bottom up stock picking approach rather than modelling or anything like that.' The one hundred companies he selects down to are those that catch his or his colleagues' attention so that they decide to visit and then analyse them for themselves. It's the 'research that comes from brokers' which provokes a company visit and which backs up the information gained at visits, he says, but 'what we *love* to do is find an underresearched company using our own intellectual shoe leather to find a good idea, and then we look to see if a share is cheap or expensive and then go with *our conviction*.'

The words 'love' and 'conviction' that Bingham was just quoted as uttering were spontaneous and highly suggestive. They give a clue as to how emotion may have functioned to select information and to make ideas salient. In the next chapter I will elaborate this idea and review neuroscientific and other findings to suggest that emotion functions as a kind of glue in decision-making, allowing individuals to commit to the decision to make a dependent relationship with the underlying entity in highly uncertain circumstances and still be comfortable about it. Certainly, it was very apparent that with all the information he had to hand about the companies he had to decide to buy, hold, or sell, Bingham needed some way to feel comfortable with his commitment. He could never know all he would like. So he was, therefore, very far from experiencing himself as the omniscient demon of standard economic theory. Rather, uncertainty and its cognitive and emotional management was the essence of his situation; he always had too much information to manage but also never enough to be sure it was enough to make reliable judgements about present or future.

Asked to describe his general approach, Bingham said he and his house were more long-term focused than others and had 'a stock-picking culture' which rested on two aspects of expertise: they thought of themselves as good at assessing the people who run companies and good at identifying long-run themes to help them select which companies to explore. 'We try and distinguish ourselves by meeting companies. It's very vital to everything we do. It's all about meeting companies'. [We are] 'looking at global themes, if you like, and I try to identify companies that will do well within that framework...'

His asset management company is now a subsidiary of a very large financial conglomerate with billions of dollars under management, but he thinks of his team as filling a niche; their portfolios are 'generally constructed of large, medium and small companies' which, he says, 'distinguishes ourselves again, because a lot of companies our size tend to focus on large and medium cap, ignoring the small cap side.' I came to think of claims of this sort as mission narratives. In doing their job, managers had to have an explanation for themselves and others which gave meaning to their situation and which enabled them to distinguish themselves and feel comfortable. Lots of others are doing what they try to do and so they had all created a story of their own about general strategy. I think this was both to make sense of what they were doing for themselves and to be able to advertise it to others.

Like many others Bingham emphasised that part of his team's mission was to make long-term investments. 'Long' was rather pragmatically defined. He first said it meant looking for stocks to hold across an entire business cycle, and then when asked what that might mean, he said it was 'three years'. I saw Bingham early on in the study. I came to learn that, while from a macroeconomic perspective this seemed an absurdly short period for a business cycle, three years was indeed a very long time in financial markets. Many managers believed prediction beyond 18 months was essentially impossible.

A lovely business

To give an example of how he implemented this mission, Bingham explained about what he considered a 'classic' long-term investment. 'What we do, we try and buy a company for the long term. A classic is *Sound Healthcare*.' He elaborated on how it was a beneficiary of a government outsourcing programme aimed at reducing infections in hospitals quickly and before there was further bad publicity. 'It's pretty much in a monopoly position ... a *lovely* business.' This was because it had 'an order book stretching forward years and a very good finance director'. That person was 'the key to this', he said. Summarising, he said, 'It's a "money-making machine" we will be 'holding it for ten or even fifteen years'. It was doing well.

Finding *Sound Healthcare* was also an example of what Bingham meant by using themes. It came about because Bingham and his team had identified healthcare companies providing essential services to government as a theme likely to pay dividends and had then found that particular company as one which could especially benefit. Themes identified were quite often companies benefitting from government policy (as above) or legislation (see below) or perhaps also some macro fundamentals they identified. An instance of the latter was oil. 'We think oil is going to be strong for a while. It'll wobble around but we think that's a long term. ... So, we try and buy companies that are going to benefit from that. ...'

Fabulous

To get down to specifics, each manager was asked to give three examples of stock decisions (to buy, sell, or hold) s/he had made in the last 12 months which s/he found satisfying. Bingham offered four, two of which illustrate what has just been set out and especially the way confidence in decisions is supported by emotional attachment. The first, still held from earlier in his career, was a UK engineering company (*Amazing Glass*) which was 'the first company I ever met' and which he just thought was a 'fabulous company'. Its core business was toughened glass for which it also had an 'amazing bit of technology' – 'a great cannon for testing – you'll see the American President in an armoured vehicle ... it's their glass'. But their 'real growth engine' is the lamination of solar panels. 'They don't make them, their skill is lamination.' The theme was 'legislation driven'. 'It's a green investment case ... and a proper company making proper profits. ...' Management impressed him. He had met the chief executive about eight times now. 'It's very much a two-way thing. She trusts us; we'll support her in good and ... well, there haven't been bad times, but we would.' So, as he put it, it was 'a management story. It's a good long-term growth story ... get to know her style. Its absolute trust what she's going to say, which is crucial. She doesn't say anything she shouldn't say, but there's trust in what she is saying, so that gives you a lot of comfort. It's our decision whether we're paying too much for the shares, and we are paying a lot, rating-wise, for them, but again, taking this three-year story, we're pretty comfortable with that. I think this sort of company is fairly unique.' With new ideas like alternative energy 'you can get these big bubbles' but 'we think, again, this is an undiscovered story and we're there early'.

Another success was *Lawsons,* a car retailer. It was identified by selecting as a promising theme companies in sectors which might benefit from changes to European anticompetition legislation. The legislation had apparently altered the balance of advantage between the car manufacturer and the retailer – meaning that although manufacturing with too much capacity did not seem a good option, retailing held out the likelihood of increasing potential profitability. 'We liked it a lot' and 'it's been a fabulous investment'.

'Fut!'

What about things that hadn't gone so well? Every manager was asked to think about the last 12 months and to identify specific decisions with which they had not been satisfied. Bingham mentioned a catering company, *Burgers for Schools*. He had known and followed the management for a long time, noticing their skill. This company was 'a turnaround situation', a situation where a management group had bought out the previous owners and now expected to do better. They did do better but to take the company over its management had taken on a lot of debt which made it unexpectedly vulnerable. 'We had put a lot of trust in them but then that top chef came out with his programme and schools didn't have burgers on the menu anymore. They went 'fut'. It made me realise how brittle the food industry is.'

There were 'issues', Bingham told me. There was 'the debt', he said, and also he had 'got the analysis wrong'. When buying in he 'trusted' the management to deliver, based on their past record. But, 'unfortunately they didn't, and we didn't get out'. Apparently, when the burger business's school contracts were lost the value of the company was cut by half. Moreover, the management company couldn't sell that bit of the business because if they did, they couldn't pay off the debt.

The example shows one of the ways careful thinking and analysis can come unstuck. What has worked before is not necessarily repeated a second time. Also, in financial markets where outcomes depend on future events, it is very hard to think of everything. It emphasises how it's a decision-making environment with many imponderables and much uncertainty. Had Bingham learned anything? He said he concluded from it that it is dangerous to buy companies with debt. One could see his point. At the same time, on another occasion borrowing might be necessary to finance a good idea and might work out perfectly well.

Cut and move on!

As in Bingham's case in two of the examples above, many managers used an affective word like *trust* to summarise complex cognitive and emotional judgements about company management leading them to enter a dependent relationship by buying the company's stock. Consequently, when their predictions or hopes did not come true, they often reacted as if betrayed. We will see that this is widespread among managers and it was the case with another of Bingham's examples of a decision that he was dissatisfied with. This was *'Leave it with Us'* – a company which helped people to get their cars repaired after they had had a car accident and exploited an 'insurance theme' Bingham had identified.

This decision illustrates another pitfall. In this case he said there had been three companies which fit the theme and two had in fact worked out – the trouble was that 'we just got the wrong one. We picked the wrong management. They were untrustworthy'. Bingham spoke as though particularly hurt that apparently the company had announced a profits warning on the very day 'I was there – although nothing had been mentioned in the trading statement earlier.' He sold his shares that day. But later he got a phone call from the company chairman to tell him he was 'wrong to do so'. 'They underperformed for two years although now they have recovered', Bingham said.

The example illustrates how important timing is in determining outcome, how difficult it is to evaluate what one is doing, and how emotions get involved. Bingham knew he had been emotional about his decision to sell. He had felt betrayed by management. In a later chapter we will see how very often when company management did not achieve what they or the fund managers calculated they would, the fund managers spoke of them as betraying trust. It was not that they had made a mistake or been defeated by unknown uncertainties. Bingham's struggle with how to evaluate what had happened and the difficulty of learning from it was then evident. 'I made a loss on those shares but it's what you've recycled into that that matters, and who knows? Would I have been better off staying with that company? It's often better for your own peace of mind to just move on; made a mistake, just move on and try and rectify it rather than having to meet people that you're not sure about anyway, and not feeling very good about. Just cut it and move on.' Again, one can see his point. But from a psychoanalytic viewpoint 'moving on' takes one away from 'bad' feelings and makes working through and learning from experience more difficult. It may also leave a residue of unresolved discomfort which may create a future bias. Some managers spoke about how after being 'let down' they or their colleagues would never buy some companies' shares again. Some of these stigmatised companies included some of the world's largest like BP or Vodafone in the United Kingdom.

The Market

Another moment in Bingham's interview was interesting because it alerted me to how price movements are treated as signals and to the anxiety they create if unexpected. Talking of price movements he hadn't anticipated, he said, 'The market always is telling you something, and one should never be arrogant enough to think, well, they're wrong. Often the market is telling you a story. ...' I had heard similar sentiments before setting out on the study when talking to a very senior and sceptical fund manager about the dotcom bubble, '...and then the head of equity argued along the following lines, maybe there is something here that we're missing. I'm not sure, maybe there is, maybe we should factor in some different criteria, change some parameters to allow for something we are obviously overlooking. The market's telling us there's something we're missing. Maybe we factor in different growth rates. ...' Such logic had led to his company investing in dotcoms along with everyone else.

Fred Bingham's interview has introduced the world of the fund manager. It will be apparent that it paints a rather different picture from that we might expect from standard economic and finance theory. It shows something of the essence of the situation my respondents faced. They had to make choices in situations of overwhelming choice, information overload, and information uncertainty. In their world it quickly becomes apparent that as far as most of the decisions they have to make are concerned, the rational course of action is by no means obvious. Rational calculation and thought play a major part but are bounded by experienced reality, human capacity, and the availability of relevant information. Conviction about particular investments has to be created. It is gained from narrowing down the information obtained to fit into themes (stories) that Bingham and his team considered promising and by engaging emotions. Whether he was describing success or failure, his emotion was a palpable feature of what can quite easily be conceived as a story of a dependent relationship with a beginning, continuation, and ending. Among the examples, he mentioned a 'lovely company', a 'money-making machine', an 'order book stretching years', 'a 'fabulous company', a 'proper company', an 'undiscovered story', an 'amazing bit of technology', a 'fabulous investment', a company 'giving comfort', 'it's about trust ... she doesn't say anything she shouldn't', and so forth. As with the last remark, he identified talented and trusted management in whom 'we put a lot of trust'. But as we have seen they can betray and become untrustworthy.

Mark Devreaux

Fred Bingham's examples of stock-picking to hold long term are instances of a manager trying to identify 'fundamentals'. The effort is a part of every stock-picking decision but does not always have the same emphasis. Keynes (1936) famously pointed out that stock market prices also depend on what other people think. So although the managers to be described in the remainder of the book all considered that stock prices depend on knowing about the underlying entity, they also thought about how to judge other people's assessment. In economic and finance theory both are 'in the price'. But to the fund managers I spoke to, the degree of information uncertainty and investors' response to it meant that this was always an open question. We try 'to pierce through the smoke and emotion and be contrary to the consensus notion of let's wait for the smoke to clear', said the next manager, Mark Devreaux. 'I mean the problem with that philosophy, I think, is you can make money but if you wait for everything to be clear you will miss most of the money to be made. In that case the market is pretty efficient and where we value investors make money is when it's smoky and there is a lot of panic and controversy. Once everything's clear, it's easy, right?'

I saw Mark Devreaux in the United States in late June 2007. He was looking for securities that other people did not see were undervalued. He had been in fund management for 11 years and had quite recently spent some time out of the industry at his own choice. He has a degree in European history and higher degrees in science, accounting, and law – all from prestigious universities. For the last two years he has been head of his team, comprised of 20 portfolio managers, several analysts and traders, as well as back office staff. The overall value of the fund he is directly responsible for is $35 billion and his funds are part of a still larger group.

Devreaux's mission strategy is that of the classic 'value manager', based on finding companies at low valuation which he judges to have considerable upside potential. He is prepared to invest in distressed situations – companies at or near the edge of bankruptcy – if there is a strategy he considers viable for turning things round. He is also prepared to be interventionist with management in such situations. His funds mainly invest in US securities but are permitted to hold a minority proportion in developed markets overseas. It is an open fund with performance data publicly available in real time with clients from individuals to institutions to intermediaries interested in a classic value fund matched against the S&P 500.

'We operate as a team...the process is "bottom up"', he said, meaning Devreaux is not making top-level macro-decisions to inform his investment decisions but making a security by security selection process. 'We're trying to buy securities that we think are trading today at significant discounts to intrinsic value.' Like any classical 'value' investor, he often looks at out-of-favour names – industries and companies that have some element of blemish or controversy – trying to buy assets at a discount to what he thinks they're worth in today's marketplace. In other words, he is avowedly contrarian but looking for steady, consistent long-term returns as opposed to 'very volatile great year, bad year and great year, bad year timing of markets'.

How is all the possible information distilled? They look at what is flagged as 'cheap' by commercial data feeds. 'We will use some screens as a starting point – what looks cheap on price to cash flow, or what's trading at high free cash flow yields, things like that.' But their speciality is to 'dig deeper'. Devreaux and his team have built up considerable institutional knowledge of lots of names, and it is the responsibility of the analysts to know what is going on in their sector. 'We have an analyst group who do our own work internally, and hopefully we have an institutional knowledge of lots of names. We start with a portfolio with stock we own and it's the responsibility of each analyst to know what's going on in their sectors – industries. We have group meetings to compare notes about one area versus another and people generally have an idea about what's going on in the entire portfolio. We are very reactive to news and developments. Portfolios are also determined after team meetings. Every stock has price targets and holding periods can be very long – over many years. There are about 200 names in the portfolio.'

In his interview Devreaux chose to tell me about three decisions in the last year with which he felt satisfied – buying, selling, and re-buying *Car*, selling *Wood*, and selling *Conglom*.

Seeing through the smog

Devreaux's team bought *Car* just over a year before the interview when 'all the news' about the company was 'extremely negative'. It was having issues with one of its biggest suppliers which seemed to be at risk for bankruptcy and which it was rumoured would have serious consequences. But would it? They 'kicked the tyres and did a lot of work' to investigate the 'true' situation before taking a very large stake in *Car* which then rose more than 50 per cent in a few weeks. Having doubled their money, 'we made a decision to exit'. A little later, when there was another series of negative 'newsflow items', involving the decision of a very large shareholder to sell stock in the company which provoked a decline in price, they looked at it again and 're-established the position'. 'It was somewhat controversial', Devreaux emphasised. *'It was not easy going against consensus sentiment'* but 'you know, when we do it right, that's what distinguishes us.'

Devreaux aims to assess where sentiment is wrong and will change. He described how such decisions start with reading lots of financial information. With *Car* it was lots of 'supplemental documentation about pension plans, liabilities, etc., etc., healthcare benefits.' To evaluate the situation one of his team made a number of trips 'meeting with management out there, some conferences, some conversations with the people at senior level, whomever we can talk to – maybe board members, etc. – to try to get as good a feel as we can as to what's going on.' When that's done, and it's 'pretty intensive', there is a team discussion. 'What makes for a good value investor is being able to, sort of, separate out the emotion (not that I don't get emotional) about things that stocks do.'

Devreaux's view is that stocks do not always trade efficiently because people get scared and stocks get stigmatised. Bingham had also made that point in his interview. People feel 'I don't want to own this', said Devreaux. 'It doesn't really matter what the price is, I don't want it.' That is Devreaux's opportunity. 'We come in and ask what that is really worth.' Of course, when there is bad news or real doubt and people do not want to own certain names, Devreaux is very aware that they may be right and his view wrong – 'things can go wrong and it's never 100 per cent.' But he feels 'you know pieces out there' – meaning that he thinks he has a grasp of relevant facts – and on that basis can work out some kind of 'true value'.

A key aspect of his approach is that he tries to calculate the potential down-side that could follow from a purchase 'and limit his investment' to situations where he thinks it is no more than 10 or 15 per cent but balanced by a much bigger 'upside potential'. This is the approach which will 'generate alpha for us' – quantify the downside so 'it's a great risk-reward for us'.

Your head spins

In the *Car* case, they thought the stock was undervalued because investors got frightened and could not manage the complexity of the information available; could not use it carefully to quantify the various complex risks that were applicable. Devreaux said it was partly because that's not that easy to do. 'You know, your head spins when you're trying to quantify healthcare liabilities…pension liabilities…discount rates and what the sensitivities are and what the management options might be', he said. A central point was *Car*'s ability to negotiate with their unions and to try to assess what kinds of concessions they might or might not be able to get. 'You try to put all those pieces together', he said, adding that he thought 'a lot of people don't get to that level of analysis'. On Devreaux's assessment the likelihood of *Car* actually going bankrupt was very limited. That meant the downside risk was capped off so that the risk – reward calculus when buying the shares at their then very low price was good, 'a lot of potential upside and a very limited downside. There was a margin of safety.' Later examples will illustrate a variety of such ways to feel safe.

You can't fall in love!

Devreaux's second and third examples emphasise his view that to be successful his approach had to be 'disciplined', which meant be very careful about getting emotional. For instance, *Conglom* was a European company which they had invested in very successfully and seen transform itself and its stock market valuation. Discipline meant setting a price target for when they would sell and also being aware it was 'not a very liquid stock', meaning that if they sold their very large holding quickly they could bring down the price and hurt themselves. Reducing the position had to be planned and gradual, accepting some loss of additional potential gain. 'You've got to have the discipline to say, what's the level at which you exit a position that's done extremely well'? He was very pleased with how they had managed that with *Conglom* – 'it was a good judgement, a good call'. 'You do get *emotional*, and you *like* names doing well, but you can't *fall in love* with the names.'

Fighting the pain and its difficulties

Of course, not all such decisions work out. Devreaux described times when his investments did not perform as he hoped and other times when he became cautious and then missed out. Two specific examples which he blamed on 'failures of process' involved *Computer* and *Energy*. He had begun buying *Computer* shares just over a year before when the share price was falling. With hindsight he described the decision to buy not as wrong but as made 'too early'. Apparently *Computer* had begun to show signs of operating weakness and its sales volumes were down. One of the analysts had the task of knowing what was happening. After team discussion they decided the market was much too gloomy about the future (too emotional) and started buying the stock. However, quarterly results and news about the whole computer sector worsened, and, with additional competitive threats also emerging, the stock kept sliding. Then *Computer* revealed it had accounting issues. By then the stock was down by a third since they had purchased – 'that's pretty painful', said Devreaux. 'Ten per cent downside is OK, I can manage that', but this was too much.

When a holding falls as much as 25 per cent there is an automatic review. The idea is to reconsider the situation and either act to back their judgement by adding to the holding or to give up. 'If stocks are coming down, if we've done our work, we should be adequately positioned. If we don't have the confidence to be positive then we've probably done something wrong.' In this case they did not and they neither cut their losses nor doubled up, which was the source of his dissatisfaction. After the review Devreaux decided to add a little bit to the position but not enough; he was indecisive. When eventually the stock did have a tremendous recovery he did not benefit enough to make up the loss. He was unhappy: 'Even though I have risked a pretty significant position it hasn't given me much upside'. Essentially he was not able to develop confidence in his thesis when the stock price kept falling. Was it signalling something? 'I was concerned about the accuracy of our analysis, whether we really had our arms around how bad the business could get. I wasn't ready to throw in the towel and say forget it but I was concerned about how bad things could go. Using hindsight we really should have doubled the position at 20... but because I was early it has cost me significant dollars (on a benchmark basis) and a lot of risk with no significant return... It's not good because we are compared to the benchmark every day.... We are judged on a daily, weekly, quarterly, monthly, and yearly basis... it's a permanent loss of capital (to the benchmark there) with no chance to recover it. That's a bad thing. If we do that too many times we will not succeed.'

Why had it happened? Like most managers Devreaux had an explanation: 'It is a company that had gone from being a growth stock which we don't tend to own, to being a good company at an attractive valuation – a value stock. But when that happens there is a dislocation of the shareholder base and for a while it's neither one nor the other.' Having an explanation is likely to be an important part of any manager's coping capacity; it allows them to feel potent even when success eludes them. I will be presenting other examples, including the development of extreme flexibility, in explanation.

They did everything possible but...

Devreaux's second example of a decision that did not satisfy him was *Energy* – a US-based coal company. Here management had let his thesis down. As usual, he had bought their shares when there was negative news, the price was falling and other shareholders were selling. They did their usual research work and valuations. However, after purchase, 'the company proceeded to basically do everything wrong it possibly could, from operational issues to safety issues, to a bunch of things. Management destroyed value and also wasted opportunities or were not quick enough to execute them and the stock got clobbered.' By way of explanation Devreaux said he was again dissatisfied with the valuation work. 'It was not as robust as it should have been. ...' No doubt he had a point; at the same time it was obviously not his view at the moment of decision. Again the important thing seems to be to have an 'explanation'.

Getting buffaloed or not!

Most managers spend a lot of time assessing management, and so did Devreaux. 'You listen to what they say, what's their strategic plan. You know, how do they sound? I mean, do they sound like they know what the hell they're talking about, or do they sound like idiots? Do they sound like they're working for the shareholders, or if they're working for another agenda? I mean, the notion of, you know, maximising shareholder value, whatever that means, there's sort of this generic concept, but, you know, is it returning free cash to shareholders? Is it... is it positioning the balance sheet to, you know, to optimise returns to shareholders, or is it more in the nature of, you know, empire building, or just, you know, wanting to own, you know, the biggest business, or... or just being obstinate about, well, you know, we've been here all along, and this is who we are, and we're not going to change? Or, is it more a sense of, look, you know, we've got these assets, and we've ... our job is to work for the shareholders, which is what we like to hear, and position ourselves to get the best value out of these assets that we possibly can for shareholders?' I have quoted these remarks at length to show the inherent suspiciousness between asset managers and company managers. Listening to them think is a bit like eavesdropping on a group of men or women talking about the unreliability and deviousness of the other sex.

Like many other managers, Devreaux sounded assertive and rather 'masculine' at this point in the interview – as he set out the situation he had to assess. 'There are no sacred cows, you know; basically, everything's on the table, we have a vision, we have a strategy, we have a good team, it's deep, here are other people, you know, here's how we articulate it. I mean, all those things ... you can get buffaloed ... you know, getting snowed, I mean, getting, you know, George Bush looking at Vladimir Putin, you know, I ... I took the measure of the man, right, and then it turns out, you know, what does that mean? So, yeah, I mean, that can happen, so I think it's ... it's not as much, you know, looking the guy in the eye, and saying, you know, do I trust you, as hearing the person out, and ... and then, sort of, comparing what they say with what they do.'

The interview, which took place in late June 2007, ended with Devreaux discussing what was then recognised as 'the current period of high values' and 'how that might end'. He did not mention anxieties about subprime, although the credit crunch was to start a few weeks later. But he did think asset values inflated. 'I think there's some risk in, you know, how it all unfolds, and what the event will be, whether it's, you know, China, or it's, you know, some economic data in the States, or it's war in the Middle East, who the hell knows, but, you know, things happen ... when you're at a [high] level of ... of optimism, in a sense, and froth, success in the marketplace, you know, you're ... you're that much more at risk for those events to have this ... this, you know, ripple effect, of ... of really damaging the market. So, you know, having said that, I'm not predicting that we have some catastrophe, but I think the better things are, you know, in some senses, you know, looking at the last [period], the better things are, the more risk that things are going to get bad. Because there is, you know ... I mean, things don't just go straight up. There are movements up and down, bad things happen, and ... and they will.' Like the others who spoke about it, he was thinking of ordinary ups and downs, not the catastrophic developments which were to occur.

Devreaux's account complements the one from Fred Bingham, filling in further details of the reality of the fund manager's world. He too was far from the calculating demon of standard theory. Assessing market sentiment is crucial to all his calculations. For him 'emotion' is a constant fact of life. It is opportunity and danger. 'Falling in love' or 'hating stocks' is what others in the market do and he tries to profit from this. At the same time, he is in no doubt of the importance of emotion in driving markets. His example of *Computer,* in which he had 'to fight the pain', illustrates how his emotions (his 'concern'), in the context of the pressure on him to perform, sometimes prevented him from acting as rationally and decisively as he planned. His discussion of *Energy* showed that he has the same ambivalent feelings as Bingham about having to be dependent on company management to deliver his expectations.

Duncan Smith

Whereas Devreaux and Bingham focused in different ways on fundamentals, the third manager, Duncan Smith, had his eyes firmly fixed elsewhere: on the mind of the market itself. As mentioned, standard finance theory treats information about stocks as already 'in the price'. It has, therefore, always had some difficulty explaining why the main financial brokerage companies (the sell side) employ such large numbers of highly paid and hotly competed-for financial analysts. If information is in the price, no rational person would pay analysts to offer expert advice on the future of companies and regions, or for issuing 'buy', 'sell', and 'hold' guidance, or predictions and analysis of company results on a quarterly basis – especially since academic finance research shows there are significant questions as to how far they are useful to predict future prices (Mokoaleli-Mokoteli, Taffler et al. 2009).

However, the approach that Smith and others like him adopt provides some hints as to why managers might pay for such services and their value. Although those I interviewed unanimously declared that they regarded the stream of views emanating from these analysts and pundits about the predicted future values of stock as prejudiced, inaccurate, ill-informed, trend-following, or merely unreliable and lazy, they subscribed to their expensive services and clearly saw them as useful. The reason, to judge by Smith's interview (and, in fact, Devreaux's comments about *newsflow),* is that managers do not use analysts and news items to tell them about the fundamentals of the underlying investment opportunities (which they think they can assess for themselves), but to help them to know what others are thinking.

In fact, one could say that Smith based his entire strategy on sensing market sentiment and predicting where it would go next – once people had digested the news he thought he had ahead of them. Smith had been in fund management for 28 years and was personally responsible for $18 billion in UK funds. Some was private client money, but most was from pension funds with different risk profiles. His funds were judged against the United Kingdom all-share index. The team to which he contributed had 13 members. Each person was a sector analyst and a portfolio manager and together they managed about

$50 billion. His university majors were in economics and maths. His sector responsibilities were in pharmaceuticals, healthcare, and oil exploration.

Like Bingham, Smith can invest in any UK company but the mission strategy he uses is to look out for change which is going to get in the news: 'We have daily meetings to discuss stocks and what things are changing, so it's a continuous process of reassessing what you hold, and why you hold it. You're looking for where things are changing for the better, or for worse, and that would affect your view of the relative attractiveness of an individual stock against others in the portfolio, or others that you don't own at all, so it's all about relative attractiveness. ... '

To make those decisions (unlike Devreaux) he starts from the standard economics idea mentioned: 'the current share price reflects the information' in the market. His mission strategy is based on the idea his company has (quite legal) access to information that isn't there yet and so can profit by being ahead. He thinks he gets this privileged position by using his prestigious asset management's firm name to talk to senior people in the companies he is thinking to buy or sell, by talking to other companies who are in similar industries, by talking to 'my colleagues from overseas who look at similar companies', and by taking a view on the economy. At the same time he looks at what is being said about these companies in the news. In this way he builds a picture of what the market is expecting and what he thinks will happen. If 'the market is expecting scenario X, but in your opinion, with all this work, it's actually going to be worse than scenario X, then the market ultimately will be disappointed and that will cause the share price to fall. So it's building up that picture of what the market is expecting, and where do we think the market is wrong.' The principle is straightforward. If Smith thinks the market is overoptimistic on a stock he will tend to sell shares (go underweight), and if he thinks the market is too pessimistic, or too cautious in the outlook, he buys shares (or goes overweight).

In his interview in late August 2007, Smith spoke about three decisions he had made in the past year which satisfied him.

They always surpass their targets

Taking the example of *Well-managed-oil*, Smith explained how he had noticed that, historically, the management had regularly forecast quarterly earnings growth lower than they actually achieved. 'Six months ago they said they thought, because they're earning between 10 per cent and 15 per cent this year, they would grow their sales 10 per cent, or 15 per cent again. When I looked through all the stock market analysts, they were all going for 10 per cent, and the management, a few months later said, well, actually, we don't think we will grow at 10 per cent to 15 per cent, it's going to be 15 per cent to 20 per cent. Next time all the analysts going for 10 per cent went for 14 per cent, or 15 per cent.' But the industry was still very buoyant and 'their momentum' was very strong.

Smith thought this pattern of always announcing less than they achieve would continue and so felt confident that at least 'they were going to beat 15 per cent'. He was right. In fact 'they actually produced 35 per cent, so that was miles ahead of expectations'. The point was he noticed how in the context of the company itself being cautious 'the analysts were being far too cautious in their estimates'. His idea was that 'when the company reported its earnings, sentiment would be pleasantly surprised, and people would upgrade their estimates', so he bought the stock before everyone else. 'The stock went up on that news … it went up 6 per cent yesterday, and it was up a couple of per cent today, and it went up the day before that.'

Asked why he thought the analysts themselves didn't see the argument he was putting forward, Smith explained his edge. He said he thought it required a more open mind. He thought growth fund managers or value fund managers were anchored on their particular frameworks or had preconceptions about the size of companies they would look at, and 'so you'll get people who will filter stocks out of their universe'. He doesn't operate like that; 'I'll look at anything, and we, as a team, look at anything, to try to decide where we think the market is wrong.'

He added that he thought financial analysts were always worrying that they might look daft. 'You'll find that City stockbrokers tend to follow company guidance, because they don't like going out on a limb, in case they're wrong. They always tend to lag the story, if you see what I mean, and that's where we can add value, by seeing where we think they're wrong. So *Well-managed-oil* is a good example – what with what the company was saying and their track record, 'the analysts were not giving them any benefit of the doubt! They'd already beaten the numbers three or four times.'

The scorecard

The 350 companies he could be investing in are those Bingham was scrutinising too. How does Smith manage the potential overflow of information? 'With the best will in the world', he said, 'it's not easy to look at 350 companies every day'. He narrows down using a summary spreadsheet device (the 'scorecard') used throughout his firm. It is prepared for them and takes commercially produced quantitative data feeds and analyses what is happening before 'flagging up' which companies to go and search into more. Smith said he uses it but insists 'he is not driven by it'. He is a little sceptical; 'like any spreadsheet of data, if you get a bug in the system, or somebody puts a wrong number in, you just get rubbish out at the end. …' But he does think it's a 'good crosscheck', a filter, to say, 'Well, that one's looking interesting. I don't own that, so I should go and speak to my analyst, and say, why is the scorecard saying that, and do you think that's wrong, so get a conversation going. Because as I say, my analyst could be a seller of the stock, for various reasons, and the scorecard makes it look attractive, but you start that conversation, so that's the way I do it'.

So although the scope of the potential information overload is clear to Smith, the company's mission statement focus on what is changing is the handle on it. 'You can't look at 350 companies every day, in detail. But because we're looking for things changing, it's easier. It's a constant process of looking at that company and saying, are things still improving?' For him stock prices are signals – he says he really has to sit down and ask what stock prices are telling him: 'is that right, or is that wrong?' If he thinks a price is wrong he will 'run the story', meaning he will try to understand what it is. One of the characteristics of financial assets mentioned in the last chapter is that their value is always in question so that valuation is a constant process. Smith keeps looking. 'You look at the valuation, and say, well, it was on 15 times, and it's now on 17 times, and is that still justified by what I think is going to happen?' He rehearses what might be happening in his mind. A management may have 'told the market they can do this, they've then updated their expectations, and is that still being too cautious? ... It's just running the whole process again, just at a different price level.'

Although telling about *Well-managed-oil* clearly indicated Smith's emotional involvement, he wanted to emphasise, like Devreaux, that any successful manager had to take emotion out from what s/he was doing. The scorecard 'uses a number of factors that we've back-tested ... to be predictive of stock price performance. ... *That takes a lot of the emotion out of it, because it's just numbers, and rankings, and all these factors are ranked.'*

Stories

Smith was just quoted as mentioning 'running the story' and like the first two managers I have described it is clear that managers make sense of the situations they encounter by creating narratives about events and that this then enables them to commit to action – cognitively and emotionally. In fact Smith used the word 'story' often. As prices go up and down he said he was constantly reassessing, as he put it, whether the stock he is thinking about is still 'a valid story'. In his thought process it seemed that one story is linked to and compared to other stories. He is always asking himself does this 'story still work' or are there conflicting or 'better stories' in which he should be investing?

The screens on Smith's desk and his 'scorecard' tell him what's moving, and if he is speaking to a company tomorrow, he says can renew his interpretation of 'the vigour of their story'. If one stock goes up 10 per cent, and another stock goes down 10 per cent, it then raises the question, well, I still like that story, but is this a better one, because the share price has moved that way. 'So it's all relative and it's like constant motion'.

This way of thinking and making sense of financial data in terms of the stories behind them seems to lie at the heart of what most fund managers do – as we shall see further in the next Chapter 5. Meanwhile, what about Smith's unsuccessful decisions? One involved a company called *Outfits* and once again assessments of management and then a sense of betrayal were at the heart of the interview 'narrative'.

A company that didn't care!

Outfits was a company Smith invested in after meeting the management. 'I thought the story was a sound one: they're a very good sports retailer, and I thought the valuation looked fine.' What he hadn't counted on was the behaviour of 'the guy who ran the business'. 'I think he is a very good retailer, but he's a bit of a maverick. He tends to still run it like it's his company, and it's not. He owns 57 per cent.' The problem was that 'he could get away with' being a maverick in the private arena (when his company was not quoted on the stock market) but not in the public one. He just acted from his own volition and would 'buy stakes in other companies and all that stuff, and I hadn't really expected that'. There were other issues too. 'Obviously the weather hasn't helped sports retailers. Also the fact that the company wasn't really helping analysts, in terms of people kept saying, I'm not sure about the numbers, but they wouldn't talk to them about them'. Creating uncertainty 'is the one guarantee for shares to fall', said Smith. He then elaborated like the other managers on how price functions as a signal that something is amiss with one's case. 'I bought stock at the IPO, at £3, and I bought more, all the way down to £2.70. But they are now £1.40.' He still couldn't believe it and can't bring himself to take the full loss. 'I've sold some, but I've still got some, but that's been a bit of a disaster, really.' Smith told me how 'you keep thinking I'll get a better chance to cut my loss'. When things did not improve, Smith, like Bingham and Devreaux, felt betrayed. He realised 'the company didn't seem to care what was happening to the share price, because they weren't communicating with us. We met the finance director and he was awful. From a finance director you expect certain disciplines, and he didn't seem to have them, and then there was the trading thing, you know, the weather has been rotten, and people are not buying sports goods. 'I just thought I don't need this.'

Could anything be learned? Smith, like the other managers, has some kind of explanation but not one from which it would be easy to learn. 'It's probably a reinforcement, rather than a learning, but investing in companies where the founder is still the majority shareholder, you have to have your eyes open that they may still consider it their company. Over the years you saw it with people like Robert Maxwell, and all these guys where it was their company. Yeah, sometimes the market operates in the greater fools' area.'

There has to be trust!

Worries about how to trust in management featured in Smith's interview, as it did in the three earlier and in most others. 'There has to be trust', he said, but quickly added 'one can be surprised'. So doubt is everywhere. 'Enron was a big example, or WorldCom. People trusted them.' He then told a story about another 'perfectly good company'. In this case the management were 'perfectly sound, very trustworthy' but then they discovered fraud in one of their divisions. 'It wasn't the management who was carrying out the fraud, but they discovered it.' He went on to elaborate how difficult it is to know what is really going on. 'With the best will in the world there are lots of people much brighter than me out there, looking at accounts, and if they can't spot it, how can I? If somebody wants to pull the wool over your eyes they can do it for quite a long time.'

Smith explained his feelings: 'You don't trust them again for a long time, you don't want your fingers burnt, and there have been companies like that in the dim and distant past, who have said one thing and done another, and you think, well, hold on, do I really want to be dealing with these guys? '

Could actually meeting management be useful? 'It's crosschecking…I mean they're not going to tell us anything that they're not going to tell anyone else, so in some ways it's how you ask the question.' But again, like the other managers, Smith becomes assertive at this point of the discussion. It must be 'you driving the agenda, and not letting them drive the agenda'. Like many of the other managers he then described how companies would come in with a big flashy pack of handouts but he and his colleagues would refuse to spend their time on that or a glossy PowerPoint. They would insist 'we just want to ask you these questions' and then try to check consistency. 'When you see them again, well, you can say well, you told us this last time and this hasn't happened, and why not? You're telling us this now and why should we believe that?' He and his colleagues have been trained on the kinds of things you can ask, and how to ask them, and that kind of thing, 'but at the end of the day you're forming a view based on, not just what they tell you, but based on your experience of them, of similar companies, and of the industry, so that's really what we do'. Smith told me quite emotionally, 'It's a challenge, but there's not a job I can think of that would allow me to meet these kinds of people…and grill them on, you said this, but that's what happened.' He found it exciting to meet the heads of very large and well-known companies and 'it makes it a fascinating job; you get to meet all these guys that run the economy, basically'. Other managers said the same and for many the human contact is clearly a key part of the experience although the 'quant' managers I saw tended to avoid it as a source of bias.

Business risk

Smith worked in a company whose funds were targeted to be in the top quartile of performers. To do this they focused strongly on what stocks were in the basket that made up the index and then made decisions to be under- or overweight in them. In doing so they were defining risk (as just implied) as the risk of being beaten by competitors. In consequence they were also operating within constraints as to how far they could diverge from the index basket set by the client mandates – the idea behind marketing funds is that clients and their advisers have different risk-reward preferences and tolerances and that the mission statements of funds provide them with options. Clients might be willing to risk doing 3, 4, or 5 per cent (etc) worse than the index in order to do 3, 4, or 5 per cent (etc.) better. Funds were designed accordingly. How were such things calculated? Smith explained that companies historically have shown volatility against the market, and so risk tolerances are devised for portfolios using statistical methods which assume normal distributions and calculate the proportions of each stock to hold so that what he ends up with has a 95 per cent chance of being either plus or minus 2 per cent, or 3 per cent.

As we will see in further chapters, working in this kind of institutional context could exert a considerable influence. For Smith, reflecting the structure in which he works, risk was relative and his performance was always on his mind even after all these years. One interesting aspect of his account, which will be taken up in a later chapter at length, was that he identified a conflict due to the asymmetrical attitudes he expected from clients.

Calculations about proportions of stock 'can't tell you whether you're going to be up or down' which he said was a problem. He illustrated his idea by mentioning a hypothetical situation where a client might take a long-term view and want his portfolio to take more risk to create the chance of outperformance – for instance being prepared to do 5 per cent worse than the index in order to do 5 per cent better. The trouble was, he thought, clients were not likely to be consistent when it came to losing 5 per cent rather than gaining it. He was not going to be equally rewarded by the risks he took. 'The risk is, if I underperform by 5 per cent' they take money away but 'if I outperform by 5 per cent' they're pleased but 'I don't get any more money off them'. He called this business risk. 'One of the problems is that people don't think of the downside, whereas we, as fund managers, have to be aware of the downside, and the business risk of underperforming. That's not to say that you don't do the things that are going to produce the outperformance, but you just have to be aware that the more risk you're taking the bigger the business risk, if you like.'

Devreaux was quoted above commenting about his performance being public 'every day' and he mentioned how this influenced his thinking. Smith hinted at the same conflict when he said that he could see his performance on screen daily but that 'I try not to look at it', adding that 'some people' are obsessed by it. He then mentioned that, in his view, clients were obsessed with the short term, which worried him; he added that he thought this could be managed if the story was right. 'As long as you can explain why you're doing what you're doing, and why you think it will work, they're not going to sack you after three months, six months, nine months, or a year. If, after a year it's still not working, it gets harder to keep saying, that will be right, that will be right, but fortunately I haven't had to do that for quite a while.' Being able to tell a story was important here too.

George Monroe

The last manager to be discussed, George Monroe, works for another well-known major international house. I interviewed him in late June 2007 in the United States. His company was also focused very definitely on 'beating' benchmark competitors so that the proportions of holdings were strictly governed by mandates.

Monroe had been in the industry for 15 years and had been a portfolio manager for ten. He was also part of a team. However, unlike Bingham and his colleagues who combined their own experience and analytical capacities with data provided from brokers, like Smith and Devreaux, Monroe and his team all functioned simultaneously as portfolio managers and expert industry sector analysts – in this case dividing up the different areas of the US economy between them. Monroe analysed utilities and consumer staples. His own portfolios amounted to over $3 billion and the team as a whole look after $35 billion. They are part of a very large financial company running several different strategies other than stock-picking.

An accountant by training, Monroe was a little withdrawn and suspicious in the interview but warmed to it as he told me his 'stories' in which he was very much involved. He says he enjoys what is hard, painstaking work.

Monroe was again faced with the information overload I have mentioned and particularly so as he was very anxious to do a lot of hard work to get the detail. His way to limit his information universe was first through his US and industry sector focus and then again by using mission themes. In his own mind he looks for situations that others will be too lazy really to look into by undertaking painstaking accounting analysis. He thought of himself as a dedicated artist. His US utility companies are selected with a regulation theme similar to that used by Bingham – which companies are going to benefit from anticipated changes in the regulatory environment? Otherwise, and again like Bingham, he looks at management. He also reads trade newspapers like *Megawatt Daily* in great detail.

Like the other three, Monroe volunteered that he takes it for granted that the market is strongly influenced by emotional factors, but his mission is to use his accounting skills to 'take some of the emotion out of it'. His financial analysis aims to assess price targets for the stock to buy or hold. It is discussed with the full team before being accepted.

Exciting decisions

Notwithstanding his argument about keeping emotion out, Monroe's examples were all rather exciting narratives. The three decisions which had most satisfied Monroe in the last 12 months involved the purchase of a supermarket chain (*Goodfoods*), a restaurant company (*Fastfoods*), and a tobacco company (*Greatsmoke*). All were performing very well and he was visibly excited telling me about them. He was clearly very pleased to be able to talk about all his very hard work but embarrassed to tell me how he would visit some of 'his' restaurants and other companies at weekends or on the way to work to 'see what was going on'.

Monroe had invested in *Goodfoods* after a visit to talk with management which had also been attended by other investors. He had followed this up with detailed arithmetical analysis of information. It was all in the public realm and it wasn't a 'complex company'. But most of his competitors had been too 'lazy to do the work'. Admittedly, he said, it wasn't easy work. It was hard and it had to be done in August when everyone else was on holiday: 'I had to pull a lot of resources together to get this report out and to make sure I understood the numbers and the trajectory of the numbers... nobody else wanted to spend the two weeks to do it... just chose not to do it'.

As Monroe elaborated, it was clear that he established very personal and special relationships to stocks. 'I felt an obligation to try to understand it... it just couldn't be this pool of dark black, this black hole... I *had* to sort of look at it.' In fact, the company's potential was not obvious at first. 'I didn't see anything.' But he had then met the management and noticed how confident they seemed to be. 'There were 75 people in the room and a 30-page book.' They seemed 'pretty confident' and it looked like 'they know what they're doing'. A bit later, in August, when he didn't 'have any great ideas in the pipeline', he did more work. 'I was invited out to see them. I said, sure, it's August, nothing's going on... it's one of those exhausting get up at 6 am... get back at 12:30 a.m. at night jobs.' He became '*wildly intrigued*' and started doing an '*incredible* amount of detailed work'. The management team 'had bought by acquisition selectively and handpicked what they felt were all the best of another company's assets.' I thought 'I've really *got* to do it. ...' But first he had to overcome doubts. 'They had published pro forma models with very high margins and I didn't really understand how the margins could be so high.' None of the competitors had those kinds of margins. But the CEO's answer had been 'when you go and you handpick stores, you can create this kind of margin dynamic'. Apparently if you went to any supermarket chain and handpicked the best stores, 'you're going to have stores with these high margin dynamics'. Monroe combined 'the pro forma of the old company with the new', a task that was complicated because *Goodfoods* didn't have calendar-year-end results and because accounting requirements forced them to recognise all of the expenses associated with the takeover transaction but none of the revenues. 'So the numbers were very, very messy'.

The hard work added to the excitement, and then Monroe went to another meeting with all the management division heads from around the country 'which I thought was impressive'. He got to talk to the person in charge of the West, the person in charge of the East, the person in charge of the North, and they 'were sort of impressive guys who felt like they would keep, keep their eye on the ball, and keep the operation sort of running smoothly'.

Along with excitement security now came in. 'The key wasn't in my mind that the business had to grow dramatically, the key was that you just *couldn't* mess it up. And, I think, they understood, that their objective was to…not to mess it up.' 'When I put the numbers down, the, the numbers worked, if they just didn't mess it up we were going to make a, a tremendous amount of money…that's what got me very excited.' He bought the stock which subsequently did very well. Monroe's other two experiences of success involved similar and excited stories full of personal involvement which will feature in later chapters.

They just left

We now turned to an example where Monroe was not satisfied. As in the case of *Goodfoods, My Utility* was a company which had acquired other companies and whose management team Monroe considered had exceptional ability. After the acquisitions they cut costs and made the acquisitions work. Others had not understood that this could happen because the accounts had some complications which it took work and skill to unravel. So the stock had been underpriced. 'There was a valuation discrepancy between this company and most of the other peers because the business model was a little bit different.' Apparently they had a training business and a small marketing business some investors judged might be more volatile, and therefore less predictable and therefore deserving of a lower multiple. 'My argument was this management team was very good and that multiple disparity would eventually close.' It all went as planned for a while but others in the market never saw it the same way and the multiple never really closed. Then 'very senior people, like, the two most senior people left, not because there was a numbers issue or anything like that' but for better jobs. 'In the span of a three-month time frame I've never seen anything like that in my career.' How did he explain it? 'It's a fault of the Board.…I don't at all subscribe to the notion that it's just sort of bad luck for the company. The Board should have prevented it from happening. You loved this management team, you thought they would do exactly the right thing for you, you thought they would extract this value. They were putting this culture in, they ostensibly have the relationships with the regulators and they're both gone…the two most senior people are both gone…it just became a slow sort of mediocre kind of name…and so that was sort of disappointing.' The stock had not 'blown-up' or 'cratered'. It was just a poor performer. 'You would never imagine.…I've never in my entire career had two senior…two of the most senior executives walk out in a three-month time frame of a company that was executing brilliantly.' Like the other three managers he was clearly feeling betrayed.

In summary, George Monroe's interview gives a picture of someone who is very dedicated to what he does and who, despite striving to use his analytical skills to make what he thinks of as unemotional decisions, actually got very excited and involved with his stocks. His success stories as well as his failures have the same hallmark – a search effort to reach deep understanding of companies and company management and in doing so to feel he has found what might be called an unrecognised story, preferably with all the risks of what might go wrong somehow divested elsewhere. Monroe was somewhat uncomfortable at revealing the depth of his interest. He contrasted his willingness to do more than those other investors 'on the Street' and was again a bit uncomfortable when admitting his view that in fact he thought he did think of most other investors as 'lazy'.

I mentioned above that Monroe thinks of himself as an artist. At one point in the interview he told me what really sums up his ideas about how he works. He said he was just at a conference two weeks before and had probably had ten meetings with different managements. Seven or eight of the meetings were 'true one on ones…just, just myself and the management team'. He then has what he thinks of as a 'true conversation'. It wasn't that he got any illegal information. It was more that he got the picture. To explain further he interrupted himself to talk about a famous photographer he had once seen. She had said something that was sort of brilliant, he thought. She was rehearsing how she had once been asked why are you…so good? She had been somewhere the week before standing with her five assistants and she had said, 'Isn't this amazing'. An assistant had said to her, 'I don't see anything', to which she replied, 'That's why you're not me'. 'I think this business is somewhat like that, I mean, even in our conversations internally I'll present on a stock…for instance I'll do 15 pages on it. I will say this is the best thing I have seen in a couple of years, and three other people on this team, at this firm, who are very, very smart can say, I don't see that at all. So, so you, you meet with these managements, they talk about their business and it's what you…what you sort of take away from that meeting that, that either makes you successful or sort of not successful.'

Emerging themes

The four interviews provided qualitative data. They reveal the key elements of the context assert managers face due to the characteristics of financial assets I have mentioned.

First, the interviews show the importance of uncertainty. Each of the four respondents was faced with very large quantities of data which had fundamentally uncertain implications. As Devreaux stated explicitly, once a choice was clear it was easy and no longer important. All four managers described the vast array of potential information they might absorb – a context accentuated in the global electronic age of minute-by-minute reporting, blogging, and opinion-guessing. The information they had was always *both* too much to be examined exhaustively and never enough to give any certainty about choices.

A particularly important source of data they used to make inferences about what was happening were price movements. In standard economic theory prices clear the market. In the financial markets to which my respondents related price changes were taken to be a signal of something happening in the market that required an explanation – a source of rumour, doubt, or excitement and an indicator of what others might be doing. So Devreaux described struggling with what the fall in *Computer's* shares meant for his thesis and Bingham told me that when prices fall he thinks 'the market may be telling' him something. Time after time unexpected price movements caused uncertainty, doubt, and anxiety in the face of which holding to their previous theses was often difficult. Upward movements in shares they did not own suggested the possibility they were missing out. Downward movements in those they did own suggested the possibility of error. Their descriptions underline the decision context created by the characteristics of financial assets. Because they are volatile, abstract, and hard to value, efforts to trade them readily engage primitive human mental functioning in which doubt and anxiety about loss are interspersed with excitement and hope of gain. We might think of observable price movements in the market as the human equivalent of the sudden movements detected by animals in their peripheral vision. On the African plains such movements or other sense-detectable changes cause edginess and possible stampedes among the herds. The descriptions have shown that to hold on to an individual thesis requires nerve and commitment. It may be easier to cut and run.

Second, the interviews show how when each of these four managers bought and sold stock it made sense to think they were making and breaking emotional attachments. Stocks were 'loved' and 'hated' as well as 'liked' and 'disliked'. Many comments implied thinking and inference saturated with emotion. Devreaux talked of 'true' prices and Monroe of 'true one on ones' to assess the worth of management – 'just myself and the management team'. For him a 'true conversation' would reveal true worth. Again, like Monroe, Bingham talked of 'undiscovered stories' to which he felt he had special access and of a 'lovely business'. Smith talked of the special pleasure in meeting the men and women who run industry. In a somewhat different but related vein Devreaux looked for companies who were 'out of favour' and Monroe about 'loving' a management team who 'you thought...would do exactly the right thing for you'. Attachment relationships were clearly potentially ambivalent. All four managers talked of company managements whom they trusted or who disappointed them in terms of betrayal. Their stories may remind readers of archetypal human stories such as the 'ugly duckling', 'frog prince', or Superman. In essence it does seem not unreasonable to think in terms of love affairs that are imagined, made, and broken.

Third, the replies from all these four managers show a constant influence from the fact that asset managers are not isolated atoms but members of human social groups. Markets are social entities in which actors orient their behaviour to others. Asset managers are institutionally employed with clients inside a culture and social structure. Duncan Smith's whole strategy was based on an orientation to what others were thinking. '*It was not easy going against consensus sentiment*', Devreaux said. Smith's situation and Devreaux's comment illustrate how the experience of all four respondents is saturated with uncertainty and consequent anxiety about what others are thinking, even if sometimes they claimed to be better at handling it than others. Price movements were one source of anxiety as we have seen, but it went much further. Managers were in an institutional context where they were expected to be exceptional and to beat the market. They had to manage their experience of the felt consequences on their performance and their choices of all kinds of news on a day-to-day basis. They were making decisions which were inherently at risk of being wrong which invariably rested on claims, expressed via their stories, to the effect that they knew something exceptional that others didn't. But they knew this was uncertain. The problem was that although they could really be ahead of the consensus, as their story suggested, they could not afford to be permanently out on a limb. They bought excellent prospects at low prices. Prices had to come back their way for it to work out. Similarly, being rational and less influenced by emotion than others was all very well as long as the market eventually came round to their view. So they knew that all their claims were inherently questionable. Others might know more than they did, or they might have been misled. And even if they were still confident when things didn't look obviously good, maybe those looking at their performance would lose faith. Devreaux said his performance and even his stock holdings were public and 'we are compared to the benchmark every day'. Such transparency is one way institutions have responded to the potential agency problems clients face with fund managers. Managers had to cope with their experience of their successes and failures themselves and also had to anticipate and cope with the experience of this on their clients. Part of this coping was to claim they had ways to 'take the emotion out' in one way or another. Another aspect was to have some ready explanations. The four just described had 'stories' about what had gone wrong or could be learned. Their analysis was 'not robust enough', we just got in 'too early', and so on. These explanations seem to perform an emotional and morale-boosting task. Conviction has to be maintained, because it is essential to do the job. An indecisive fund manager would be as much use as a pilot with vertigo. So Smith, for instance, could weave stories that he could use to trump other competing stories. More generally, managers found tales to tell which supported them in the necessary belief that they could continue to be exceptional, and also stories to help them to explain and manage failure. They often blamed themselves *ex post* for things when it was often hard to know what they could have done about *ex ante*. But to do otherwise might cause a loss of nerve. It would make the next decision very difficult to make at all. The four managers' explanations of failure were not convincing if studied carefully. We can see, if we view the explanations as *covering stories*, that is as efforts to organize discordant facts to make them feel what they are doing makes sense, that what they achieved was to allow respondents to maintain their morale and to shift aside difficult questions evoking potentially uncomfortable feelings.

Fourth, as the last point just made emphasises, all four respondents made sense of their situation by telling stories. Stories about their overall approach protected them from information overload by trying to define what information they could legitimately ignore and therefore the terms on which they are evaluated. All the managers and all asset management companies have public investment strategies which they advertise. Sensing that they could not absorb all information and focus on every asset in every market, their stories were a frame which enabled them to convince themselves about the validity of what they chose to concentrate on and to feel comfortable. They were doing what human beings mostly do. They create narrative rationales to bolster and support their selective search focus. Such rationales made sense of their selections and thought processes and appeared to enable them (and, in their minds, also those of their superiors and their clients) to *feel* that what they were doing was coherent. It cut the universe of information about which to be concerned down to a manageable size. Thus, asked how they thought they could be successful in a competitive market on a consistent basis, they outlined to themselves and others what was their public narrative.

Stories also support their individual actions. They provide the conviction necessary to hold a position through time and changing events and become part of an imagined relationship they establish to assets stretching into the future. Some common elements can be noticed in these stories. The scripts, for example Bingham's about Amazing Glass, tend to provide support for the idea a particular asset is in some way exceptional and also a secure choice.

The picture these four interviews paint will be elaborated in later chapters and tested for wider validity by presenting findings from randomly generated examples from the other interviews. The picture depicted is of a context for financial decision-making creating ongoing uncertainty and so inherent and ongoing cognitive and emotional conflicts for the individuals and institutional systems concerned. It seems likely a range of interdisciplinary thinking may help to understand this context better. Before going further, therefore, the next chapter will focus on subjects that have not hitherto attracted much attention even from behavioural economists – namely what sociology, psychology, and cognitive neuroscience can tell us about how narrative, groups, and mental states influence human thinking and decision-making, particularly under uncertainty.

3
Narratives, Minds, and Groups

This chapter offers a rather brief review of what we currently know about the role of narrative in everyday life and how emotion and feeling states influence how we think, particularly in groups. The treatment can only be frugal. The issues involved range across several disciplines and are immensely complex so it is impossible to do more than sketch out some possible lines of thought.

Narrative in everyday life

My four respondents had to commit to action in a situation where outcomes were uncertain. The fact that they supported their actions by telling stories weaving together reason and emotion to feel comfortable will, therefore, be unsurprising to many psychologists and cognitive scientists, let alone to social scientists or psychoanalysts. The word narrative has two etymological roots – telling (*narrare*) and 'knowing in some particular way' (*gnarus*). The two are so intertwined they cannot be untangled. Bruner (2003) uses this point to summarise the importance of narrative particularly for giving us ready and supple means for dealing with the uncertain outcomes of our plans and anticipations – citing Aristotle to note that the impetus to narrative is expectation gone awry – *peripeteaia*, or trouble. Among other possible functions, narratives provide a vocabulary of meaning to support and legitimate action (Mills 1940) and to deal with misfortune.

The extensive academic literature on narrative ranges from modern cognitive neuroscience, through developmental psychology and studies of artificial intelligence, to social anthropology and literary studies, as well as to psychoanalysis. It is clear that telling stories is a fundamental human activity whose importance is increasingly recognised. In fact it is so automatic and so much part of human life that the 'ways of telling and the ways of conceptualizing that go with them are so habitual that they finally become recipes for structuring experience itself' (Bruner 2004). I shall draw attention to a few central points about storytelling that may help in thinking about the findings from the last chapter and those to come.

First, from the narrative perspective the psychological concepts of selective attention and perception underlying the experimental results drawn on for the heuristics of behavioural economics should not be understood as evidence of error or faulty thinking. Current thinking across disciplines suggests the world is not out there waiting to be correctly represented inside us. Rather we find it as we act. We see the world as we set out to find in it what we are motivated to look for and much of the time it works (Berthoz and Petit 2008).

Second, the key point is that telling stories is part of planning. Plans are stories projected into the future. The case that they should be viewed as *the* elementary neuropsychic unit of human consciousness and action is not new. It was made 40 years ago (Miller, Galanter et al. 1960). Of course, planning clearly requires moderately well-established expectations about how nature works and, even more important, how others will respond. Plans, like the decisions Bingham and the others made in the last chapter, can succeed, become modified, or fail. When it's the latter it's either because we didn't know enough or because of the way we knew things.

Third, the psychoanalytic concepts of the *phantastic object* and *ambivalent object relationships* that I have suggested are useful to understand behaviour in financial markets have at their heart the idea of unconscious phantasy. Looked at closely this concept is very close to what Miller and his colleagues mean by a plan. Unconscious phantasies are the basic building blocks of mental life conceived to exist on the boundary of biology and psychology (Spillius 2001). They can be thought of as providing an inner template of the stories we tell ourselves about ourselves and others and what we are doing and planning to do beyond immediate awareness. Beneath the surface of consciousness individuals are always imagining (enacting unconscious phantasies) of what is happening in their *object relations* with others. They conceive the imagined actions they are taking towards others or others are taking towards them. Unconscious phantasies accompany and help to endow with meaning experiences of gratification and frustration or indeed anticipations of either. They form the basic template for action whether in actuality or only in imagination. In *object relations* we are representing ourselves as doing such things as loving, hating, beating, fearing, humiliating, admiring, blaming, criticising, and envying others, and, of course, also imagining them feeling all such things towards us.

Fourth, the extent to which the mind works through narrative, in a metaphorical sense at least, now appears to be more extensive even than psychoanalysts conceived. The neuroscientist, Damasio, suggests that even our brains should be thought of as 'natural storytellers' (Damasio 2004). This is because, as in narrative, neural processes are dynamically and continuously organising our perceptions and memories by, as he put it, putting one thing in front of another over time, based both on what is happening and what is learned or known. In this way the brain is active, constantly organising elements into a 'narrative' in a structural sense very similar to the way we tell ourselves stories. It corrects and builds up the 'story' by fitting it to existing conceptual categories and changing concepts. Adjustments are made all the time through a process of continual readjustment, building concepts and conceptual categories by manipulating the memories we have of objects or situations. He makes the point that concepts are not abstract entities. They are always based on the experience of unique events which are then pulled together on the same axis – for example, as sad events or exciting events. He makes the point that proof that changes in concepts are taking place all the time beneath consciousness can be demonstrated in a simple fashion by asking people to think of an aeroplane or car and noticing how the image that comes is most likely of a specific recent model. As cars have changed we have been rebuilding our concepts of cars, modifying them without realising it.

Fifth, beyond the way our brain and basic, cognitive memory and perceptual systems work in what can be thought of as a narrative way, interesting studies have shown not only that people think in stories all the time but that stories function in a fast and frugal way like a language. Extensive research by Roger Schank (1990), for example, shows how people understand what they apprehend in the world in terms of the stories that they have already understood. New events or problems are understood by reference to old, previously understood stories and explained to others by the use of stories. We typify situations according to social and cultural norms and then fit the appropriate 'scripts' to them. These make mental processing easier because, for example, instead of having to figure out how all the details of what to do every time you enter a restaurant, you know the restaurant script and only have to play your part. Fitting events to existing stocks of stories is, therefore, a fast and frugal way to recognise what is happening and 'know' what to do.

Sixth, narrative also serves to establish identity. Bruner argues that stories lay down routes into memory not only for guiding the life narrative up to the present but also for directing it into the future. 'A life as led is inseparable from a life told', he says, or still more bluntly a life not 'how it is' but how it is interpreted and reinterpreted, 'told and re-told' (Bruner 2004 p708). Like Freud's concept of psychic reality, Bruner's idea of narrative formulates the role of subjectivity in action. Reality is constructed according to narrative principles (Bruner 1991).

Seventh, the fact that emotion, intuition, and gut feelings functioning well below consciousness are powerful influences on human decision-making has now become commonplace. But it would be wrong to imply either that decisions are irrational (at least in the broad sense of pursuing means-end relationships rationally) or that we do not also use reason. In fact an outstanding and controversial question is exactly how to conceptualise the way judgements (thoughts) are based on reasoning, on the one hand, and intuition and affect, on the other. One traditional way of thinking is to suppose there two opposed systems within our mental architecture as supposed in both standard and behavioural economics which contrast rational and irrational. Another is to think that these are merely different modes available within the same toolbox we call the human mind.

Evidence of the complex systemic linkages observed extensively between different parts of the brain over the last 15 years (some of which I will review below) suggests that the notion of dual mental systems is likely to mislead. Rather than posit two separate mental systems, it was Bruner (1986) again who proposed that two modes of knowing are available, reflecting two ways that the mind makes it possible to interpret the signals of reality it notices and to decide things are true. The first mode of knowing, the narrative mode, is context-rich. In contrast, the second, the paradigmatic-abstract mode, aims at being context-free – as in economic models. The narrative mode is based on the spatial and temporal ordering of experience, whereas the paradigmatic mode aims at superseding the limiting dimensions of time and space. The power to render tangible basic dimensions of experience in narrative is in contrast with the power to generalize beyond them in logic. It orders observation and emotional responses and serves to establish conviction about truth – 'truth-likeness', verisimilitude, or believability. Like Gigerenzer (2007) with his idea of gut feelings, Bruner stresses these are not inherently contradictory or opposed processes but complementary ones using their own operating principles designed for a specific ecology – the narrative mode being particularly adaptive and effective in situations of uncertainty or in relations between human beings. The idea, in fact, is that evolution has provided us with two different but essential toolsets to evaluate data according to context and that social norms will determine which is more appropriate in which situation (see Keren and Schul 2010).

In summary, this brief review of thinking and a wide range of other writings in sociology, social anthropology, cognitive science, and developmental psychology suggest stories are one of the main ways we give meaning to life and make sense of and judge the truth about our observations of an inherently uncertain world. They suggest a very different way of thinking about what to do than present in either standard or behavioural economics. Stories pervade our daily lives, from the rumours that might be true or false spreading around the financial markets, to the plans told to friends and relatives, or to dreams in the night and daydreams between human chores. In short, 'narrative including fictional narrative' gives 'shape to things in the real world and often bestows on them a title to reality' (Bruner 2003 p8). In this context it is not surprising that my respondents had as many stories to 'explain' why their selections hadn't performed after the fact as they had to recommend them to themselves beforehand. In Bruner's words, 'Narrative is a way to domesticate human error and surprise' (Bruner 2003 p29). So it seemed to be for my four fund managers. It is, we should recall, stories that matter in courts of law where competing accounts of events are adjudicated, ultimately based on the sense of truth created in the minds of the jury. It seems a reasonable hypothesis, based on the material in the last chapter, to suppose this is what might be a useful way to think about what happens in financial markets too.

Minds, states, and thoughts

The idea that emotion and mental states play an important part in effective human thinking, and the evidence that intuition and gut feelings can be reliable guides to successful decisions and action, has been growing. Gigerenzer and his colleagues provide useful reviews and evidence (Gigerenzer, Todd et al. 1999; Gigerenzer and Selten 2002; Gigerenzer 2007; Gigerenzer 2008). George Soros, one of the most successful investors of all time, told me he learned to use his occasional backaches to identify unease and to retreat from his positions until he could (logically) explain his doubt. He found this useful.

I have mentioned how it now seems clear our human biological endowment provides us with a variety of tools to use in particular social environments to make particular types of judgement and that among these states of mind are highly influential. Such views have become commonplace as evidence from cognitive neuroscience about how minds work has expanded exponentially. Growing knowledge about how brains work is not the same as knowledge about how minds work. Nonetheless the evidence is suggestive. It rests on the long history of working out which parts of the brain seem to do particular things (for example, by noticing what is and is not possible when certain patients have damage to particular parts of their brains) and much more recently in several new methods of observing blood flows and electrical activity while at the same time conducting various psychological experiments. Research of this kind is expanding and shows the way specific brain systems react very rapidly under certain experimental stimuli.

For example, functional Magnetic Resonance Imaging (fMRI) data[1] shows which parts of the brain are using energy when specific actions are taken or when certain perceptions and feelings are stimulated and experienced. They produce apparently 'real' pictures of flows of energy between parts of the brain, but it is important to keep in mind that these are in fact the result of complex statistical computations – computer representations. In particular they show nothing whatsoever of the singular content of the psychic reality of a specific person, just as the letters of a book reveal nothing of its content. At the same time it is a fact that, offered ten words to read, it is possible to predict with 100 per cent accuracy which word a person is thinking of by computing the observed pattern of energy use. It is also easy to determine from such patterns whether or not a face or an environment is familiar to a person.

What is interesting concerning these functional brain images is what they show about how much of what influences us is unconscious. During acts and perceptions, many previously unexpected neural circuits are active *without ever reaching a conscious level*. I will mention three main sets of findings.

First, in the old mammalian brain (common to all mammals) there is the basal brain, with the limbic system and the amygdala – deep and evolutionarily old cores of grey matter which play a major role. They contain patterns that are general, but run fast and can be life-saving because of their quick and dirty mechanisms. Primitive inherited reflexive functioning and learned automatisms are to be found here, like the implicit memory of Ledoux (Ledoux 1998). Emotions, especially the negative emotions and primary judgements about trust, anger, and sexual attraction, of obvious interest to understanding financial markets, are generated in this area, but it is not an area of which we can become conscious. The patterns there are preverbal and just like emotions. Patterns in this zone can only be changed by new experiences.

Second, there is the neocortex. This is the superficial layer of our brain which is evolutionarily younger and is implicated in most activities that we can be conscious of – categorisation, adaptation, and giving meaning. Activities in this zone are much slower than those of the basic brain structures but the results are more complex and differentiated. They help in adapting to changing environments, making it possible to relate external events to oneself and to make judgements. The acquisition of language plays a major role here, but it is assumed that many of these categorising activities leading to consciousness were already present long before language came into being. Since language came relatively late in the evolution of man and developed itself rapidly in a short span of time, it is assumed to be a function that builds on already existing functions. In fact for neuroscientists it is not entirely clear what consciousness is. Today it is essentially seen as a complex system that slowly limps behind and gives meaning to decisions and actions that have already taken place at an unconscious level.

Third, there is the cortical zone: the prefrontal cortex, characterised by a dense network of connections. Activity is noticed in this zone even when no special task is being performed. Neuroscientists used to think that it was a default setting of the brain, but currently the activity is believed to stem from the continuous formation of associative connections (in a kind of narrative) rather along the lines fundamental to the psychoanalytic notion of unconscious phantasy I have mentioned. Interestingly the effect of this activity on concentration and creativity is greater when one is conscious of it (in fact when the frontoparietal cortex is also involved), rather than when there is a spontaneous wandering of the mind of which one is not aware. While logical thinking is inhibited by emotional stress, this spontaneous formation of lateral associative connections is more active when new things are presented and when a certain amount of stress is present. It is the zone which is active in creation, as in jazz playing and 'aha' experiences.

The main point to make about mental functions based on this fMRI data is that they are organised in vertical, functional, hierarchical units with links between different levels. Crucially, it seems that the kinds of complex conscious actions that interest economists cannot occur without the working of and feedback from the more primitive basic zones and vice versa. For instance, the amygdala is regulated by higher cortical mechanisms, which it overrules in many instances – bringing thinking to an end by action, so to speak. Flight responses are critical here. Since Freud's revision of his theories in the 1920s the experience of anxiety (as of other core affects) plays a central role in psychoanalytic thinking (Tuckett 2007). One human characteristic when we look down from high places is to feel at least a little anxious. It is also a regularly observable characteristic of human functioning that in situations of excitement and euphoria (whether situations of love or hate) the resulting states of mind can interfere with thinking, particularly with calculation and due diligence.

The brain responds very similarly to internally simulated experiences (in effect to the unconscious phantasies mentioned before) as to actual external ones (Damasio 2004).The emotional circuits go through the amygdala and the ventromedial prefrontal cortex (Dietrich 2004). The cognitive circuits pass through the lateral prefrontal cortex, which is linked to spontaneous thought processes, and emotional and cognitive information is reintegrated at the dorsolateral prefrontal cortex (which is linked with planned actions and control) (see also Fonagy and Lutyens 2009). On the other hand, the brain also continues to function in zones that are not always integrated; there are perceptions that go directly to more basic and unconscious zones, bypassing the classic perceptual pathways.

The speed with which neuroscience enquiry has developed has been astounding and will presumably continue to be so. For our purposes my main point is that the psychoanalytic postulate of psychic reality expressed in unconscious phantasy that I have introduced is clearly no longer an unreasonable narrative for thinking about what we know. It is entirely possible something very like unconscious phantasies are created by self-regulatory mechanisms of the brain as the subject interacts with the environment, involving a complex neuronal mapping. These self-regulatory mechanisms are linked to consciousness and language, but interwoven with evolutionarily older mechanisms that at the same time can short-circuit them. One useful analogy offered is to compare the conscious content of psychic reality to the GPS system in a car, which has no contact with what happens on the road nor with the nuts and bolts of the engine, but which may guide a driver by relying on maps and a satellite system to determine the position of the car. The conscious mind is unaware of 95 per cent of the elaboration of sensations, feelings, drives, and perceptions that is going on. But it matches all that with complex maps, which are adapting slowly and giving meaning to perceptions and decisions that have actually already taken place at another level (Bargh and Morsella 2008; 2009).

Since Freud the term unconscious has been used as it was above to denote that of which the mind is not aware and to capture a second aspect – dynamic processes through which perceptions, thoughts, feelings, and so on are actually removed from awareness. This dynamic unconscious is conceived not so much as a lack of awareness but more as an active (defensive), shifting, and potentially unstable process of avoidance. Used in this way, the concept of the dynamic unconscious provides a metaphorical narrative which allows us to theorise how people can have conflicting thoughts and experience but stay unaware of it and not realise it for a long time.

The term *divided state*[2] plays a central role in my argument. It is a concept designed to highlight the dynamic, unstable mental situation routinely described by psychoanalysts in which ambivalent or conflicting thoughts and feelings about relationships can somehow reside in the mind and have consequences but are not always equally salient for proper realisation, reflection, and nuanced resolution. The term seeks to comprehend the switches in affect and concern that take place because conflicting thoughts and perceptions resident in individual minds seem to be there but not available for curiosity and investigation. Concern with default risk, liquidity anxiety, and awareness of uncertainty more or less vanished in much of the financial community before 2008 and a report on risk assessment and incentive systems suggested this pain was still being avoided well after the crisis (Senior Supervisors 2009). Obviously people at some level knew and know. But, instead of using what they know to think, which might cause them conflict, frustration, or panic, they turn a blind eye.

Since Freud's seminal papers (Freud 1911; 1914) psychoanalysts have been developing a theory of thinking based on the idea that it is both the product of human emotional experience and an influence on it (Bion 1962; Fonagy and Target 1996). Put simply, thoughts are meaningful because they have emotional consequences. They make us feel good (pleasure) or bad (unpleasure). It is particularly true of relationships in which we are highly invested. If we think 'realistically' about such relationships the result is likely to produce ambivalence – good and bad feelings. Some thoughts that do not create pleasure may be about things that could worry us, cause doubt, or make us suspicious, feel embarrassed, guilty, or ashamed. They create some degree of psychic conflict for the mind to manage. This can be done to produce a more or less *integrated* state in which individuals are more or less aware of the reality of their thoughts about another person or project, or a *divided* state, where they are not. There is a general tendency to manage thoughts that produce mental suffering and spoil pleasure by avoiding them or the situations that might produce them. Daily clinical observations show thoughts can be quite easily ignored, pushed away, or rationalised out of awareness so individuals can have no idea they have them for very long periods. This mental 'evacuation' is not completely effective so that sometimes residues are left, such as some uneasy feeling, quick temper, stomach-ache, backache, or headache. Such diffuse phenomena remain as signals but without their meaning for the moment.

Humans have the ability to process information and experience in different ways in a *divided* or *integrated* state of mind. This is probably functional. For some purposes, such as the single-minded pursuit of a goal in battle with no thought for the consequences, or creative endeavour with little thought for consensus thinking, the *divided state* may confer significant advantages to the group of humans as a whole. But, generally, the pursuit of reward is tempered by the fear of loss, producing anxiety, which is a signal of danger. The psychoanalytic account of human development describes how, as we all mature from infancy, experience teaches us the limits to single-minded (omnipotent narcissistic) pursuits without attention to constraints. Most of us, therefore, develop integrated-state thinking for much of the time and so are usually aware of the potential conflict between the possibility of reward and the risk of loss. Experience has taught us about the possible consequences of taking risks. However, the constraints we apply to ourselves due to our awareness of consequences are not always welcomed. The fact of human ingenuity and innovation means that historically many constraints have been overcome. We can always argue that this time 'might' be different. In this situation 'saying no' and relinquishing an idea in the face of a realistic judgement that it is not going to work feels unpleasant. The possibility of loss and the steps taken to guard against it are felt emotionally as an unpleasant cost; situations that cause anxiety and frustration are then resented.

When individuals pursue excitement with no thought of loss (or, conversely, are preoccupied only with loss to the detriment of the opportunity for reward) they are thinking within a *'divided'* state of mind. Reality is then not objectively perceived but distorted. In this way a state of mind acts, so to speak, as a frame. Within the frame of mind, rather than experiencing emotional conflicts directly, individuals cut themselves off from direct awareness of them – they 'make' them unconscious. They can then be excited about something and no longer feel frustrated or anxious about it in any usually obvious way. In consequence they can engage in what is actually risky behaviour and feel excited by it without any conscious awareness there might be a problem. They are not anxious about possible consequences and have no doubt or other 'bad feeling' about what is going on. In a *divided state*, therefore, conflicting perceptions that could give rise to anxiety or frustration are 'split off' from consciousness. Quite simply they are 'not thought' and so are not available to prompt thought.

We can apply the concept of a *divided* state to the *object relationships* we establish – whether these are actual or imagined. In a *divided* state of mind, opposed or conflicted feelings towards the people and objects about whom we tell ourselves stories in our thoughts are split into more or less entirely separated serial relationships of love and hate. Individuals or objects are then hated with no awareness that they may also be loved. They may be dismissed out of hand or entirely 'forgotten' with no awareness that they exist and may be essential. In such states of mind, which once again might be highly functional if, for instance, we were required to live in solitary confinement or intolerable conditions, individuals are freed from the awareness of ordinary reality. In that state of mind they can then almost exponentially exaggerate either a person's or an object's positive attributes or their deficiencies. In that state, we might then be aware only of either our love for the object (or person) because of its extraordinarily good qualities or our hatred for it because of its perceived terrible faults.

It is important at this point to make clear that all of this makes sense only if we recall we are talking about what I mentioned above as *psychic reality*. Mental states alter awareness consequentially. But when perceptions of reality are made unconscious the world hasn't changed. It is only the way it is perceived and thought about that is altered, albeit with powerful implications. What we take to be real determines our responses. There are, however, some further interesting consequences. First, maintaining a divided state of mind in the face of 'the facts' requires a great deal of ongoing unconscious mental work selectively to continue to perceive and assess only those aspects of matters that an individual can bear to perceive. Psychoanalysts call this *'splitting'* (Laplanche and Pontalis 1973). It is a normal state which is never absolutely complete even in abnormal cases of outright insanity. Reality keeps offering data. Individuals are, therefore, continually forced to engage in mental operations to deny what doesn't fit, in order to keep pushing away the emotional consequences they would otherwise face.

The more that processes such as we have been discussing are in operation, and the more that 'phantasy' and reality get divorced, the more extreme splitting must become. One consequence is that anxiety (in other words the split-off perception of what is being ignored) may break through and make itself 'felt' in the form of physical symptoms, unexplained jitters, unease, or nameless dread. All may be felt, but without being connected to their cause and so (unless interpreted and given meaning) unavailable for thought or rational action. *Splitting* thus lays the foundation for catastrophic reversals in confidence or trust in people or objects, such as we see in the panic phase of an asset price bubble. A significant problem is that the nature of splitting means that reversing it gently is difficult, partly because it is often resisted. Because it involves both the unpleasure of giving up the excitement which will then be spoilt, and because facing worries and concerns about what may happen is actually unpleasant.

All this makes clear that it was not very surprising to find that Fred Bingham and his colleagues routinely used gut feeling (such as unease) *and* logical reasoning to form their agenda, imagine futures, and make their decisions or to find them sometimes dealing with the emotional conflicts their job entailed by taking up *divided states*. But the evidence also showed how they were also routinely and unavoidably influenced by their institutional context. It is to this social-psychological context I now turn.

Groupfeel

The evidence that human information processing is not atomistic and certainly does not take place in an isolated ether is overwhelming. It suggests the judgements we make, the feelings we experience, and the behaviours we engage in that I have just been describing are situated in a rich social, psychological, and biological context, which includes context information 'stimuli' or signals that are immediately present, remembered, or constructed on the spot. As founding fathers of economics like Pareto and Marshall began to recognise (Parsons 1937), people make decisions not just through calculation but because they *feel* right in social contexts.

Sociologists and social anthropologists have compiled a large literature on the way cultural and structural contexts create norms and values that influence meaning and behaviour as well as the presentation of the self. It is so well known and available it will not be reviewed here. The general point is that social contexts serve to legitimate some actions and ways of thinking and knowing at particular times and places or to stigmatise others. They create different contexts for social actors to construct reality and 'what passes for knowledge' with different results (for example, Berger and Luckman 1966). Social contexts, therefore, influence such matters as the changing significance to be attached to differences between men and women's perspectives or to whether 'narrative', 'intuition', or feeling are 'heard' and attended to as a significant source of knowledge in psychology or cognitive neuroscience 'stories' of the world. Variations in the paradigms we use to assess 'scientific' truth are no exception (Berger and Luckman 1966; Kuhn 1972; Habermas 1971; Gadamer 1975; and see also Lawson 2010).

Social context, therefore, such as the structure of the organisation in which they worked and the norms and values prevailing, provides one background to understand what my asset managers told me. And psychologists have also done a great deal of research over the past 50 years or so on how psychological context shapes judgements, feelings, and behaviours – including our sense of what is true. A particularly powerful instance in all communities recognised in psychology is the influence of context on thought in the social-psychological process I will refer to as *groupfeel,* for reasons which will be made clear below.

Research has described two general context effects which apply to groups: assimilation and contrast. At its simplest, the conclusion of this large body of work is that judgements as to what is right or what to do change according to context, that is, depending on whether others are experienced as hostile or anxious, particularly peaceful or apparently highly competent or otherwise, and so forth (Mussweiler 2007).

Collective decision-making failures have often been attributed to group members' unwillingness to express unpopular opinions. Incident investigations frequently name lack of dissent as a causal factor (Sunstein 2006). Long-standing psychological explanations rest on decades of research into social influence, social identity, and group processes and refer to Janis's model of what he called groupthink (Janis 1982).

The ubiquity of observations about the strange things that happen in groups has meant that Janis's idea has been widely accepted as a valid and verified phenomenon by many academic psychologists (Fuller and Aldag 1998; Turner, Pratkanis et al. 1992) and also validated using fMRI investigation (Van Bavel, Packer et al. 2008). It seems to explain how situations arise where those in a group become so identified with each other's feelings and beliefs that they cannot think properly about other possibilities, such as in the 'planning' of failed military adventures.

Sometimes, when Janis's concept has been looked at in detail, however, and the various individual predictions he set out about what caused groupthink have been subjected to laboratory test, results have not been conclusive (Baron 2005; Packer 2009). For one thing, group pressures are not automatic. It is experimentally demonstrated that under certain conditions strongly identified group members (perhaps those who care about organisational aims they feel are threatened) may not conform to group pressures but challenge them (Packer 2009).

The implication is that while Janis was right about the symptoms of group-think and their relationship to decision-making – the suppression of dissent, polarization of attitude, and poor decision quality – he was wrong in specifying the specific antecedent conditions that led to them. It seems likely that the reason for negative findings may be a function of demand characteristics of the experimental situations – in other words, the way the experiments were set up. It seems also that the general prevalence of the underlying phenomena (consensus seeking, group polarisation, out-group stereotyping, and the suppression of dissent) are so close to 'ceiling levels' in almost any group brought together for research purposes that experimental manipulation of antecedent variables under laboratory conditions had little effect (Baron 2005). The group behaviour noticed, therefore, is not the product of particular leadership styles but of a general tendency in any group that has a sense of social identification through a linked purpose – something which can apply to virtual groups as much as to physically propinquent ones. As the results showing that some people can resist group pressure show, it can also be overcome.

When I introduced my term, *groupfeel,* in the preface and subsequently, I did so because although I have been using the term groupthink, I came to realise that to capture the underlying issues that are relevant for economics a new term might be more useful. Thinking and feeling are highly correlated notions and all the research makes clear it is the feelings generated in a group that influence thoughts. Janis himself, were he alive, might agree. He mentioned in his book his concept was partly inspired by observations of the psychoanalyst, Wilfrid Bion. *Groupfeel* certainly captures what Bion had in mind better than *groupthink.*

Bion (1952) distinguished between what he called Basic Assumption and Work Group functioning. He considers them as two ways any group can find itself functioning (two tendencies as it were). Both types are based on an elaborated psychoanalytic theory of mental states which I have been discussing using the terms *integrated* and *divided.* It was Bion, in fact, developing the ideas of his mentor, Melanie Klein, who played the leading role in this theoretical development.

The essence of Bion's approach to groups is that what matters is the effect of feeling on thought and then the effect of thought on feeling in an ongoing dynamic. Following his thinking, *groupfeel* seeks to capture that what happens in groups is first and foremost a feeling state, not merely a cognitive one. Bion had reasons for his ideas in his own experience. He became a psychoanalyst only after he had been a senior and innovative army officer in a tank regiment in the First World War, and then after extensive work with officer selection and other groups during the Second World War, as well as in many institutional settings. In elaborating his thoughts about groups, he stated that he hoped to show that in his contact with 'the complexities of life in a group' the adult resorts to mechanisms described by Klein (1935; 1946) as typical of the earliest phases of life. He saw all this as based on the human necessity to make contact with the emotional life of the group in which he was brought up (the family) and considered the task to be as 'formidable to the adult' as the early and very emotionally charged relationship of the infant to the mother and her body. That relationship is characterised by powerful feelings of love and hate and states of overwhelming satisfaction and anxiety, including very paranoid anxieties and insecurities. Bion suggests that 'the belief that a group exists', as distinct from an aggregate of individuals, is fundamental and is associated with beliefs (unconscious phantasies) about its intentions and attitudes to the subject and between its members. In a basic way (as the research mentioned confirms), being in a group means there is some loss of individuality; there is some sense of something above. A stranger walking into a room in which a group that has existed for some time is assembled 'feels it'.

Bion argued that any group meets to 'do' something and that in this activity, according to the capacities of the individuals, they cooperate. Usually they have specific skills or training to work together. Insofar as the activity is 'geared to a task', it is related to reality, 'its methods are rational', and, therefore, in however embryonic a form, it is scientific. Insofar as a group functions in this way it is a 'work group'. But work-group activity is regularly observed to be obstructed, diverted, and, on occasion, assisted by other mental activities 'that have in common the attribute of powerful emotional drives'. He thought these features spring from 'basic assumptions common to all in the group'. Powerful among these forces are more or less hidden beliefs that the group (or leader) will sustain the members of the group, that 'pairing' is taking place (in other words that parents are imagined to be present who will look after members as their children), and that the group has either met to fight or take flight. The point about all three features is that membership in the group feels good and exclusion from the group feels bad. In this way, when individuals are involved in *groupfeel* in a basic assumption group they do not each process any available information about events in external reality individually (for instance, to reflect on the risk and reward they anticipate and to arrive at different conclusions). Rather they aim to feel like everyone else. In this situation evidence from outside about what might be factual and not tends to be treated merely as background noise. What makes members of such a group feel secure is not any consideration of facts but the fact that they are all doing the same thing together.

Bion went on to argue that there were several other interesting features of basic assumption groups – in particular that time plays no part (they are outside time) and therefore there is no development; the initial situation, the reason for forming the group, must remain forever. The other crucial feature concerns curiosity. 'I know of no experience that demonstrates more clearly' that a basic assumption group experience is active than 'the dread with which a questioning attitude is regarded' and particularly towards the group itself (Bion 1959 p162). His theory about that is blunt. 'My impression is that the group approximates too closely, in the minds of the individuals composing it, to very primitive phantasies about the contents of the mother's body'. He means, in fact, to anxieties which are held in what I have called a *divided state* about the imagined damage hate has wrought on the mother's body and her capacity to provide – anxieties which are fundamental to early infancy in the Kleinian theory. These anxieties necessitate beliefs in magic and omnipotence, characteristic of the *phantastic object*; indeed it is fear of cruelly causing damage beyond repair and hence despair that requires the object to be built up as so phantastic. Extraordinarily powerful processes occur in groups which generate emotions like wildfire.

Psychoanalytically based ideas, such as Bion's, come from psychoanalysis as a mainly clinical discipline able to provide a systematically integrated set of theoretical approaches to subjectivity. They are useful insofar as we are obliged to take subjective experiences like suspicion, trust, doubt, enthusiasm, and conviction seriously. The theoretical framework cannot be proved in the laboratory by any methods currently available and for practical reasons clinical work based on it is not easily subjected to randomised controlled trials. Moreover, the subject matter is easily at odds with the main trend of scientific thinking in the last century. Historically, the opportunities for endless reinterpretation potentially offered by psychoanalytic argument can potentially lead to a kind of perverse thinking where anything can be made to mean anything else. This is a real concern in psychoanalysis as in other social sciences. The nature of the subject means it is difficult to replicate findings. Its value is built on a narrative rather than logical form of knowing, but with the additional problem that psychoanalysis postulates that important causal factors are dynamically unconscious. In the clinical setting these difficulties are potentially overcome by the daily opportunity the psychoanalyst has to use his feelings and capacities to try to distinguish between a 'selected fact' and an 'overvalued idea' (Britton and Steiner 1994). And in fact theories about clinical technique (see, for example, Widlocher 1994) and about individual patients have changed due to this kind of dialectic. Nonetheless, with its detailed theories becoming modified with the aid of experience rather than subjected to formal test, psychoanalysis has largely existed as a clinical discipline outside universities.

In consequence, conclusions about the importance of dynamically unconscious processes, ambivalent object relationships, unconscious phantasies based on infantile sexual drives, divided and integrated states, basic assumption groups, and working through – that is, the core concepts used in this book – presently rest on clinical conviction and such feelings of verisimilitude as those who use the theories, including those reading this book, actually sense in the situations to which I will suggest they apply. But there are signs that new attitudes and new means of observation may be about to create change in the epistemological landscape. For example, the Nobel Prize–winning biologist, Eric Kandel (1999), has argued both that psychoanalysis revolutionised understanding in the first half of the twentieth century and that modern developments in neurobiology and other research fields should increasingly make its propositions more testable, if psychoanalysts have the stomach and resources to attempt it. Or, again, the eminent Cambridge historian, Quentin Skinner (1985; 2008), has argued that it is important to revisit the grand historical theories but to build them on the basis of human agency – the subjective situation of the human agent taking decisions. He acknowledges what he calls the hidden and unacknowledged role of psychoanalysis in helping to bring about many current intellectual developments.

Summary

In this chapter, following my description of what Fred Bingham and the others told me in Chapter 2 about their situation, I have aimed to introduce some ideas from sociology, psychology, and cognitive neuroscience which provide a basis to understand how narrative, groups, and mental states might be expected to influence human thinking and decision-making, particularly under uncertainty. I have elaborated on the concepts of *groupfeel* and *divided states*.

The next four chapters will explore how far the findings about uncertainty and narrative from the first four interviews are replicated across the sample and, particularly, set out in more detail the various ways the decision-making context asset managers experience seems to stimulate a search for *phantastic objects* and generate both *groupfeel* and *divided states*.

4
Divided States

The remarkable fact about the events leading up to 2008, when many of the world's financial institutions created unsustainable financial relationships between themselves, was that they appear to have done so without anyone really realising it. This was not because it was impossible to know, however, but, according to later investigations, because somehow almost everyone turned a blind eye.[1] With a few exceptions (Lewis 2010) they did not think about what was going on and they did not investigate what was going on. Whether they ran the financial institutions that were at the centre of the new developments or analysed and invested in them, those who could have been curious ignored explicit warnings and warning signs and also flew in the face of history.

I have suggested that lack of curiosity and real investigation is usual in asset price bubbles because during them there is an apparent change in the financial market's sense of reality towards a *divided state* of mind. Although financial institutions are staffed by very highly intelligent and knowledgeable people, both thinking and memory apparently fail regularly. The aim of this chapter is to understand better the way the context of the asset managers' tasks were structured and the effect this seemed to have.

I argue that what fund managers told me about the context in which they work (and particularly the incentive structures within which they were contained) could very well predispose financial actors to be selected into their work because they are rather easily able to adapt themselves to thinking in a *divided state*. This state may help to make the experience of their work more acceptable and less anxiety provoking. However, at the same time, because it may dull anxiety about the likely consequences of action, it may also create a dangerous institutional context.

The data suggests that the everyday financial markets in which my respondents worked were accentuating rather than mitigating the human potential for developing *divided states* of mind. In part this was because there was a potential misalignment between the incentive systems in place and its effects on the way they worked. The findings might have wider implications for understanding how the state of mind of those running banks and investing in them can quite regularly become '*divided*'.

The pressure to perform short-term

The fund managers I studied mostly operated inside the large corporate entities which now dominate financial markets. Their task is to invest clients' money. But the underlying objective is also to help those institutions gather assets and so to earn the fees with which they are associated. These twin objectives have the potential to place them in conflict, particularly if we bear in mind the characteristics of financial assets as volatile and abstract and recall that assessing investor performance is near impossible. As I talked to them, it became clear that conflicts around performance, agency, and feedback are a reality. Like the managers mentioned at the end of the Chapter 2, most respondents had a mission strategy based on the idea that they should make decisions based on their long-term expectations. But the systems in place to market their services meant that managers also actually felt under intense short-term pressure to be seen to be performing exceptionally. It was a structural situation which might militate against taking a long-term view and intensify the emotional pressure on them when the medium- or long-term expectations underlying the investment theses to which they had committed were the object of uncertainty due to price movements.

Among the fund managers I interviewed it was taken for granted that their competitive situation meant that they should perform exceptionally and that successful asset gathering (and the huge fee rewards that follow) requires visible short-run investor performance. They were highly intelligent and thoughtful people who were dedicated to what they were doing. Nonetheless, despite their knowledge that short-term volatility does not predict long-term movements, despite the doubts about whether investor performance is really assessable, and despite a widespread belief that short-term movements were likely to be 'noisy', few could 'resist' at least daily use of the statistical packages with which they had been provided to monitor how they were doing. In other words, they spent a lot of time anxiously looking in their rearview mirror. In some cases they looked many times a day. In either case this suggests a form of temporal myopia in which it is reasonable to think their long-term aspirations were at least to some extent somehow divided off from their actual behaviour.

In fact, because my main focus in the interviews was on describing decision-making, at first I did not realise what I was seeing. Direct questions about remuneration and performance assessment were not included in the interview until, as the issue of short-term pressure became apparent, more systematic questioning about performance was finally included in the last eight interviews.

Fortunately many of the managers earlier in the sample had mentioned the pressure they were under and had made spontaneous comments about it when talking on other subjects. So when this material was collected together and looked at systematically after the interviews were over, just over two-thirds of all those interviewed (n=36) had given enough answers about their behaviour in checking on their performance to allow a minimal estimate of how wide-spread it was.[2] Of these individuals, more than three quarters (n=28) had said they checked out their performance situation either *every few hours* or at least *daily*.

Four managers, in fact, mentioned they checked both their absolute and relative performance every few hours and 24 did so at least every day. The comments of both groups revealed how performance pressure weighs on their minds, hints at how difficult it is to sustain bad news, and indicates how mixed (divided) they feel about their behaviour; they needed to offer rationalisations to try to remain comfortable – that is, to attempt to present an explanation that was logically consistent and ethically in line with the attitudes, actions, ideas, feelings, and so forth, that the subject has and whose true motives are not perceived (Jones 1908). Here are seven brief examples drawn at random:

It is very hard when share prices are falling very, very fast, and the screen is all red. You know, it's very difficult to work out what's confusion, and noise, and what's a good opportunity. ... I have my own spreadsheet, and through a variety of very clever little links I can see how my portfolio is doing. I can see every single company, and weight it, so I have that on a daily live basis. (Chuck Bronsky)

As a global investor you've got to make hundreds of decisions unknowingly, every day. You've probably got hundreds of share prices on your chart, on your screen. ... So many things get thrown at you. ... We review our perform-ance in quite a lot of ways daily, which is probably a bad thing. It can become very focused on short-term performance. (Brian Anderson)

What we look at every day, *first of all*, is our performance versus our bench-mark for the trailing day. So yesterday we lost 9 basis points versus our benchmark, but up to date we're still up 77. So we'll look at that, how we're doing versus our benchmark. (Andrew Smythe)

Unfortunately, one of my funds is publicly listed ... or there's a price for it on Bloomberg, and it's the worst thing that could have happened, because I now look at my price daily. What it could do is make me more reactive, and it could speed up my decision-making, er, because I feel more under pressure, or less under pressure. It really ... makes or breaks your day. And therefore I've got to stop looking at it. (Colin Menton)

Every day! I know you shouldn't. But it's important to know sometimes how your portfolio is responding to market movement and feel whatever, because sometimes however much you know, it's still useful. ... It doesn't affect my decisions that much. (Sol Abram)

All day every day we sit in front of screens that tell us what the prices are ... we've got systems that estimate performance on a daily basis. So we're very aware of performance all the time. (Daren Cook)

This is not attributed to me, right? Every hour, maybe! I started in this business back in '93, as this junior guy who knew nothing and I worked with this guy who was very smart. Every time I was there he was like, 'Oh! My God! Hilton is up three cents. Hilton is up five cents. Oh! We're up three basis points today.' I thought this is the most ridiculous thing I have ever seen and now I do the same thing. (George Monroe)

We will return to the embarrassment that George Monroe's comment makes evident. But first it's worth noting that among the purely quantitative managers the proportion looking at their performance at least daily seems to have been even higher than among the stock pickers. Six out of seven were doing so even though such managers suggested during their interviews that quantitative strategies enabled them to protect investment decisions from short-term emotional volatility and also stressed how in general they had limited their ability to intervene. Perhaps they were just more screen-attached. But the reasons offered were interesting. For example, Jeremy Swanson looked at his performance daily. What was the point if his process only allowed him to change it monthly? 'That's a fair question!' he said, showing he could see it was a bit illogical. But he developed the answer quickly. 'I think [you do it] in the spirit of understanding what risk you are taking on, you have to kind of live the performance a little bit. It's all very well to look at a sheet at the end of the year and say okay, it was good or it was bad, but that wouldn't give you much colour on the sorts of days you were winning or the sorts of days you were losing on. An important part of the job is communicating with clients too, so you have to know where you are.'

Was Swanson rationalising? A fellow hedge fund manager, Simon Reeves, revealed the pressure to take up a divided state beautifully. He made clear he was well aware of the research that showed 'if you look at it every hour or every two hours or every day, you make yourself unhappy' and therefore it is better not to do so. On the other hand, he laughed, 'one of our clients' wants a daily e-mail with performance details and this has to be done. He said he had evolved his own approach to not looking very often when he is doing badly. 'I do this even though it's such an obvious ploy to trick myself', he said, laughing. He then added, 'having said all that, whether I look at performance or not, if my performance has been shit I know it; for instance my wife can tell from my body language that I have had a bad day in the market. I call this one of the downsides of doing this job'.

Another 'quant', Julian Edwards, showed a similar subtle awareness of his attempts to rationalise – again punctuated by laughter. He looked every day 'for two reasons'. He thought he 'should really kind of know where it is', he said, laughing, and 'it's the only way we can understand if there's particular stocks that are being adversely affected' to see 'if we need to go and make adjustments'. Like Reeves, Edwards could see the contradiction, following up this remark by saying, 'I will say that I no longer have portfolio performance on my computer screens any more'. It had made him look at it 'all the time' which was 'bad and inefficient'. 'So I have my assistants have it,' he laughed. Another hedge fund manager, Warren York, did the same.

These quotations elaborate the statistical findings. It seems many managers certainly felt under considerable short-term pressure to deliver and showed signs of being in conflict about it. If so, this is likely to be a fertile ground for the development of *divided state* thinking and rationalisation. By August 2007 when the final round of eight interviews was conducted, I had become sufficiently aware of the existence of such pressure to perform short-term and its potential significance that I modified the interview to take care to try to get every respondent to elaborate more fully on the performance pressures they faced. To illustrate the findings from this changed approach I will start using material from the last but one interviewee I saw, Leonard Frost, whose discussion on the subject was particularly articulate. But, as I will show, the analysis of all eight interviews (one of whom was Duncan Smith whom we met in the Chapter 2) demonstrates that Frost's replies were not unusual. Frost was particularly forthcoming and what he said was particularly evocative, but what he said was said by all but one of the others. In essence it is clear that the managers looked at their daily performance and worried about it because in reality both bonus payments and their futures in the job were at stake if performance stuttered even for a short while. Competitive pressures mean that those who survive long-term have adapted to living with it.

Leonard Frost

Leonard Frost had been a traditional stock picker for 20 years. When interviewed he was heading a team of nine people whose task, like most of the others interviewed, was to attract assets to the firm by achieving exceptional investment performance and to go on doing so year after year; his stated obligation was to ensure the team's investment results consistently beat the return of the average fund in his category by at least two per cent, an ambitious target.[3]

He was directly responsible for investing $4 billion into the UK market and the team for $35 billion.

Frost spoke in a frank and direct way of what he felt certain was the pressure most fund managers felt under to perform in an exceptional manner and the ways they try to cope. As a seasoned veteran he had learned to take the rough with the smooth and to believe he could do it. In his view he had succeeded. He had outperformed for two out of the last three years as he had two-thirds of the time for most of his 20 years. 'This year has not been good, '05 and '06 were brilliant.'

His comments revealed that he had adapted to the pressure of having to be exceptional by developing a degree of hunted cynicism, including some hostility towards those he felt had placed him in his situation and who, he believed, had 'no clue, frankly'. 'Most people seem to think you can outperform, not just every year but every quarter or every month but they're living in cloud cuckoo land, these people.' Such cynical pragmatism suggests someone who had developed a picture of himself as a slightly resentful and lonely individual battling against the odds – perhaps using resentment to gain the strength to maintain his conviction under adversity (see Steiner 1996). 'Very few people actually understand what this industry really does in the real world ... (but) ... If you outperform two years in three, you're going to give your clients a good return. We've outperformed two of the last three years ... if you can deliver two out of three months, two out of three quarters, two out of three years, you'll do what the client wants you to do. And I've been around long enough to realise that. ... '

It was palpable as we talked that, as in the attitudes just expressed, and despite his long record of success, Frost's fear of underperformance and getting the sack was never too far away. In fact, in response to a question about whether it could really be true that he felt so insecure, he used simple statistics to argue that even managers performing above average 65 per cent of the time will on average probably have three poor years in a row before 17 years are up, and he did indeed believe this would trigger the sack. 'The survival rate is actually quite low', he said, underlining his seriousness by referring to me by my first name at this point and then elaborating that when he interviewed graduates who were thinking of joining the firm he would ask them a very blunt question: 'Why on earth do you want to go into an industry where you're almost doomed to failure, even if you're good?'[4]

The pressured picture described by Leonard Frost is not surprising looking at the investment mandates he and my other respondents had – those of the four respondents in the Chapter 2 being rather typical. Almost all of my respondents were mandated to outperform a combination of their rivals or an index – as is common in the industry. Only a handful of interviewees were not explicitly charged with being exceptional and even these all gave some indication of pressure. This finding is consistent with what is generally believed about the industry.

An analysis of the last eight interviews showed that in seven of them (one was Frost and another Smith) interviewees volunteered clear references to pressure and revealed that the pressure of underperformance and the resulting anxiety was palpable. The exception was Brad Johnston, who worked in a team with an unusually long-time horizon in which remuneration was largely team-based. He maintained he did not feel individual performance pressure despite interviewer probing – and in his interview certainly demonstrated a considerable capacity to stick to his decisions. In August 2007 he was heavily committed to maintaining or even increasing his holdings in the finance and banking shares on which he was an expert, at a time when those shares were falling significantly.[5]

The picture of a significant daily pressure on fund managers to be exceptional emerging from these last eight interviews is supported by many other comments from the sample. David Allen, who invested $1 billion into global markets, was one of the first interviewees I saw. His team was under very great pressure and has subsequently been disbanded. He elaborated much of what has been said already and made clear the great difficulty he had maintaining the official strategy of holding stocks for the long term. In his interview he gave several examples of losing his nerve. He also said his 'growth' style of trying to select quality companies which could be held for the long term was 'out of fashion' with clients and their advisers. They were literally fighting for their assets. 'We try to focus people on more than three-year numbers because that's the time horizon we're looking out at when we're buying stocks. Unfortunately we live in a world where you get measured on a daily basis. ... Next year, if we have a year where growth stocks work better than value stocks, and we're still under, I think that's going to be a tougher explanation and it'll put a lot more pressure on us. In a year like we just had, no one's happy about it, but there's some level of understanding, and compassion ... so, yes, there's definitely a certain amount of pressure. It affects morale, it affects your sleep, a lot of things.'

Dominique Lyon invested $1.5 billion into global markets. He also mentioned how expectations about how clients will respond weigh heavily on his thought processes. He volunteered, 'when we talk to clients we always tell them the investment horizon is about three to five years. However, if you underperform substantially over a 12-month period, you can already be in trouble.' His point about being forced to be short-term was supported by Colin Menton, who invested $3 billion into global markets. 'As much as I like to be long-term, I'm as short-term and shallow as everybody else,' he said. 'I'm bummed if my performance is bad.'

Many managers had thought about their situations but felt caught up in a system they were powerless to do much about. Nigel Sheraton, who invested

$1.5 billion into emerging markets, was emphatic. 'It's completely inappropriate in my opinion for managers to be assessed on performance...if I was given my choice, I'd make it ten years.' He knew, however, that this wish was unlikely to be fulfilled. 'It's really a function of the tolerance of the marketplace for underperformance', he said. 'Frustratingly, that's gone down as years have gone by and even your institutional clients are irritatingly short term. The reality is', he elaborated, 'if you underperform for two consecutive years, new business will dry up very quickly, and by the end of the second year, you'll start getting some of your shorter term clients throwing the towel in. There's increasing intolerance for any period of underperformance,' he concluded, confirming the presence of myopia.

I will be elaborating further on fund managers' experience with clients and its implications in Chapter 7. Warren York ran a large quantitative hedge fund risking $50 billion using complex mathematical trading algorithms, investing only in derivatives. He was quite clear on his experience with clients. 'The underlying problem for most of these processes is if you get into the state where underperformance starts to last longer than you have some easy way to explain'. In other words, you have to have a story. At that point, he said, 'you get into the psychology of clients' and also those responsible for advising them. 'Often the people that we are investing for are not the owners of the assets; there is an agency relationship between them'. Advisers have to 'explain things'. York's point is pertinent in that it highlights the chains of agency relationships to which managers are subject. On every link of the chain the characteristics of financial assets I have mentioned are pertinent – prices are volatile, values are inherently uncertain, and performance is hard to measure. Confidence is inherently brittle.

Quentin Matthews, with 20 years in the industry, invested $600 million into European markets outside the United Kingdom. He was emphatic, detailed, and sophisticated in articulating the inherent conflict between what might be rational in terms of the investment strategy a 'good' fund manager might attempt and what was rational in terms of commercial survival. Matthews pointed out that the difficulty for a lot of fund managers was that they not only have to convince themselves they are on the right track as time unfolds, but they also have to convince employers and clients. 'Even if you were completely convinced you are right, even if you don't panic', he said, 'your employer might panic or your clients might panic'.

I have suggested that the market in financial assets is inherently uncertain and volatile and that the signals coming from it make it difficult to sustain long-term theses and create the potential for panic. Matthews made clear how that works. 'If you are lucky enough' your 'theses work out to establish' you 'a reputation which earns you the right to have confidence and to inspire confidence'. 'But if not', he said, 'to be honest, bad luck! You just happened to start in a wrong year and tough. If you'd started maybe in a different year, you'd have got to that critical point and then you could have gone on investing in that way.' He told me he had 'certainly seen' plenty of examples. He could think of people who actually 'had a perfectly sensible way of doing things'. But if they had started off at the wrong moment and 'it went badly for whatever reason' they would fail and lose their jobs. 'We all know', he said, 'let's face it, it's short-term numbers' but as 'any academic' look at it can tell you, 'that's noise'.

Making clear the problems implicit in modelling financial market decision-making as 'rational' or not, Matthews said, 'People aren't stupid. Commercially it's sometimes very difficult to behave in a way that's rational. In a long-term sense what's rational in terms of investment behaviour may not be rational commercially. That's the problem.' Operating a behavioural finance–influenced strategy, he also saw it as an opportunity for anyone with confidence and the ability to resist pressure. 'Many, many players in the market don't have the luxury, if you like, of taking a long-term view, even if they think they ought to. They know commercially they can't or maybe they're wrong but they perceive that they can't. So, they talk about being long-term but in reality are staring at every month's performance, trying constantly to buy something that goes up tomorrow and all the rest.'

Unease and ambivalence

I have mentioned that the psychoanalytic concept of *ambivalence* refers to a situation where individuals have fundamentally conflicting feelings about a proposed or actual course of action to engage in a relationship. Being aware that these conflicting feelings exist creates mental pain but also offers the opportunity to determine how best to resolve it. Not being aware, being in a 'divided state', may allow one to pursue an activity without direct mental pain (and thought) but produces symptoms of unease, such as the embarrassment of feeling found out. Earlier in this chapter I quoted George Monroe as embarrassed when talking about how often he checked his performance. Other respondents would laugh nervously, perhaps signifying a degree of mixed feeling and so perhaps the internal emotional conflict some managers felt over the betrayal of their long-term aspirations and accompanying mission statements by short-term anxiety, an indication in fact of a 'divided state'. To try to explore this emerging possibility a brief analysis was undertaken to see how many signs of embarrassment, anxiety, or discomfort seemed to be present in the interview transcripts at those moments when discussion of performance monitoring was taking place.[6] To do this properly every manager would have needed to be asked about performance, other questions should have been designed to probe, a rating scale should have been developed before the study began, and raters should have been trained to use it reliably. As none of this could be done in the kind of exploratory study undertaken, the results to be described from this rudimentary effort should be treated as hypotheses for investigation rather than conclusions.

With such caveats the analysis was interesting. In over half of the cases (7/13) where we judged that data was available one way or the other (nervous laughter, a comment about not wanting to be quoted, or, alternatively, an apparently very relaxed and confident set of responses), it seemed that respondents did show signs of nervous unease when answering questions about how they reviewed their behaviour. This may be some confirmation of the idea that managers not only feel the burden of their obligation to achieve regular exceptional performance, but also feel uncomfortable about an implicit conflict between the public strategies they are obliged to adopt (and in full measure attempt to implement) and what they think is actually realistic.

Certainly managers experience the emotional consequences of being in the front line of the way investment markets now function. They have to deal with the emotional ambiguities implied by the way the asset management industry sells itself. It is, therefore, they who have to reconcile the conflicting demands, for example, of an official long-term strategy with the difficulties clients and their advisers have in tolerating uncertainty if short-term performance signals are poor. It is they who must reconcile the official risk parameters set for their funds with the fact that to achieve exceptional performance actually requires some form of contrarian behaviour. Being contrarian always entails the risk of being out of touch with market sentiment or mistaken about one's information. Gordon Hamilton, discussed above, made this point rather clearly. In one example he spoke about how he had decided not only to be contrarian in holding an unfashionable stock, but also had to 'stick out his neck' considerably because the stock was not within his institutionally determined area of expertise: 'I did it at a degree of personal risk. ... I think, really, people run with, it's safer being in a pack. It's very uncomfortable being outside the pack and actually going against the flow, and being prepared to step out of the crowd. Because the common view is that if you're wrong, and everyone else is wrong, well, that's okay. If you're right, well, that's what you're expected to do. But if you're wrong, away from the crowd, *then you are out there on a limb!*'

Turnover

There are two further grounds for thinking that the pressured situation described by the interviewees in this chapter is widespread among professional investors in the market, which suggests the widespread existence of at least the precursors for a *divided* state.

First, the fund managers were realistic about the personal risks they faced. Fund managers do get fired and do move on. According to a survey recommended to me by the UK Financial Services Authority (Investment Solutions 2007), the turnover among UK equity managers during the period I was interviewing had been high and rising. 'Staff turnover has increased yet again, with the figure for the three year period ending 30 June 2007 reaching 72.7% (24.2% per annum) for UK equity teams and 78.2% (26.1% per annum) for UK fixed income teams', the report concluded. Drawing out the implications, the authors state that 'in the case of UK equities, if a team of 10 were in place three years ago, there would have been 7 changes, which may have been three leavers and four new joiners, for example'. But they stressed that this did not mean all teams are changing. 'For both asset classes, companies surveyed ranged from stable teams with no turnover, to teams where there has been more than 100 per cent turnover over the past three years.'

Second, available data does suggest an ongoing conflict over time horizons, with short-term perspectives regularly winning out. As one of the interviewees pointed out, trading statistics do show that on average fund managers trade a great deal and hold stocks for relatively short periods. They also show that holding periods tend to be shorter than managers advertise. For instance, a study of managers using 991 long-term equity strategies conducted by Mercers and the independent IRRC (Mercers and IRRC Institute 2010) reported an average turnover of 72 per cent. If average holding periods were in line with Fred Bingham's three-year rule of thumb for having a long-term strategy, the figure should be half that. Additionally one-fifth of the firms studied by Mercers turned over all their holdings once or more within a year. Furthermore, the authors report that nearly two-thirds of strategies had turnover 'higher than expected', if actual holding periods were compared to the formal mission statements as to managers' intentions. Some strategies actually recorded more than one and a half to two times higher turnover than intended. In other words, the data shows that although formally managers may try to seek to take a somewhat long-term view, in practice they are often unable to do so.

A later chapter will pick up Warren York's point above and explore the relationships fund managers had with clients and how they tried to manage them. Here I want to stress that insofar as fund managers are in conflict and placed in a *divided* state, they are not alone. This is a widespread phenomenon in financial markets.

The characteristics of financial assets that I have been underlining mean that clients and their advisers are in the same situation and suffer the same experience. How do they know, when things are not going well short-term, how things will turn out if left undisturbed in the longer run? In this situation, exiting from one fund and entering into another is the quicker and perhaps emotionally easier choice and also gives the impression of doing something. When they are dissatisfied clients switch managers, and when they are dissatisfied managers change stock holdings. As Nigel Sheraton said above, it seems that the tolerance for underperformance in the market is low and getting lower. He argued that when things aren't going well new business dries up. Even institutional clients, he said, are 'irritatingly short-term'. Just as the pressure managers feel to find something that works is reflected in their turnover figures, so the pressure to find successful funds is reflected in the way clients change funds and asset management firms change the managers they employ. Lowenstein, a strong critic of mutual funds, studied three very well known leading US funds in detail. He found that turnover rates of 200 per cent to 250 per cent were not unusual in the ten-year period ending August 2005. But, very significantly, he also found that these funds were themselves bought and sold by their clients at not dissimilar rates (Lowenstein 2008 p61–3).

In later chapters I will elaborate on the systemic pressures throughout the market to adopt a short-term focus and the impression many had that these pressures were growing. I will describe the inherent problems that financial market actors faced managing their experience in financial markets as they are currently organised. As a background for those ideas, some aspects of the way financial markets have come to be organised are worth a brief examination.

The way the market is organised

In their early history financial markets were heavily speculative. Reports about them are full of intoxicating and colourful descriptions (Mackay 1848; Dale, Johnson et al. 2005). Crazes of one kind and another were regular and taken-for-granted. In many parts of the world to this day little distinction is made between gambling and investment. This contrasts with the gradual development of financial institutions in developed countries as the main vehicles for managing savings for retirement and other objectives where the main purpose appears more prudential.

The change from disrepute to respectability can be studied in the United States. There, typically, investment was speculative activity and was either unlawful or morally reprehensible for a long time. The sociologist Preda (2005) has described how gradually during the latter part of the nineteenth century all that changed; the prevailing view of the 'investor' was reconfigured so that his (it was male) image as a speculator and gambler gave way to an image of the investor as a technician and to investment as 'science'. Whereas before about 1870 financial dealings were carried out in back alleys and gardens and much of what was happening was either actually illegal or strongly condemned as immoral, there was subsequently a process through which investing in financial markets gradually became first prudential and respectable and then in the last 30 years or so even came to be seen as high 'tec', high IQ, high profile, exciting, and glamorous. At the same time the managers of money were more and more highly paid. This process, which in recent years has escalated further, has resulted in financial services accounting for very large numbers in employment and financiers being represented as brilliant and innovative superstars, with banking and financial management activities more highly remunerated than any others.

Accompanying this change in profile, financial markets themselves have also changed in their organisational structure, particularly in the last 30 years. Investment companies employing professional fund managers go back a long way – one of the earliest was the Foreign and Colonial Government Trust founded in London in 1868. It was created for the purpose of investing in various governments' debt. Trading government debt was a major activity and the main purpose of all financial markets for many years. Gradually shares in 'joint stock corporations' were traded as well. Many small investment management companies were then set up by groups of wealthy citizens. For example, the Massachusetts Investment Trust was set up in Boston in 1924.

Initially such investment trusts consisted of groups of investors paying a local adviser (a fund manager) fees to manage their money. The adviser was legally obliged to act solely in their interest, in return for a fee. Gradually some of these trusts came to be set up as corporate entities. Then, in the United States, following a historic court ruling given in favour of the managers of a California investment company in the 1940s, there was a significant change. Managers won the right to sell on the corporate investment trusts they had created to someone else to manage and so to profit beyond just earning fees. As a result, instead of remaining fairly small and local entities managed as 'trusts' solely on behalf of the depositors, management companies have increasingly become profitable earners in their own right. They have gradually been bought out first by each other and then by the very largest banks and financial corporations, aiming to profit from the management fee income and economies of scale that come from owning them. At the same time, and increasingly, money management has migrated from localities to a small number of major centres.

As money management has become big business, the fee income to be earned has inevitably become sought after. The 1967 Nobel Laureate, Paul Samuelson, is said to have observed shrewdly, 'there was only one place to make money in the mutual fund business – as there is only one place for a temperate man to be in a saloon, behind the bar and not in front of it … so I invested in a management company' (Bogle 2005). Given the theory of the random walk and the difficulty achieving consistency, Samuelson's point was that whereas fund performance is bound to be uncertain, the management fees accruing to management companies are guaranteed. They were, for example, payable even over the spectacular periods of declining markets in 2008 and 2009. It is thus for their fee income that very large organisations bought out fund management companies and those working for them and paid high premiums to obtain them.

Given that asset management was becoming a very large and profitable industry, the next step, inevitably, was that the promotion of the products of asset management companies also became big business. Funds have been marketed seductively as is the case with any other commodity. Consumer-appealing tags and flavours abound leading to the proliferation of a dazzling array changing like any other consumer product according to fashion. From 300 US mutual funds in 1980 there were roughly 4,800 US funds in 2008.

It is important for my overall argument to note that at the heart of all the promotion is the selling of a dream. Typically what is offered is the opportunity, via investments in funds with star-performing managers, to join the ranks of the exceptional – to be in a fund with unique insights, a superb record, especially secure methods, or particularly brilliant research. Full colour advertisements in Sunday and other newspapers and all the skills of the advertising industry have been widely employed. Barsky cites as a typical example a full-colour advertisement in the *New York Times* for American Financial Futures. It featured a sexy blonde in a translucent white suit, and the page read, 'It's not just about where your dreams will take you, it's where you take your dreams' (Lowenstein 2008). Another advertisement in *Baron*'s featured a lighthouse against dark clouds. 'Not every storm shows up on weather radar', it read. 'Look for the right Lighthouse. Van Kempen' (Lowenstein 2008). In the run-up to 2008 similar advertisements could be read in Sunday colour supplements, on the walls of the London Underground or bus shelters, or blazoned on the side of London's black cabs. They contributed an atmosphere of glamour and excitement to what was 150 years ago a highly stigmatised industry, shunned and outlawed, taking place in back streets.

The success of this reconfiguration of the asset management industry is emphasised by its growth. It is estimated that mutual and related funds in the United States now have $10 trillion in assets under management – from $135 billion in 1980. These are not easy sums to imagine. But even one per cent of $10 trillion is very large and the global total is $22 trillion. Such growth in funds has in part been driven by legislation moving individuals from passive recipients of defined benefits towards potentially active involvement in investing their defined contributions. 401(k) pension plans in the United States have meant that about ninety million Americans are now invested in mutual funds (Lowenstein 2008) and there have been similar developments in the United Kingdom and elsewhere.

Summary

I began this chapter asking how it might be that markets get caught up in risk-shifting. I hypothesised it could have something to do with the resolution of ambivalence by developing ways of relating to reality characterised by *divided states*. After elaborating what psychoanalysts mean by that concept I described how, although they tried to be long-term investors, my respondents were nonetheless very preoccupied and anxious about their short-term performance. They sensed their behaviour was contradictory and were embarrassed and even resentful about the situation they were in. The main point to carry forward is that it appears current arrangements mean that the institutional competition for assets to manage has become increasingly active, highly visible, and exciting and that this has consequences for those who work in the market. In the process expectations have been raised and marketing claims made which create pressure for exceptional performance – as experienced by the fund managers I interviewed. Whereas once fund management was apparently a rather stodgy slow business, mostly carried on by well paid but largely cautious professionals, who mostly held stocks for long periods and were mainly organised as private partnerships outside the public gaze, it has become exciting and very active.

Crucially, whereas once risk-taking was shared equally between managers and clients, this is no longer necessarily so. As is frequently observed in discussion of the aftermath of the 2008 crisis, bonus payments reward success but do not equally penalise failure, especially if based on short-term results. Losses may lead to termination of employment but they do not have to be paid back. Agency relationships have, therefore, changed fundamentally. In the view of at least some significant industry insiders the process of institutional change – from partnership to share-holding institutions – has altered the incentive structures which once constrained risk-taking (Perella 2010).

The pressure to be fantastic and the changing nature of agency relationships between them can de-couple risk and reward expectations. They create the conditions for divided states.

5
Finding Phantastic Objects

This chapter will develop what I started to describe with the four fund managers in Chapter 2. They told stories about what they did. In this chapter I will argue it is useful to think that what they were doing was telling stories about their efforts to find phantastic objects.

I introduced the concept of phantastic object in the preface. Developed with Richard Taffler (Tuckett and Taffler 2003; Tuckett and Taffler 2008) to capture the particular attraction of dotcom stocks, tulip bulbs, and other objects of financial mania, it brings together two of the most central ideas in psychoanalysis: unconscious phantasy (discussed in Chapter 3) and object.

The notion of 'object' is used in this formulation in the sense traditional to the history of philosophy and psychology. It is a way of distinguishing the representation of a thing, person, or even idea from the thing itself. But in psychoanalytic usage an object is not just any thing or person. It refers to the inherently attractive – to whatever it is in the world 'which attracts' individuals by offering gratification or frustration.

Combining the terms phantasy and object, phantastic objects, therefore, are powerful psychological attractors, acting beneath consciousness, which excite phantasies of gratification or frustration. They are based on a template of the earliest emotional experiences and what they evoked – experiences laid down in the mind in what psychoanalysts call 'memories in feelings' (Klein 1961; Matte Blanco 1968; Sandler and Freud 1988) and cognitive scientists have come to call implicit or procedural memory. The latter operates at deeper levels than actual (declarative) memories and requires no conscious retrieval (Fónagy 1999; Fonagy 1999). Phantasy opportunities fitting the template do not offer just satisfaction or gratification. They provide, so to speak, imagined scenes of exceptional and ultimate satisfaction or the threat of unbearable pain or deprivation, like the pictures in Dante's Inferno or Milton's Paradise Lost.

As I mentioned in Chapter 3, unconscious phantasy is like storytelling. It makes sense of experience and orientates the subject to action. It is the equivalent in psychology and modern cognitive science to narrative. Both disciplines view the human mind as an 'information-processing organ' with remarkable capabilities as both a pattern recogniser and pattern completer (Pinker 1997). In particular, apparently facilitated by the functioning of mirror neurones in the brain (Damasio and Meyer 2008), humans can regularly derive good enough conclusions very rapidly from incomplete data. Storytelling (whether to others or oneself, and perhaps in some sense even beyond consciousness-processing systems in the nature of brain-functioning itself) is part of that ability. It is so integral to cognition and memory that there has been a developing consensus that narrative is the 'inescapable frame of human experience' (Young and Saver 2001).[1]

With this background I was not surprised, therefore, that Fred Bingham, George Monroe, and the other fund managers introduced in Chapter 2, remembered how they had made their decisions by telling me stories without notes and, when I probed, in great detail. The other managers were the same. From the first pilot interviews this was how they spontaneously chose to explain their decision processes – beginning with phrases like 'well, the story with this one was...' and then organising details in classic narrative form along the lines of a beginning, middle, and end. They even narrated when they wrote up their notes, some of which were provided to me to examine.

Stories seemed to be drawn on to explain things to colleagues, superiors, clients, and themselves. In this way we can think of the narratives they told me[2] as clearly both an implicit rationale for others and a justification for themselves. They served to tell me about what had happened, allowed them to make sense to me in the interview and at the same time made sense to them. Certain themes in these stories seemed both common and significant.

Convincing features

When I listened to the stories Fred Bingham and George Monroe told me what came across from my psychoanalytic viewpoint was a picture of how they had built up and developed in their minds a dependent yet satisfying relationship – in their imagination and based on their feelings as well as cognition. By an analogy actually used in the industry one could easily understand the various processes described in those decisions to purchase stocks as the steps taken in entering into a marriage accompanied by a supporting story, one whose function might be seen as providing a cognitive and emotional basis for what managers, like lovers, imagine will be future ups and downs. It is a characteristic of financial assets that they are volatile and can betray; in consequence the experience of anxiety and emotional conflict is anticipated. Similarly, there is an expectation they might be undervalued because others have come to be prejudiced against them and hate them.

Beyond this picture of a developing relationship were there any consistent features in the story scripts that might suggest what fund managers find attractive when presented with opportunities to buy stocks? Looking through just those stories told in Chapter 2, I quite quickly noticed, when doing the analysis after the study was over, something I had only had some inkling about when doing the interviews. Certain persistent elements stood out time and time again. Some of them seemed to create grounds for believing exciting and exceptional rewards might be on offer and others grounds for feeling secure.

Fred Bingham, for example, attributed to *Sound Healthcare* the opportunity to own a company which had monopoly pricing in the context of transparent evidence: there was an 'order book' generating revenue stretching far into the future. In the case of *Amazing Glass* he suggested there were opportunities from its amazing technology or amazing star appeal (a product used in the US president's car), from its very trustworthy CEO (meaning someone who doesn't say anything she shouldn't and in whom we can therefore be confident), from its being a 'proper company making proper profits', and from it still being a largely undiscovered story. In the case of *Lawson*'s, Bingham was attracted by the security for the company's future profitability being backed or guaranteed in some way by government.

A feature of George Monroe's stories, on the other hand, was that he seemed to be particularly impressed when he felt able to see through black holes that others were fooled by. In the case of *Goodfoods* he also imagined himself to be getting hold of handpicked (cherry-picked) opportunities with above-average returns looked after by a management which 'just couldn't mess up' so that there was 'no real downside'. It was also impressive that how Monroe described his relationship with *Goodfoods*, in his own mind, was governed not by emotion but reason. He thought very firmly that it was a decision so thoroughly investigated he had been 'able to take emotion out of it'.

Mark Devreaux told a story about *Car* suggesting how he thought he could see 'through the smoke' (for instance, financial 'details which can make your head spin') by talking with Board members, 'separating out the emotion', overcoming prejudice, and estimating that (quantifiable) downside risk was limited. Duncan Smith's story about *Well-Managed Oil* emphasised the management's good record and his being able to 'maintain an open mind' when the minds of all those around in the market were presently closed.

Sensing a recurrent set of themes in these accounts I began to suspect the stories managers were telling me were actually being generated by something like a common script. I hypothesised there might be some common elements on which they were drawing – themes apparently making financial assets attractive to my fund managers.

To look systematically at this idea, and then to test how far the hypothesis might go, the details of all 165 'buy' stories were carefully examined by two

Table 5.1   Six characteristics of 165 buy decisions

1. Truth seen through to by exceptional ability or effort	• Mentioned in at least 75 stories (45%)
2. A company or sector with exceptional opportunities	• Mentioned in at least 65 stories (39%)
3. Limited opportunity for bad surprises	• Mentioned in at least 45 stories (27%)
4. Proven, solid, or able management	• Mentioned in at least 43 stories (26%)
5. Decision reached because particularly able to manage emotion	• Mentioned in at least 18 stories (11%)
6. Company with monopoly or related market power	• Mentioned in at least 17 stories (10%)

research assistants working independently.[3] Both were asked to write down what they thought of as the key features of each story and to comment on what they thought important about them. They did this very successfully and compared notes. It turned out that one or more repetitive features could be discerned within each of the 165 stories I had been told. In fact on further analysis it became clear that at least one, and usually several, of six particular elements was always present, as set out in Table 5.1.[4]

To understand what is implied in each category I will discuss each one and illustrate the kinds of stories which contained such elements by drawing on three randomly selected examples from those rated as falling within each category.

A special ability to see the truth

As many as 75 stories were told in which the manager's confidence in his or her decision emphasised his or her ability to see through available information; he or she was able to recognise a situation with much more potential than the market currently recognised. The precise reasoning varied but the stories interviewees told that were placed in this category were about how some situations were not well covered or analysed by others or how they involved situations which others in the market found particularly bemusing, mind-dazzling, 'smoky', or smelly. In consequence these stocks were the victim of other people's prejudices or ignorance, or even ones that others did not dare to hold because they were felt to make the 'street' or the 'city' panic. We met an example of this kind when Mark Devreaux was describing *Car*, and other examples were at the basis of George Monroe's strategy when he said about *Utility* that there was a 'valuation discrepancy' between this company and most of its peers because for others its business model was a little bit different and the company a bit too 'complex'.[5] Tristan Cooper summed up the situation in a way many managers would do: 'The judgement of the market on management and on the quality of the company is not very objective and a lot of the time is very unfair. People look at the stock price and that's how they judge the company a lot of the time.' Three examples of all the stories drawn at random from those containing this feature are as follows:

Fastfoods

Describing his decision to buy this company, George Monroe said he had an initial feeling the market was 'getting into that sort of black hole kind of area' where no one had looked at the company enough. The company had not hitherto been 'aggressive' enough in 'leveraging' its balance sheet and so was underperforming. He did lots of calculations and studied lots of accounts and worked out the company would outperform by 10 per cent but this was not in the price.

NewishAir

Ed Morse remarked of this stock purchase that while others panic he can see through the smoke of emotion. *NewishAir* operated in an emerging market with rickety infrastructure where an 'awful accident' had caused all airline valuations to collapse. Based on extensive calculations he believed the outlook was 'still rosy' on a three-year investment horizon and therefore the fall in price was an opportunity 'to pick it up extremely cheaply'.

Lend

Duncan Smith identified that *Lend's* profits and share price had been performing badly due to the low profits it had made because risk premiums were being compressed due to the availability of easy credit. In August 2007, the beginning of the credit crunch meant that there were going to be rising rates and new opportunities for the business to make profits. Smith decided to invest before others reviewed their prejudices about lenders. 'I dug into it a bit more and I thought, I'm going to buy that.' He supported his decision to invest by detailed discussions with the management of the company to whom he had access and felt quite excited that he had also been able to persuade a colleague to change his opinion on the stock – that colleague had 'wanted to sell his shares' in the company because it was underperforming but had now 'decided' to invest 'some more'.

Exceptional or even amazing

When George Monroe was talking about *Fastfoods* he became rather excited. Looking at me rather sheepishly he told me how he would 'pop in' to their restaurants on the way to work (armed with his carefully worked out knowledge of the profitability of each menu item) and see which products were selling. 'I'm not afraid to get into the trenches and stand in a restaurant line to see what everyone is ordering.' The *Fastfoods* story was not only an example of a company found by a special ability to peer through to the truth, Monroe also had grounds to believe its financial performance would be exceptional and was very excited about it.

In fact 65 stories of that kind were told. In them the fund manager's confidence in his or her decision seemed to be based significantly on a belief that he or she had found something with quite exceptional or even amazing prospects – something to 'love' even. Such companies might have a unique business model, amazing or very new technology, or some kind of star support or appeal. Sometimes the circumstances in which they were discovered was exciting – via access to very top board members or during very personal visits to 'see for one-self'. In other examples managers talked about opportunities in emerging countries with 'wonderful assets other people need' and 'absolutely full of coal, hydro carbons' and with a 'lot to offer'. In still others, stocks were about to benefit from 'catalysts' and 'kickers'. Typically the situation in these narratives was that they were very much 'undiscovered stories', suggesting true love rather along the lines of the Princess and the Frog. As well as the story of *Fastfoods* mentioned above we had already been given an idea of this kind of thinking when we encountered the managers talking about *Amazing Glass, Goodfoods, Sound Healthcare, Utility* ('I loved that management'), and *Well-Managed Oil*. Three further examples, drawn at random, illustrate all the stories placed in this category.

Newspaper

This was a story told by George Hamilton about a company trying to modernise itself by 'monetising their content for the internet' and in the process spending a lot of money. Others were prejudiced and profits were therefore falling as elsewhere in the newspaper industry and the share price had fallen by over 50 per cent. Hamilton thought he could see through to a brighter and exciting future. 'I knew what tends to happen in such businesses'. First they 'have got all the spend and none of the revenue and none of the profits. So the market extrapolates' from this 'this terrible trend'. But he thought of it as like a pharmaceutical company investing in research and development; 'eventually one gets paid very handsomely, at which point valuations will rise a lot'.

BasicResource

This was a story Roman Bone told about a company stigmatised because of market expectations about future losses due to falling prices for the basic products they produced in turn caused by the anticipated recession. But Bone didn't agree. Looking 'further afield' he described the 'fabulous growth' of the Chinese market – 'which is where the prices for what they produce are all coming from these days.' Also we 'looked West and we see that in Canada and the US, capacity is changing hands at twice the price per ton as implied by the price *BasicResource* is trading on in the stock markets'. Bone saw an exceptional unrecognised opportunity which excited him – especially when the value of his stock doubled within the year.

CarEngineering

Leonard Frost aimed to find companies which were near monopolies or with pricing power which put them in a special position of being able to raise prices and profitability. Generally auto manufacturers were 'not very attractive'. But one company was different. Only '4 people in the world' make catalytic converters for cars and to do so 'you need to have access to platinum.' *CarEngineerng* has just that. 'So if you want to invest in the auto industry it's an attractive place' and one getting more attractive due to the prospect of litigation 'in terms of pollution limitations' and government regulatory action. Moreover, they 'were in there because the management was superb'.

Lots of security

When talking about *Sound Healthcare* Fred Bingham told me about how it had a 'transparent order book stretching far into the future' and that it was a 'proper company making proper profits'. 'Their order book goes out for a huge number of years,' he continued, 'they've got a very good Finance Director, which is the key to this, and it's just a money-making machine.' George Monroe described *Goodfoods* as having 'no real downside' and Mark Devreaux said the same thing about *Car* – after his very extensive investigations. Forty-five stories had such features. The narratives contained some element allowing the manager's confidence in his or her decision to be based significantly on a belief he or she had found something exceptional because the possibility of unusual upside existed while the prospects for nasty surprises or miscalculation were limited. An above average return was promised with less than average risk. The investment felt secure.

Investors telling stories considered to include this feature had a range of ideas about how and why their companies' prospects were secure. For instance, they could see that the companies' products would be 'in demand for years' or that revenue flows were very 'transparent' rather than opaque, or that effectively the future was underwritten by government or government regulation. They might refer to analogous features of a company's situation about which the manager had tried and tested experience; they felt secure because they had seen this situation work out before. Another feature might be that a company was 'underleveraged', meaning that if things went a bit slowly or unexpectedly they would not be forced into premature action. The general idea, present in all narratives of this kind in one way or another, therefore, was that in effect downside risk was taken out or quantified and the companies just couldn't really 'mess up'. Once again, here are three examples of such stories, selected at random from all those categorised as having this feature.

RealEstate

Ashley Crawford's story about buying stock in *RealEstate*, a financial and retail estate company in Japan, was based around his belief that he had identified a 'young' company which 'in five or ten years time' would become a big company and which, unlike many property investments in Japan, was protected from risk. He said he had 'a lot of confidence that's the way it's going' and considered that among a range of 'young' real estate companies in Japan, *RealEstate* was unique because it had established a near monopoly in a specific sector of the market where there wasn't much competition.' What was particularly attractive was that this sector was particularly low risk 'due to the local government's political commitment to reducing levels of 'nonperforming loans'. 'I think it's almost impossible to change that course they're on' because 'we would have had to have a complete change of political regime and that doesn't happen there'.

Cigs

In this somewhat unusual story Quentin Matthews described how he was very worried about investing in nearly all the stocks in a particular country but had to select some due to mandate constraints. He had to hold something. The solution was *Cigs*, a major tobacco company, whose products were always in demand so it was safely profitable.

GovTel

Ben Hann told stories about how he fulfilled his mandate to purchase risky 'lower grade' bonds in small- or medium-sized companies by finding companies where the risk seemed to be 'capped off'. Telling the story of *GovTel* he said that he liked it for two reasons: as an IT company it had a risky rating because that market was 'project based' and 'in a normal IT business risk is priced quite high'. Close inspection, however, showed that the business had a 'good product' and 'good position'. Specifically the communication devices it manufactured were mainly for the police and similar services of a major government. In his view neither that demand nor that government was going to 'go away'. Therefore, the company seemed to offer security as well as unusual return. 'Sixty per cent of the turnover was in that country and about 90 per cent of that was in the public sector.' The security of government contracts was felt to guarantee reliability and safety.

An imaginative, proven, exceptionally solid, or just very able, management

Feeling safe was also a feature of another group of 45 stories where the source of security was felt to derive in one way or another from the management team in charge. Confidence seemed to rest on the fund manager's belief there were good grounds to think he or she had found a company with excellent management. It might be that they had done it all before (as, for example, when Colin Menton described a telephone company expanding into a new country), it might be that the management history and profit records of the company caused it to be described as a 'proper company', it might be that the CEO or CFO was particularly trusted, well known from a past company, or even a star from previous roles, evidence perhaps of the recognition heuristic (Gigerenzer 2007).

As with other story components, management qualities overlapped with the reason some companies were seen as amazing or low risk – as in George Monroe's description of the management of *GreatSmoke*[6] or *Utility* who just always seemed to be able to 'do it' even if he was not sure exactly what they planned, or in Colin Menton's description of a South American entrepreneur: 'He has a history of being good to minority investors' and he 'understands very clearly'. This last comment is a particularly interesting feature of some stories of this kind. Fund managers like managements they thought understood them and their requirements – those who had an understanding of 'what shareholders needed' as in the case of Mark Devreaux who, when assessing company managements, asked himself, 'Do they sound like they're working for the shareholders, or if they're working for another agenda?' Again three examples of stories with such features have been selected at random.

EasternBank

Colin Menton's story about why he invested in EasternBank (a Western bank which had recently expanded its interests in Eastern Europe) emphasised the importance in such countries of of 'strong' and 'aggressive' management who would seek out investment opportunities, capacities that the management of EasternBank had demonstrated before and that made them a more attractive prospect than their nearest competitors. 'What I'm looking for is strong management who are aligned with minorities, um, and I'm looking for excess returns.' 'We came across this management team' whom they had 'met personally' which gave them a 'massive belief'. He called this 'private information', not 'inside information', and it was built up by 'meeting management'.

EasternLux

Alan Thomas told another story about an Eastern European country (perhaps indicating that 'trust' is a vital commodity for feeling secure in emerging economies). He had bought this utilities company because it was going to benefit exceptionally from the abolition of price controls. 'The regulator, basically, freed tariffs where people were going to pay market prices for electricity and not put a cap or a ceiling... that offered this company 50 per cent annual returns over three or four years.' Others knew about the company, but 'basically, I bought into the idea more than others'. This was because he thought it was 'a well managed company' with 'significant tangible cash flow generation' with 'responsible management'. These last three aspects give precisely what the security managers look for while at the same time seeking exceptional returns.

Houses

Roman Bone told a story about a company run by a 'fascinating chap' who was 'orphaned', 'brought up in a gypsy caravan', who 'can barely read or write', and who had become 'the most successful up-market house builder in the country'. According to Bone's story such success was not recognised by many financial analysts because he was something of a recluse it took an effort to search out and also because 'they can't hold a spreadsheet conversation' with the chief executive.

Being able to manage emotions

Like those described in Chapter 2, many of the fund managers included in their narratives comments about how on this particular occasion they were pleased as to how they had been able to use their rational cognitive capacities to manage their emotions. Their success in doing so, which they thought had allowed them to perceive an otherwise unseen opportunity (as indeed to reject a flawed thesis), was a feature of several 'buy' stories across the sample – as indeed the capacity to make 'objective' decisions not influenced by emotions was at the heart of the 'quant' appeal discussed in the same chapter. In his story about *Goodfoods,* for instance, Monroe described how the 'basis of this and every decision was I try to keep it mathematical, I assign a valuation, and, and I try to take, you know, some of the emotion out of it'. In another story, Francine Taylor told me how when holding *GoodResource,* she had noticed how she had become nervous and had begun 'inching back' her holding of a stock because the price was falling, but then got hold of herself and decided to 'stop' and 'to take time' to 're-evaluate' and to control her emotion. She was pleased about this. 'I think most, most of the time, most people will not go back... you're then in this cycle of always kind of missing it,' she said.

As we will see further in the next chapter most managers had an experience to tell when in the face of adverse information they had 'lost it' and been unable to maintain a thesis (which subsequently did prove correct), and so ended up in trouble. I had the impression that it was to counter such anxieties that in at least 18 'buy' stories managers spontaneously suggested they had felt confident in a particular buy decision precisely *because* they felt they had been able in some way to control their emotion and stay rational rather than give in to excitement or anxiety; it would be different 'this time' they implied. These narratives therefore included the idea that on this occasion they thought they had been able to be more forensic and so would be able to hold on longer, be more patient, or be more rational than others. The prided themselves on the fact that they had been able to overcome initial prejudice and so could view situations objectively and where appropriate change their minds. Sometimes they suggested team structures could facilitate this attitude. Certainly, those who included elements of this sort in their stories clearly derived some confidence from them. Here are three randomly selected examples of stories including such elements.

NotKnownResource

James Talbot told a story in which he expressed considerable satisfaction at being able to buy *NotKnownResource* despite at first rejecting it. He had been prejudiced against it because he felt there was something 'fishy' about the available analysis, which was mostly secondhand. 'We just couldn't get the confidence in the numbers we were being given.' However, the stock then went up a lot. He felt regret but what pleased him was that the missed opportunity did not become a 'bias against the stock'. He had engaged in more thorough research of his own and now more people were 'covering the stock'. 'So suddenly in our model we started getting concrete numbers that we had a lot more confidence in, and, yes, lo and behold, it was very cheap, it had fantastic growth, it had fantastic news flow.' Talbot was a behavioural finance enthusiast. 'Did I anchor on the fact that I'd lost 60 per cent?' 'No', he said, although 'a lot of people would have done. I said "I've missed it, I've missed the boat."' But 'we sat down and we got it and four months later it's doubled. So that's a good example of not anchoring on price levels but anchoring on fundamentals.' He said, 'You can argue that I let my emotion get in the way initially', but he was now very pleased to have a process that then 'overcame emotions'.

GreatSmoke

George Monroe told a story about deciding to hold on to *GreatSmoke* (and to persuade his colleagues to do so) when there was a lot of emotional pressure on him to sell. 'I allowed the numbers to sort of guide my investment decision. I felt very, very firmly that the business was very good.' Based on his analysis he didn't believe the negative value implied by possible outcomes from various court cases and 'bad publicity' and was certain 'the market' would also eventually 'realise that *GreatSmoke* really has value'. Everybody had told him it was time to sell but he said, 'let me read to you the press release and the transcript of the conference call from last quarter: "I don't know how they're going to create value but they will. They're smart guys." We revisited that thesis, and I went back and I re-visited my price targets. I really try to take most of the emotion out of the process. Discipline and process is incredibly valuable as long as you adhere to it.'

VeryLargeCo

Chen Chang told a story about deciding to buy into one of the world's biggest industrial companies because they had appointed a new CEO with the mandate to stop cost-getting, get the scientists back to innovation, and get back to basics. He was in tune with the core of the company and had a 'fairly good' track record. But what was crucial for this decision was the willingness to withstand short-term fluctuation. It might take time and needed calm. Chang said, 'We've got more patience' and 'with our long-term perspective we look at things a little bit differently'.

Companies with monopoly or market power

Several of the earlier stories suggested that what was attractive about particular companies was the strong market position enjoyed and the pricing advantages that came from it. Fred Bingham's *Amazing Glass* was an example. As he told his story, one of the things that made him very confident in this company was what he called 'its proprietary toughened' glass and its recently acquired expertise in laminating fragile solar panels (actually made by another company); 'their skill is to laminate these very brittle beasts.' Such skills put them in demand and were not easily copied. Similarly, Alan Thomas's *Easternbank* had a strong presence in fifteen emerging European countries with a network which had built up market power, and Leonard Frost's *CarEngineering* was one of only four companies both making the crucial catalytic converters required for modern motor engines and the platinum to make them. Stories like these, in which the key feature was the way a company's position or skill allowed it to enjoy a competitive advantage in the value chain, or to benefit from named franchises and branding, or to exploit the barriers to entry other firms would face, were features that regularly figured in 'buy' stories. They made a manager's thesis about a company exciting and exceptional as well as going some way to providing a reason to feel secure with the risk.

At least 17 of the stories contained such elements. Here are three illustrations, again selected at random from all those stories containing such features.

Asian Telecom

Charlie Fraser bought *Asian Telecom* shares because they owned the second largest cellular operator in a large emerging country. This ownership gave them a semi-monopoly position and great prospects; barriers to entry exist in cellular telecom markets and the potential for expansion in this country was very large. An additional feature of this story was that there was a technical factor.

The company's advantageous position within the country where it was operating was amplified by the fact its shares were listed on an exchange outside the country which made them much more liquid and so potentially more valuable because everyone could buy in without restriction. The shares of other competing companies inside the country had foreign investor limits, so their shares could not be bought and sold freely, increasing the attractiveness of *Asian Telecom*. Fraser expected 'to be able to unlock the value' once all this became clear to others and the shares went up.

BrightComputer

Andrew Smythe told stories about his ability to see through to the deeper truths. Therefore, he thought he could 'add the alpha' where fundamentals were strong and he was confident also that that valuation or sentiment was 'way off base' and so prices depressed. The story he told about *Brightcomputer* had these features and also included a great amount of admiration for its products which he personally admired. To his mind some were 'way ahead of the competition and will be', he thought, for some time, giving them market power. Like George Monroe, he thought 'The best thing you can do with retail and consumer stocks is to go out and walk the stores, walk the mall; you have a sense of whether it's a good product or not a good product. If you go by the store here you just see that it's packed, every time you go by. Some are 24 hours a day, seven days a week, every day. Christmas, New Year's, whenever you want to be there. It's phenomenal. They have great product design and great products. You can compare their computers to a regular computer, and just the ease of use and everything related to it is remarkable'.

BrightStore

Novak Jones told a story about buying this company because it was a publicly quoted franchise of a very successful furnishing company in Europe opening in a hitherto undeveloped European country. The franchise would have all kinds of advantages against local competition and there were 'a number of macroeconomic factors creating the wealth necessary to buy houses and furnish them'. He was confident in the management of the company and the way the franchise adapted: 'You have the security of a world-class franchise in an area with very high expected growth.' It was what he called a 'double whammy'.

Generating confident scripts

Novak Jones's 'double whammy' is perhaps a summation of the ideal-typical script found within the stories the fund managers told me. What it seems really attracted them when they were assessing investment opportunities with a view to buying financial assets was consistently a combination of two features: security and exceptional expectation.

Analysis of their stories in terms of the six categories just elaborated suggests that on the one hand managers liked to be convinced there was some cap on uncertainty, some offload of risk, or some guarantee of visible and substantial future income streams. The elements labelled monopoly and market power, limited opportunity for bad surprises, proven and solid management, or their own conviction their analyses were calm and unemotional, all seemed to have been essential to underpin and make potentially secure fund manager conviction. It seems likely that stories with these four elements in the script removed at least some of the anxiety which one can expect to be consequent on commitment to a dependent relationship with an uncertain future. They are, so to speak, evidence of one's fiancé's and his or her family's reliability.

Stories only became compelling, however, when coupled with another feature: the prospects of exceptional returns they had identified *and* others had not seen. In other words, there had to be the existence of grounds for exclusivity and 'true love'. In fact in as many as 123 out of the 165 stories (75 per cent) analysed, the stories managers told *either* contained the belief that their exceptional way of seeing through all the data to the truth was going to pay off, and/or that what they had found was rather exceptional in the sense that the company or sector held out exceptional opportunities.

Looking a little deeper in different guises the stories fund managers constructed seemed to need scripted elements that functioned as attractors, with features which *pulled* them towards a feeling they had personally and exceptionally captured something with exceptional returns. But they also needed to script elements that gave them security, helping them to *push* away uncertainty and so the potential feeling of anxiety about making a possible mistake when entering a long-term relationship.

I will argue further below that an essential property of narrative is that it allows diverse elements of fact and interpretation to be woven together in scripts so that they coalesce meaningfully and emotionally to provide a sense of conviction and truth. Their narrative accounts thus made managers' decision-making sensible and coherent, underpinning their conviction about their choices. They seemed to be producible within their minds (at least in nascent form) for every decision, and by combining the elements of attraction and security within the scripts, seem likely to have functioned to help them build enough conviction inside themselves to feel comfortable enough to act; to commit to buy and to take risk. Stories do make sense in the telling. When they were asked to elaborate they recounted what happened in such a way that they seemed to live out what happened and to take me with them. In doing so they conveyed memorable pictures which remain in my mind to this day – the 4 a.m. early rising on a very cold morning to catch a plane to the middle of nowhere, the chance encounter, the exciting meeting, the employee overtime notice indicating increased product demand observed pinned just inside a factory in India, and so on.

Exceptional but safe

Up to now in this chapter I have deconstructed the 'buy' stories managers told feature by feature and then shown that at least three-quarters of these decisions, told me as part of a wider account of both their satisfying and unsatisfying decisions, contained both the attracting and security elements identified. As some managers told me more stories than others, and also because some satisfied decisions or dissatisfied decisions involved selling rather than buying, it is possible the analysis just carried out is weighted by a few managers – some of them turned up quite a bit, despite selection being random, because with more stories they had a greater chance to be included.

Another way of analysing the data to explore the hypothesis being developed about the basis of confidence and commitment was to look not story by story as I have so far, but at all the stories told by each manager which they considered had a successful outcome. Are the same features present if we analyse the data differently in this way? To answer that question I looked at the buy narratives of four of the stock-picking managers, selected at random. All of their successful decisions will be examined within the context of their overall investment strategy.[7] The managers so selected were Alan Thomas, Frances Shaw, Gordon Hamilton, and Leonard Frost.

Alan Thomas

Alan Thomas's account fully supports the conclusions just reached and even elaborates them. He worked within a team managing $550 million invested in undeveloped markets and even his mission statement has the attractors we have been discussing. He wanted to find exceptional companies benefitting from newly adopted European regulations and from situations where the gap between consumption levels of the established and newer European economies was presently wide. Such companies would have market power and be expected to grow much faster than others elsewhere. Among companies with such potentiality he then aimed to 'pick' 'the best managers', running quantitative analyses to find out 'how much we should be paying' for them. This emphasis on quantitative discipline included the comment that he didn't just 'invest in stories' but also wanted to be sure to 'dig deep' and 'to know the story' inside out, indicating how he tried to feel secure. To do so he wanted to 'identify the risks' and 'find out how much' he should be paying for it'. Interestingly, while he thought his ability to do this was because he looked 'five years ahead', at the same time he liked to be a bit cautious and so liked the security of transparency – he said he'd like to see something 'visible' happening within 'three to five years'. This long-term outlook was clearly not easy emotionally because he then added rather ambiguously that 'three to five years' in 'these days' could be a year.

Thomas discussed four examples where he felt satisfied with what he had decided and all had similar features: the 'story' including some of the previously identified elements. One was *Consumol*. It was an unknown story discovered by personal contact with an impressive entrepreneur added to which there was the security from both the quantitative analysis and the awareness of management as to how to keep shareholders happy. He was buying a stock that nobody else 'knew about' and so had 'no confidence in it', Thomas said. He spoke 'for an hour and a half' personally with the 'chief executive' and in the call found out 'how well he knows the company and the industry'. The quantitative analysis showed valuations were attractive. Thomas reported that the share price more than doubled over a year, which was satisfying, but it wasn't just that – what satisfied him especially was that 'I managed to take that risk'. What convinced him eventually was his sense that the management had the 'ability to know exactly where they are and where they want to be'. They knew the nature of the industry and 'they explained it very well'. They knew the size of the 'addressable market' and were 'targeting locations'. They were 'capital responsible' and so shareholder friendly – 'they didn't just want to be big in buying bits of companies as they made money; they just wanted to stick to their bread and butter.' One might say the management had the capacity to convince that it understood what investors wanted; 'if you're a public company, you want to be forthcoming with your shareholders' and 'sensitive to returns'. On top of all this they 'had a track record'; 'a two-and-a-half, three-year track record'.

His second story about a company called *Property* had the usual exclusivity and exciting features (in this case management quality featured high) but was also particularly important because it felt very secure. This had allowed Thomas not only to buy the company but also to resist the well-known tendency to sell 'winners' too early. Management was 'always able to do two things'. They had a portfolio of real estate holdings and 'the value of their company was basically driven by interest rates going down'. Every time interest rates went down their capital appreciated and so they had capital gains. But what was 'special about this management' was that they 'monetized' the gains they were getting. Thomas explained that instead of just 'booking paper gains' as appraisal showed their property values rising, they actually sold them and bought others and so cashed them in. Such actions 'gave a lot of credibility to the capital' and also they kept acquiring real estate plots for development in different nearby countries that were less mature than their own and that also gave higher upside.

To summarise, Thomas's narratives contain just the features noted above. He has reasons to be confident in management who 'know' what they are doing, finds companies not so well known by others, and finds various grounds for believing these investments secure.

Frances Shaw

Frances Shaw's account also confirms the thesis. She was one of three women in the sample and the head portfolio manager of a team of five for an insurance company. She was required to invest money for retirement funds valued at $25 billion and the context in which she worked was rather different. Her mandate gave her precise financial targets based on the insurance company's obligations and prevented her doing much buying and selling so that her investment philosophy, which was to hold securities for the long period, correlated with her situation. She wanted to invest in 'very high quality companies' and to be able to earn 'good value for long-term investors'. She strongly believed that the creation of value is something to be built 'over time' and that the best thing to do was 'to identify the factors that create value over the long run'. In this way she felt she was very different from most other fund managers and financial analysts whom she saw as concentrated on short-term valuation, that is, on the results from the next quarter and their benchmark performance pressure.[8] As a consequence she thinks that companies exist that can be totally unknown, unidentified, and undervalued by ordinary managers whose situation, in short, makes them far too impatient.

In telling me about how she found companies, she said she does not consider quantitative screening with commercially produced data of much use 'because we don't trust the data and because we think screening is for bad [fund] managers who have no ideas'. Her ideas, she says, are found everywhere: reading a newspaper, participating in seminars, receiving managers. The nature of her decision-making meant Shaw made rather few decisions. The main story she told me about an investment with which she was satisfied concerned a company called *Road* – in fact introducing it spontaneously when explaining her general approach: 'I remember a story', she volunteered. She had visited the company, an infrastructure company building freeways, in 2003. It had been a public company but a 'government had decided to privatise' part of it. Apparently no fund manager was interested at the time because there was an avalanche of information, lots of debt and very high interest rates so it was at a very low price.

In this way Shaw's story follows the hypothesised pattern. It's a narrative containing the script about seeing through to the truth by exceptional effort. It then has the next element. 'We met the management' and were 'impressed'.

Then the script contains 'exclusivity'. 'Only one other investor was interested' in buying shares on privatisation. That company was *Builders* – now another very large and very well-known infrastructure company. Both *Builders* and Shaw bought large holdings. She said she had realised that *Road* had concentrated for 35 years on investing in highways and all the accumulated debt would be paid by 2017 – 14 years away, which in her institutional situation was not a problem. This script element contained Novak Jones's 'double whammy'. There was safety from foreseeable cash revenues and excitement from how large they would be. After 2017 the situation was going to be exceptional – 'a wall of cash, a wall of cash' and 'with no new large projects', she said. To this element she added to the story a further element of exclusivity. 'When we spoke about that with our friend fund managers or analysts, they said, "My God, you are not...it's not sexy."'

The end result of this story was that Shaw finally sold out her holding for 40 times its original value to *Builders*. The story contains the key elements of the scripts I hypothesise allow fund managers to commit – a balance of excitement and security and exceptional return with low risk. As with Thomas's, above, a secure future flow of cash (a 'wall' of cash) was a particularly attractive feature of the story, as it visibly mitigated the risk of unpleasant surprises.

Leonard Frost and Gordon Hamilton

We encountered Leonard Frost in the last chapter. His story about his decision to buy *CarEngineering* was also described above in this chapter and very much fits the script already discussed. He will not be discussed further.

The final manager against which the hypothesis is to be tested, therefore, was Gordon Hamilton. He worked on a team in which everyone is both analyst (his responsibility is Health Care and Utilities) and portfolio manager. He has been in portfolio management over 20 years and the fund for which he is responsible was worth about $1 billion invested in securities throughout the developed world. His mission statement required him to hold long (three to five years) and his approach was to focus on a list of core companies in his domain and to use an analysis of each company's strengths, weaknesses, opportunities, and threats to rank them as sell, hold, or buy. The team has a standard modelling system which specifically sets out to identify companies with 'market power' with a position within the 'value chain' giving them the power to negotiate down suppliers prices, to negotiate up their own selling prices, or to benefit from other monopolistic-tending factors.

An interesting story which fitted the script found in the other stories was one Hamilton told me about his satisfying purchase of *Engineering* – his satisfaction deriving in part because it was his own idea and also because he was not the analyst for that sector! The core of the story was that he thought himself especially able to evaluate the company's legal liability. He was 'the only person' on his team who 'bought the stock' because he had past experience on which to draw. He thought he knew about such situations because he had encountered them before 'with another company who'd had a similar scare' four or five years earlier. Calmly able to carry out a disciplined analysis, he concluded the stock was a buy – 'it was the classic, going against fear'. In a script combining the usual elements providing both excitement and security he told me how the 'rest of the market and his colleagues' could only see negatives. They 'couldn't conceive of the possibility that the company could get through this difficulty' and did not realise the market had written off the prospects of any new products ever coming through and were making 'wild and unsupported generalisations'. Hamilton's other buying success, involving the opportunity to benefit from the possibility of exceptional growth from renewable energy, also combined exception, the security of government backing, and technical features of the asset, along with careful analysis to control emotion. Although companies in the sector would be new and so have no track record to give security about future performance, his approach had been to invest in an index product and so reduce selection risk. 'I was able to find a product that was able to do the work, and I was able to get a fairly large amount of money invested in this product...in a sensible and risk-adjusted way.'

Here again were narrative scripts combining sensible secure features we have come to expect – a long-term predictable income stream, government legislation, semi-monopolistic positioning, an area of investment out of favour because 'the market', the Street, or the City are prejudiced or don't look in enough detail, and a significant price discount if one invests with a long enough horizon. Such narratives clearly create the *pull* of conviction and like all the others discussed in this chapter also provide protection, a *push* against the emotion of anxiety fuelled by uncertainty, thus making it possible not just to buy securities but to go on having a relationship with them; holding them over time. Together, the analysis of the stories told by the four randomly selected managers confirm the proposition that investor conviction rests on a combination of developing a sense of exclusivity and excitement while trying to contain the uncertainty and insecurity which comes from commitment.

Validation

The interviews I have been reporting come from a developmental study where the aim was to develop ideas so that the hypotheses grew out of the analysis rather than preceding it. It is, therefore, clearly desirable that the work be repeated and the hypothesis that fund managers tell themselves and others stories about their decisions with scripts so far discussed undergo further test. However, in the meanwhile, there are a further set of grounds for believing the conclusions I have just set out are sound.

I mentioned at the beginning of the chapter that some managers had offered me copies of their internal notes, filed in their systems. Because these notes existed for another purpose, to provide institutional records of the basis for decisions and were collected before it was even known they would be studied, their content provides another independent window from which to examine the basic thesis, that fund managers build conviction by telling stories and that these stories contain specific repetitive elements so that we can think of them as following a predetermined script. Such scripts establish conviction both that something exceptional is available and it's safe to invest in it. Hypotheses supported by different methods, and particularly those supported by unobtrusive measures, have a stronger claim.

The notes I have are from five managers only one of whom has been quoted so far. They appear to support the points already made. Brian Anderson, for example, wrote of a meeting he attended with the management of *Outfits,* that 'I was excited before I went in and I left feeling more excited'. Why? Because the company was selling replica team sweat shirts at manifestly highly profitable prices ('only' sixty dollars). He wrote that the shares were 'easily' worth 40 per cent more than the top price they were likely to be offered at and could support that without being 'too creative' with his statistical analysis. His Excel model was attached and he wanted to get his order in 'the next day or so'. A second note on the same company dealt with an attempt to understand the fall in share price. The manager was able to 'post-rationalise' and wrote that 'nothing has changed my mind we will make a lot of money', adding, 'I am even more certain in my belief'. He puts the fall down to the market – 'but more importantly the press' sensationalising and offers a detailed analysis for his viewpoint which was written as a long and intriguing story describing the prejudice that was enveloping the company and all the efforts the CEO would be making to meet people in the City and calm their fears. Other notes on other companies are full of phrases such as 'the market is clearly waiting', 'limited downside', 'being missed by the market', 'investors will probably focus on', 'to conclude I am comfortably conservative', and this situation is a 'similar one to the one we saw with', 'this is a stock I will always have trouble being passionate about'. While this analysis of notes is far from definitive it appears to be describing the same world I have been describing in this chapter. Notes tell stories and the same features are present in them and the interviews.

Summary

The investment managers I interviewed told me stories about the decisions they had made because narrative is the framework within which they thought. Their stories combine cognitive and emotional elements and appear to be pre-formulated into scripts. The emotional content of their stories and the way they were building up imagined internal relationships to the companies and those who ran them is obvious from the stories. So also was the implicit search for at least the precursor of a *phantastic object*. Although these stories do not all have the extreme quality of the love stories and covering narratives of those told at the time of the dotcom or about the benefits of asset-based derivatives, their quality was similar. Usually they were telling me and themselves how and why they had 'felt' they had got 'on to something' exceptional that their peers had not seen and which, to a considerable extent, they thought was secure; at the time they had reason to believe their thesis was likely to *go on making sense to them* even if subsequent price movements threatened to undermine their theses. The stories, in other words, were about exceptional opportunities to gain reward at much lower risk than usual for such gains.

I mentioned in the first chapter how it is their characteristic that short-term volatility on most assets is greater than long and that there are significant transaction costs attached to chopping and changing. It seems likely, therefore, that to act, to make the decisions I have been describing, managers must both overcome any initial emotional conflict – setting aside anxiety – and have ongoing ways to keep doing so. Even the word 'conviction' features significantly in mission strategies. Those who cannot commit enough will get the jitters and then by chopping and changing and incurring transaction costs without compensating gains will be likely to destroy their portfolios. Maintaining the analogy of making a marriage, managers who can't, so to speak, get to the altar and stay wedded to their stocks at least in some way, are unlikely to succeed in the industry for long. At the same time managers who are too wedded to their ideas may equally face disaster. We will return to such conflict.

What is especially interesting about all this is that in the traditional language of financial economics the stories I have been outlining effectively claim that managers could find ways to get exceptional rewards without too much risk. Thus fortified and convinced, managers could commit to action.

6
Experiencing the News

We have just seen how in telling their stories about buying stocks the fund managers I interviewed seemed to be speaking to a deeper shared script; they were recounting in one way or another how they had found something – an object of desire – which was both exceptional and so extremely exciting, but also safe. We also saw how my interviewees' stories contained much evidence of searching and investigating. They processed a great deal of information, checked and double-checked, and undertook extensive calculations. In meetings they put forward their theses and then defended them against the counterarguments made against them by colleagues. But, finally, they bought the stocks and the hitherto imagined relationship began.

This chapter aims to look at the relations my respondents had with their stocks after they had purchased them and, therefore, at the issues of managing quality uncertainty and maintaining trust through time. At the point my respondents bought stocks they bought an expected relationship with an imagined path, but as time played out this reality had to be experienced through actual time. The nature of financial assets meant that future reality must be inherently uncertain.

Psychic reality and object relations

The rock on which Freud based psychoanalytical thinking was the idea that it is useful to distinguish between ordinary reality – what we might collectively agree are the facts of a matter – and psychic reality – how we subjectively interpret our experience or what we subjectively believe reality is actually telling us. Imagined relations of the kind that investors have with their stocks take place in psychic reality interacting with the facts as they become available.

Starting from Freud's work, later psychoanalysts such as Klein (1930), Winnicott (1945), and Bion (1962) conceived of human thinking in terms of 'object relationships', using the term 'object' in its philosophical sense to denote a representation (be it of a person, an idea, or a thing), and using the word 'relationship' to denote an emotional mental connection between the object and the thinker, the subject. Bion (1962) postulated different kinds of imagined object relationships, governed by the different core emotions of L (loving), H (hating), and two states of emotional perception, K or –K (knowing or anti-knowing).

What matters in this view is that knowing about something establishes an emotional relationship and not merely a cognitive one. Experiencing the reality of objects, therefore, necessarily implies a relationship with feelings. It became manifest when respondents described their experience of holding stock and having to process news about its developing fortunes. 'I love that stock' they quite often said to me about ones that had been or were becoming a success, or 'I hate it' about others that were not. Expressions of this kind were spontaneous and common and are well recognised in financial markets.

We can suppose that from a psychoanalytic viewpoint those who think to purchase financial assets create imagined (mental) relations to them. They picture a relationship with an object with consequences for reward and loss which induce feelings of pleasure and pain as they construct possible scenarios in their minds – not unlike a marriage contract, as I suggested above. As in a marriage, once the purchase is complete, expectations start becoming reality. However, unlike in at least most marriages, the relationship to financial assets is not proximate. It is carried on at a distance and news about it is filtered so that a great deal of what is transpiring is uncertain. It is, so to speak, news of stocks and possible implications of that news that reaches the investor, not their actuality. The news comes by all kinds of indirect inferential routes – including by observing the thinking and behaviour of 'rivals' around them and imagining their motives. The consequence is obvious. The holders of financial assets are in an uncertain dependent object relationship. They experience that relationship and are reliant on it for loss or reward day by day, month by month, and year by year. Therefore, as part of that ongoing experience they inevitably continue to imagine outcomes which generate emotions, as we will see below. I will elaborate in a later chapter on how psychoanalysts and neuroscientists consider emotion and imagination to equip humans with the capacity to find what they need and to make sense of events. The incoming news about stocks is sifted and filtered for meaning. What is relevant and what can be trusted?

Trust

Trust takes place in relationships – imagined and real – and is fundamentally subjective. Its converse is distrust or suspicion. Not very far away is paranoia and persecution. From a psychoanalytic viewpoint, all, quintessentially, again depends on psychic reality. Consider as a simple example a child who has just woken from a nightmare in which his mother has turned into a witch. As every parent knows, for a little while perhaps the child's dream will persist. During that time as far as s/he is concerned Mother *is* a witch. At such moments it is psychic reality, what we believe, that counts.

Trust develops through early infancy. With enough good experience to allow the inner world in which s/he exists to become predictable, the child learns to overcome doubts. Mother comes back, the food will come, a dark bedroom is safe enough, those black specks in the food are all right. Suspicions can be tolerated, investigated, and overcome. Reassurance can be given and received. But according to psychoanalysis that journey is long and never complete. It involves an ongoing passage through *divided* and *integrated* states[1] gradually more or less adjusting to reality. *Divided* states manage persecutory feelings by abolishing them, but also then make them potentially worse by creating an ongoing state of generalised doubt, unease, and suspiciousness.

Trust in a *divided* state, therefore, is not easily sustained and easily turns to doubt. It is based on idealisation – seeing only the good qualities of the object and exaggerating them while eviscerating any causes for anxiety or doubt which are felt as threatening. Trust in the *integrated* state, on the other hand, is different. It is based on realistic assessment and is therefore much more robust – depending on the outcome of curiosity, trial and error, learning, processes of mourning, and evidence to set doubts properly into context.

The extent to which individuals manage to develop trust of the *integrated* state variety depends on the extent to which actual experience has equipped them with a willingness to entertain doubts and to look. Some people don't want to do that. For instance, they may have reasons to feel guilty about being greedy and invasive towards others. They may have cheated rivals if they had a chance. If they recognise this they can accept the fact and feel a bit guilty or anxious about possible retaliation or feel sorry. But if they push doubts off regularly then they take up *divided* states. They flee from 'bad' feelings by 'splitting' them off and 'projecting' them so that in complicated ways they then unconsciously experience others to be persecuting. *Divided* state attitudes of this kind enter a cycle of recrimination and revenge[2] and make uncertainty much more difficult to tolerate. We would, therefore, expect decisions arrived at in *integrated* states to be more robust than those determined in *divided* ones.

Responding to news

Stock markets are full of news, rumoured news, and interpretations of the news and also inherent uncertainty and anxiety. The news has the effect of promoting doubt and excitement, and its volume and extent perhaps also exists as a way to try to manage their consequences, to create a sense of being 'in the know'. News and opinion is in the financial press and comes via wire services and a host of commercial electronic data feeds and commentaries all avidly studied and competing for attention. The growth of information and opinions about that information in this area has been fantastic and with the recent addition of social networking and other sites (providing more and more avenues for news) seems likely to increase at a still faster rate. In this situation where the meaning of information is uncertain, which itself results from the fact that financial assets are volatile and generate excitement, anxiety is endemic. The central question for everyone is always the same: what news in this deluge of information is real and consequential and what is mere noise?

I suggested above that my respondents were like someone who has just got married but cannot see or meet her husband because he is far away and also receives only very vague details about him and his behaviour. It is obvious this is a predicament which will challenge her state of mind and the solidity of her prior decision-making. By analogy, once my interviewees held stocks the scenarios and outcomes about which they had originally only imagined now became a possible source of worry. Their careers were now dependent on the stock performance. Concern that their original stories could be contradicted by new information was inevitable. To make matters worse, in anticipation of a potential effect on expected stock values, any news and its consequences had to be processed very fast. At the heart of the problem (particularly given the common feature of their buy scripts that they had a privileged view) was the fact that fund managers could suddenly find themselves in a state of information disadvantage. Having bought stock thinking they were in the advantageous and exceptional position of being the exploiters of information they now had become the exploited.

For example, Fred Bingham's interview was discussed at length in Chapter 2. One instance was the new situation he faced when he saw that the share price of *Burgers for Schools* began to dip. Its future profitability seemed to be under threat following the intervention of a celebrity chef whose campaign for healthy food for English schoolchildren seemed to compete with the company's fast food–based menu contracts. This quite unexpected development faced Bingham with an eventuality he had not previously considered. More attention to school meals might mean more or less profitability depending on how the story unfolded and how the company responded. What might happen? Because this threat interacted with the fact that the company managers had taken on a lot of debt to take it over, Bingham sold out, thinking his thesis was blown.

In a second example, Bingham described how his predictions for the future profitability of *Mr Sugar* were frustrated. The company announced one day that one of its core products was not being taken up as successfully as it hitherto hoped; leading to a fall in the share price. Again this spoilt the imagined likely outcome of the story Bingham had developed for that investment, which he had been holding on to for some time.

In a third example, Bingham had spoken about the falling share price of *Leave It with Us* and about the anxiety and distrust induced in him by yet another adverse price movement. He then started to get information about the management which caused him to become doubtful about his prior investment thesis and eventually to sell that holding precipitously. Having lost trust in the management he was prejudiced and decided to ignore the company chairman's warning that he was making a big mistake. In fact the company subsequently did well. But selling seemed to have provided an exit from uncomfortable experience and Bingham took it. 'It's often better for your own peace of mind to just move on; [say you have] made a mistake, just move on and not try and rectify it rather than having to meet people that you're not sure about anyway, and not feeling very good about. Just cut it and move on.'

These three examples indicate how in the uncertain world of financial markets news of price changes is a signal. Falls create an experience of anxiety and an urgent need for explanation. They made Bingham review his theses and the information they had originally been based on. His reasons for concern in each case can be put down either to the fact he had not sufficiently imagined what might happen, and then attached enough weight to those possibilities to cause him to act differently, or to the limitations of the information he had been given by the relevant sources, particularly management; in other words they created doubt as to how he had used the information or about the information itself. In the *Burgers for Schools* case he had just not thought to imagine the particular threat existed. In the case of his *Mr Sugar* investment, his thesis depended on information from a previously reliable and trustworthy source (a broker) and he had not thought it necessary to check further. In the case of *Leave it with Us* he had trusted the capacity and skill of the management team and their story for the future. Interestingly, in this case, as with *Mr Sugar*, he came to feel they had let him down – with obvious emotional discomfort and dislike characterising the second experience which prompted him to want 'out' fast.

The previous chapter showed how judgements about the quality and reliability of enterprise managers were a key feature of most 'buy' scripts. As we just saw when discussing Fred Bingham's experience, stocks which are bought then have to be held while news about them filters through. When news emerged to challenge his underlying script, forcing him to imagine he might have been in error so that he then faced either a loss or at least having to forgo an anticipated gain, Bingham, like other respondents, got emotional. In these circumstances we can postulate that the imagined 'object relationships' turns from those of L (love) to those of H (hate). Stocks that had been loved were now hated.

Two related observations support this hypothesis. The interviewees did not seem to have responded to their disappointment with much empathy for the reality of the situation faced by enterprise managers. Instead they were angry or critical. So, when learning of adverse developments in the companies in which they had invested, I can recall no fund manager I talked with making a comment along the lines that commerce and business is difficult – perhaps that it's an uncertain world and that neither production costs nor consumer demand for products is controllable or completely predictable, so that with the best intentions enterprise managers cannot always deliver all of the time. Obviously they knew this but rather than talk about it like that, they spoke about managements much more personally and emotionally – especially when the stories they had committed themselves to when purchasing the stock did not come to their expected fruition. They invariably spoke of suspicions, stupidities, and breaches of trust. Specifically they had a tendency to suspect some degree of motivated inaccuracy. In other words, not only do my respondents seem to have conceived of their relationship to the stocks they bought in object relational terms, they also seem to have come to hate those stocks which, once loved, had let them down. 'Suspicion' was a feature of all such conversations and perhaps explains the preoccupation with security in the 'buy' scripts.

Quality uncertainty and emotional conflict

Suspicion is more difficult to test in a *divided* state. My interviewees constantly faced the experience of quality uncertainty and with it the information asymmetry discussed in Chapter 1. What was significant about it was the experience. Relating to someone who knows more than oneself about something of vital interest was inherently emotionally uncomfortable and gave rise to suspicion. Those with privileged information, like the management of *Leave It with Us* from whom Fred Bingham 'moved on', created doubt in my respondents' minds. Having once trusted them, they were quick to imagine that such enterprise managers might have misled them deliberately. They thought of them as having self-interest in doing so.

Perhaps it was because the ongoing relationships between fund and enterprise managers were necessarily asymmetric that my respondents not only found their dependency uncomfortable but also seem to have had a rather fragile and moral emotional framework within which to think about it. In the case of *Leave It with Us*, for example, Bingham described selling his stocks by saying he 'hadn't wanted to hang around any more' and, as he put it, 'meet people that you're...not feeling very good about'. In that case it was true that the management did have an interest in the company's share price and might want to talk it up. But subsequent events did not actually bear out a suspicious view. It turned out that managers had not been using their position to mislead. Eventually results were good and the share price went on to do well, as Bingham had originally anticipated. Overcome by uncertainty and then embracing suspicion and abandoning his holding, Bingham and his clients lost out.

It is an inevitable fact of financial markets that much of the information about stock prospects comes from that released by enterprise management in the structural situation of information asymmetry and potential moral hazard, as just described. As we have seen, good news did not remove uncertainty. Perhaps for this reason my respondents also paid a great deal of attention – not entirely consistently given normal volatility – to price changes in their stocks. Rises or falls in share price were news that 'something' was happening. This quickly created excitement or anxiety. Underneath the beliefs in the ability and willingness of enterprise management to deliver the imagined outcomes they had formed when buying the stock lurked anxieties about being dependent, and confidence was inherently fragile. Going back to infancy humans get anxious when dependent and especially insofar as they are in a divided state, and so half expecting bad news without knowing why or from where.

The way their tasks were defined provided a clear context for fragility. In standard economic and finance theory (of course known to all my respondents) uncertainty is tackled by the concept of risk and risk is calculable and so 'in the price'. The task of my respondents had required them to assume otherwise – and as we have seen this was also true of the mission statements they worked to and the buy scripts they used to justify their actions. Of course, without uncertainty and doubt about to how to interpret the information available in financial markets, there would very likely be no possibility of information advantage, much less activity, and no stories about special insights and relationships. 'Once everything's clear, it's easy, right?' George Devreaux said. My point is that for these respondents, the essence of their task was to manage information uncertainty. For them being on the wrong end of an information advantage was an ever-present risk due to the potential agency conflicts in their relations to enterprise managers, the possibility they could be the victims of deliberate deception or just errors of one kind or another as well as bad luck.

So how did they do it and what did they describe? First and quite naturally respondents anticipated the risk that they might have been misinformed before making their buys. As part of looking for the secure element in buy scripts they attempted very elaborate projections and calculations about future values all based on imagination and assumptions. But once they were holding stock they had no alternative but to experience dependency; they had to wait and to 'suffer' living with the risks that followed what they *had* done. Bingham's examples already showed how much this is an inherent part of owning financial assets and similar issues could be seen with many other respondents and particularly with one of the others first discussed in Chapter 2, Duncan Smith.

The specifics of Smith's mandates had been written very precisely to assure his clients about potential agency problems between them. This defined how far he could take benchmark risk. Within these constraints his approach to constructing his portfolio was based on the belief, congruent with standard economic theorists and interesting in the context of this chapter, that the future price of securities is based on the information the market has about them. At the same time he also believed that by using his and his firm's contacts and analytic powers he could 'build a picture' of the fundamentals and the future news about them, which would allow him to anticipate changes in market sentiment for or against particular stocks and so future changes in price. In other words, he thought he could profit from being better informed about the fundamental situation and the markets' future behaviour. The successes and failures he described are instructive,

In the case of *WellManagedOil, Lending,* and *Helping Oil,* Smith had purchased stock and (it turned out) correctly anticipated the fundamental situation, the news it would generate, and the resulting market sentiment and its effect on price. His theses were confirmed. But in the case of *Pharma, Outfits,* and *Special Pharma,* this was not the case. Although the supporting arguments for each of these theses had seemed to him to make just as good sense, the future unfolded to show either that Smith's view of the fundamental situation had not been correct or that he had misjudged the market reaction.[3] Prices moved in an adverse direction.

Comparing the scripts for his stories about satisfying and unsatisfying decisions in more detail highlights the problem. For instance, the script underlying the *Helping Oil* and the *Outfits* stories was similar. *Helping Oil* involved the very successful launching (IPO) and subsequent performance of a new company whose management had been able consistently to grow the company faster than the stock market analysts expected so that profitability kept increasing and the price of the shares kept rising. *Outfits* also involved a new launch. It also seemed promising because it had a management with a successful track record of raising profits – using a new business model of pricing and marketing cheap but celebrity-branded clothes at high prices to generate more and more revenue per article, which had been very successful in other countries. But in this instance, as matters developed, market sentiment did not shift in the expected direction. When unseasonal weather conditions required the new company to explain some only slightly poor sales figures, the management had apparently treated the business press and market analysts rather arrogantly. This appears to have inflamed feelings and suspicions about what was really going on with the consequence that its share price began to fall. 'What I hadn't counted on was the impact of the guy who runs the business. I think he is a very good retailer, but he's a bit of a maverick. He tends to still run it like it's his own company, and it's not.' Smith stressed how the company wasn't really 'helping analysts' and so did not build favourable sentiment. 'People kept saying, "I'm not sure about the numbers", but they wouldn't talk to them about them.' As Smith pointed out 'uncertainty is the one guarantee for shares to fall' and they did. In this way, although the buy scripts for *Helping Oil* and *Outfits* were similar, the outcomes were completely different.

Much the same was true of another pair of decisions also based on a similar script involving management. In the case of *Special Pharma* Smith lost confidence in the thesis on which he had bought shares because he had lost confidence in the ability of its management to convince the market they were going to do better. Like Fred Bingham with *Leave It to us* he then sold out before allowing time for his thesis to play out and the shares then went up a lot. The problem, he emphasised, was that he had got to the point where he just couldn't trust the management enough to go on holding their shares. 'The goalposts seem to move quite a lot', he said, explaining his suspicion. 'I thought, well, I'll take my money and run.' He then elaborated the difficulty in interpreting financial results from large complex companies and how he then had to rely on what he was told at meetings with managers. 'You know, with these companies there are big moving parts, so that's fair enough, but again it's checking back on what they told me the last time, and it's not always exactly the same story. So it's nothing you can really put your finger on, but just that's not what you told me last time...it was to do with costs...some of the kinds of costs moved about quite a bit.'

The point is that Smith hoped to profit by being better informed than the rest of the market. But this strategy was intrinsically precarious causing significant material and emotional consequences. The very features that made what managers thought a good story were also associated with a bad one. Others might know more than him both about the fundamentals and the market's reaction. Information asymmetry works both ways.

Looking across the sample many managers were constantly on alert (if not suspicious) about being caught in a situation where they were the ones at an information disadvantage, because the information they had relied on to advance their thesis was not accurate or was not having the implications they hoped. As in the case of some of both Bingham's and Smith's examples, such concerns often included the anxiety that they had misplaced their trust; in significant ways the information they had been given might have been misleading or had been massaged by managements or alternately that managements might, subsequent to their buying the shares, have reasons of their own not to stick to the plans they had unveiled or be unable to execute them. Most respondents talked in one way or another about the difficulties of relying on the information they had and in this connection more than half of them specifically elaborated a fairly extensive story about the difficulty of maintaining faith in the management of the companies to deliver, especially if anything happened to create suspicion.

Blaming management

When I looked through the sample to find all the respondents who talked to me about how they thought about any new information coming to light which had implications for their stock holdings, I found that 28 managers had between them told me 68 stories about why things went wrong with their theses and that in about half of these the difficulties they volunteered involved problems in anticipating and evaluating information from enterprise management.[4] So respondents told me how they lost patience with managements when expected results were not forthcoming, or how they became concerned when strategies were changed or when explanations for new developments seemed inadequate. They told me how they came to feel managements no longer deserved trust because they had lost important contracts or lost sight of the goal posts, or run into competition. They told me about companies which discovered fraud in their accounting or who unexpectedly revealed altered expectations of the profitability of certain product lines or failed to warn shareholders of possible 'bad news'. Other doubts started from managements who turned out to face greater problems than anticipated or who had decided to acquire another company with 'predictably' bad results. Others had got ahead of themselves and invested poorly, some 'did everything wrong they could', and others none of what they promised. Some changed their whole strategy, others didn't take the trouble to look as though they cared about shareholders, some couldn't adjust to market conditions, and still others went on 'ego trips'.

Respondents talked about management on many occasions with great suspicion. In fact they tended to imply that it was they (the enterprise managers) who were responsible for how their buy decisions had not worked out. Such accounts provide a window into the complex dependent object relationships my respondents had with the stocks they had bought. As stated, the underlying problem for everyone was that the future story they were trying to anticipate was neither calculable nor predictable with any definable probability. They could not know. The situation created an experience that was not easy to bear. Because imagining and comparing possible future scenarios necessarily and usefully engages anxiety and excitement and all their biological correlates, emotion is at the core of taking action. In this way to act, to continue to back a judgement to take risk in conditions of information uncertainty involved much more than calculation. For my respondents it was an ongoing emotional conflict.

The interviews, therefore, lead to the conclusion that daily management of news is the daily management of the emotional conflict it provokes. However, I had not formulated this idea when designing the schedule and so the data is less systematically conclusive than it could be. With hindsight I could have directed attention to price changes and then explored systematically how my respondents had responded to them and related news items on a day-to-day basis – especially instances of potentially bad news about their companies. Because I did not, the data I have is only what came up spontaneously about bad news in the 68 stories about decisions they made which had proved unsatisfying.

In addition to Bingham and Smith 11 other interviewees included in their stories information about how they managed the situation when either the price of the stock they had purchased fell or it had stagnated. Price falls can be understood as threats to the security of a manager's thesis from the point of view of the possibility that he might take an absolute loss. Price stagnation, on the other hand, is likely to be a threat to the exceptional or excitement dimension of their expectations threatening relative loss. In both cases what was happening was that share prices were signalling potentially bad news for the story – in other words, for the object relationship my interviewees had been having with their 'buys'. I will discuss examples of the two types of threat separately.

Threats to security

Although each interview account has its own individual features there was a clear pattern in the narratives I have suggesting that when a share price fell interviewees responded by doubting their previous take on information and then quite quickly began to be suspicious about what managements had told them. They then had to struggle to balance their reasons for wanting to hold on to the stock (based on their buy script) against the anxiety they now experienced that it was all going wrong. As many of the examples already given have suggested, the situation was then one of emotional conflict. In the face of suspicion it became difficult to maintain their 'good' relationship, hold their nerve, and keep confidence in their thesis. Sometimes they then found that 'after exiting' the relationship because they were suspicious, the share price began to go up. I have described how this happened to Fred Bingham in the case of *Leave It with Us* and Duncan Smith with *Special Pharma*. Stories from Chuck Bronsky and Tristan Cooper provided two further examples.

Chuck Bronsky bought shares in a small company called *Lap Wireless (LW)* whose share price then began to fall. He discovered that apparently two major international rivals had begun to compete with *LW*'s products 'out of nowhere' producing what he called 'an unjustifiable panic' in the market. When the price first fell Bronsky called the Chief Financial Officer 'the same day' to ask 'what's this, what does this mean?' Apparently he was told 'nothing has changed as far as we're concerned, we've still got the same orders, we've still got the same customers'. 'Why don't you tell me what it means', the CFO then countered. Based on this conversation Bronsky then 'took it' that the company 'didn't really understand their competitive landscape very well'. He decided that in thinking it 'a good investment story' he must have made a bad decision. He sold. Later he found this was wrong. Nothing had really changed. Later it became clear *LW* 'still occupied something of a niche position and held a large number of contracts'. The stock price recovered. But like other fund managers, in many situations Bronsky had found it difficult to judge the company favourably once in his mind it had become stigmatised. He couldn't bring himself to get back in. 'It's very hard you find' to go back in and 'buy that, you know', he said.

Tristan Cooper ran a niche hedge fund. He described a purchase in *BigConstruction (BC)* as a very exciting investment, about which he was now 'ashamed of' himself. The essence of what happened was that the share price fell when *BC* had 'a wobble' because a large operation in one of the countries in which it was located ran into problems – so that *BC* had to issue a warning about a possible impact on profits. Faced with that news, Cooper went back to meet management. 'I sat down with the CFO, to try and get a sense of what kind of guy he was. He came up with a very decent explanation'. Cooper then did his 'rational' calculations once more and worked out that given the overall size of the company even a '60 million' loss 'shouldn't matter a lot'. He decided the stock was still cheap and because the company was 'doing some interesting things elsewhere' decided to hold. However, a few months later a further incident took place involving an accounting scandal on another of their large projects. The stock fell 14 per cent on the news and 'I just sold it'. Cooper said he had panicked. 'From a strict, mathematical standpoint, I should have said, fine, that's another fifty million, it doesn't matter'. But somehow, 'probably because I trusted the guy' he felt he had 'been fooled' and he didn't want 'to hear any more about it'. And then 'guess what? It's been a super star'. Cooper was furious with himself. He had let himself get 'distracted' with 'feelings about the CFO'. Cooper added something interesting at this point, reminiscent of Fred Bingham's comments: 'It also came at a time, I guess, where I was having a lot of bad time on another side of the portfolio, so my tolerance for my own mistakes was very low.'

Other stories I was told suggested the same kind of emotional conflicts. Mark Devreaux's story about struggling with share price falls in *Energy* had led him to question previous assumptions about management. Another manager, Gordon Hamilton, actually told me two stories of this kind. In both narratives (as he now saw it) share price falls made him realise he had been taken in by what managements were promising and had become foolishly overexcited and over-optimistic about their prospects. He couldn't sustain his confidence and sold out. One story concerned *ResProp* in Japan. He had 'met the management' and become 'over-influenced' by 'some exciting future expansion plans' involving the carry trade to 'lend at margin, almost like in a riskless way. 'I had this image' (of boundless success it seemed) and 'I knew it had been done before at the turn of the century' when people 'borrowed here in the UK' when on the gold standard 'at 4 per cent and built out the US railroads by lending to them at 8 per cent.' When the share price fell he realised 'I just got it completely wrong'. In keeping with other managers he blamed 'their accounting' but also 'my analysis'. But not exactly: 'It wasn't really my analysis. I had trusted and believed in the analyst.' The second example with *Photos* was very similar.

As further examples, Novak Jones, Frances Shaw, Morris Lawn, and Leonard Frost also told me stories about how falling stock prices led them to doubt management competence or even integrity – placing them in emotional conflict and leading them to the abandonment of their theses. Frost's *Advertising* revised its anticipation of US growth down which knocked 20 per cent off the share price. He said his view on the management was 'severely diminished' and he sold out. Frances Shaw lost confidence in a medium-sized European company called *SIM*. It was what she called an 'edgy', 'growth' company and she was usually willing to ignore volatility and hold long. But in this case the price kept falling. When she met with the company to discuss technological developments and rumours they denied they were in difficulty. But the price kept falling. She now felt she was not told the truth by management and began to believe there were fundamental uncertainties as to the sustainability of profits. She was left wary of future 'tech' investments. 'We don't really like to invest in the 'tech' sector because you don't have any visibility.' Then Novak Jones told me how his expectations, based on an initial belief in managements, could not survive share price falls. In this instance a plan their management had to make *Conglom* much more profitable was dashed by that management. Instead of running down their shipbuilding side and as promised concentrating on their apparently more profitable tourism franchise, they suddenly took advantage of low interest rates and boom conditions to ask investors for money to build a fleet of new ships. He revised his opinion of the company and sold 'simply because there was really little basis of trust, little knowledge of where this conglomerate was going and clearly little heed paid to third-party shareholders and what they stood for'. Finally, another manager, Morris Lawn, explained how when the share price fell he had 'bitten the bullet'. He had bought *Drains* in an IPO. In an emerging market it had appeared very attractive for many reasons, including that they appeared to be about to get a major contract with a large oil company. But when the contract had not come through the share price fell and despite their much more general case they didn't add to their holding. As Lawn put it, 'management's reputation' had been tainted; 'what they said in the offer' hadn't 'materialised'. Discomfort with feeling let down by management rankled. He spoke about how perhaps we were 'taken in a bit by management' and how he had learned that 'a contract is only guaranteed once it's been signed.' In fact the shares then went back up.

Five other managers are interesting in that they also suffered the emotional conflict but reacted by determinedly sticking to their original idea – with hindsight not wisely. Sol Abram, for instance, saw his ready access to the topmost management of the largest companies as one of the main bases of his competitive information advantage. He bought *NewBank* when its price was attractive because in 2007 others were worried about the worsening credit cycle in the United Kingdom and thought banks might suffer. His meetings with them told him the bank had a good new management team. He found they were 'upbeat actually' and that 'the market' had underestimated them. However, the shares did not 'come up' and looked like falling further. Apparently despite 'management optimism' the new marketing strategy they had put in to gain business 'did not work'. Abram explained that 'We wouldn't have been able to see that' and that by the time it was clear the shares were 'quite low'. He wasn't prepared to throw in the towel. 'They've still got some upside', he thought, and 'when people relax a bit' it may 'improve'. He was still holding.[5]

Leonard Frost told a very similar story about responding to the falling price of *Housebank* and Brad Johnston was confidently adding to holdings in other bank shares as they were falling in September 2007 convinced that the market was 'just panicking' unreasonably. Another respondent, Mike Brown, told me a story about seeking out and hanging on to a financial service company using its AAA credit ratings to package local authority loans of BBB quality in the thick of subprime and other derivative loans.

It seems possible the decisions by Abram, Frost, Johnston, and Brown were emotionally path-dependent. All four decisions involved banks, which, until they went wrong, had performed very well for these respondents and given them a great deal of kudos. Their confidence was, perhaps, based on extrapolating that success forward prior to realising just how problematic the banking industry had become.

Peter Ross was another very confident respondent but in a different sector. He had been very successful year after year and had no intention of giving in to anxiety when under emotional conflict. He told me a story about having a large holding in the shares of a large construction firm (*Construct*) whose share price went into 'free fall' when it discovered fraud. Ross had no intention of selling up. Rather he said he used his strong shareholder position to place considerable leverage on the company's board. 'The share price goes down – what do we do? Don't panic. Go and see the non exec and say, right, it's a yellow card. Once more and you're off....' Not satisfied with this reaction he voted all his shares against a current director at the next AGM. 'All we want is an investment where everyone is facing the same direction and no one's going to run off halfway through with the money.'

The price falls I have just described challenged the relationship my respondents had established with 'their' stock by threatening loss. Some reacted to the emotional conflict created by doubting management and their whole thesis – sometimes abandoning it by selling out to their disadvantage and sometimes not. Others refused to panic which sometimes lead to success and sometimes not. In all cases what was evident was a painful emotional conflict and how to change their stories to manage it.

Threats to exceptionality

Other respondents reported the emotional conflicts contingent on another type of news, apparent price stagnation. Stocks were then 'disappointing' or had become 'boring'. That experience created frustration with initial theses which then dampened and eventually destroyed all the initial excitement, leaving the underlying relationship mainly filled with anxiety. The fact that price immobility was experienced negatively was particularly evident in these interviews. When it was discussed they used various rather emotional words which spontaneously appeared in the interview narratives. Stocks which had a stable price were referred to as not 'doing much' and even as 'lazy'. Treated as a potential signal of a broken thesis, the consequential emotional conflict was then dealt with by turning against management. Love (L) perhaps turned to hate (H).

Telling me about *LargeMedia* (who ran a cable franchise), Andrew Smythe said that 'the' problem with the company was 'they've never made any money'. They had been 'building out the systems' and having to 'upgrade them'. In the past they had explained this time and again by saying 'the money's going to come tomorrow' and his investment case to himself was that at last 'this time might be different'. He purchased stock cheaply in the belief there was a 'window of opportunity'. But two years after buying stock, the anticipated upsurge had failed to materialise. He said that at this point and perhaps because his own performance across his portfolio was not what he hoped he 'lost patience' with its own thesis and sold. He said it has just taken 'too long to play out' so that, despite his official three-year horizon, after two years he said, 'forget it' and 'sold it', putting the proceeds into 'something better' he could not immediately remember. Afterwards it did do a bit better but he said he was so dissatisfied with what he called the 'slowness' of 'management and the market' that he couldn't wait any longer.

Alistair Topp became equally frustrated with *Rings* – an international jeweller which, although a low-quality company ('not a Tiffany'), he had purchased because it was cheap and because management had convinced him they were going to 're-structure' by pulling 'out costs' and getting 'earnings up'. But it never worked. 'The argument has always been they can' but 'there's always some reason why it doesn't quite work out'. The stock 'stagnated' and did 'very little in two or three years' and he concluded 'it's just crap' and 'not a well run company; nothing like as well run as we thought it was'.

David Allen's story described a similar scenario. He invested in *Store* on the basis management had a real opportunity in their market but didn't hold on long enough to benefit. Financial results were taking time to fulfil the thesis and the stock price seemed 'dead'. 'It really didn't do much and I had to ask 'what are we doing in this dead stock, that's not moving and that doesn't seem to have an investor base?' Worrying why others weren't buying it, he began to wonder about the management strategy. Nothing obvious came across but the stock was in 'purgatory'. Well before his three-year time horizon he got frustrated and sold following a small dip. 'Their reported earnings on the stock were down 3 or 4 per cent, so our analyst at the time came to us and said, you know the stock we've been thinking about, well, it's time to sell today. We did it out of lack of patience and frustration.' The stock then did very well, as they had originally forecast.

It seems likely that the need for dynamism comes about from a combination of the pressure to be exceptional noted in the Chapter 4 and the difficulty managers had trying to maintain their beliefs in their exciting stories about relationships whose outcome was uncertain. Time creates impatience and anxiety in a condition of being overseen. Most of my respondents gave the impression they did not have time to wait. They wanted a quick confirmation of their stories and when things were not moving definitely one way or the other most become uncomfortable.

Summary: Ambivalent object relationships and emotional conflict

This chapter has focused on the experience my respondents described after they had made a decision to 'buy' stocks and then had to hold them. It was an experience of managing their emotions and thoughts to maintain trust and keep away suspicion in the context of ongoing uncertainty mediated by information asymmetry. I have suggested that buying stocks anticipates what psychoanalysts call an object relationship and that holding them continues it.

Sixteen managers and 23 of the stories they told me about their experience of holding assets that gave them cause to doubt have featured so far in this chapter. It was notable that in all cases unfavourable stock price changes were treated with suspicion, as potential signals that their investment theses might have been going wrong. As some respondents emphasised, managing price signals and associated news is a time of anxiety. Although respondents were contradictory on the point most believed that asset prices are ultimately set efficiently in the market, so that when things did not work they worried the market might be 'telling them' something. If the market did not behave as they hoped they could quickly lose confidence in what they had (at the buy stage) appeared to know. They became anxious and asked themselves what did others know that they did not know? Falling prices create an experience of uncertainty and then discomfort which created feelings that were not easily managed by cognition and calculation. Feelings often focused around a loss of the previously confident belief in enterprise management and other aspects of the safety component of 'buy' scripts. They became sceptical and critical of managements – even showing signs of hate. In this situation the exciting element of the buy script could not survive and some then sold. They then might discover things went well and their original thesis had been correct or not. If so, of course, they then missed out on any benefit.

One interesting group, mostly investing in financial services, tended to dismiss bad news more easily. They hung on to their confidence – in each case able to draw on features of their personality and their investment case, perhaps aided, as in Johnston's case working within a firmly set five-year framework, by the institutional structures in which he worked. His and the others' holdings, however, were those at the heart of the 2008 crisis so that their confidence may have been seriously misplaced. Dealing with short-term doubts by having the overconfidence to ride them out is no more the solution than panicking.

The main conclusion to draw at this stage is that investing in financial assets necessarily creates just the inherent emotional conflicts that were mentioned as a consequence of the various characteristics of financial assets introduced in Chapter 1. These conflicts are permanent and can be known and worked with or not. 'Buy' scripts are an initial attempt to manage the conflicts sufficiently to create that 'spontaneous urge to action' that Keynes (Keynes 1936) described as an essential feature of making long-term investments. But the assets still have to be held in an ongoing emotional relationship in conditions of uncertainty and asymmetric information. This relation is what I introduced in earlier chapters as a dependent *ambivalent* object relationship. It necessarily involves conflicting feelings to the 'object'. The experience of buying and holding stocks thus creates an ongoing context where *divided* states of mind and relationships governed by –K are a constant temptation.

7
Divided Masters

One sociological way of looking at asset management is to see my respondents in a structured situation where despite individual differences we can ask what elements in their situation are common. What sorts of things normally happen, what has to occur, and what are the aims in the situation? By abstracting features of their institutionally defined roles (what they are expected to do and how they should relate to others) it may be possible to create a model of what happens in order to understand more effectively what can go wrong or cause confusion. Social roles and what is considered normative within them can also structure both the experience and the expression of emotion (Turner and Stets 2005). In this chapter I want to look at the structure of my participants' roles, particularly at aspects of their relationship with their clients and the implications it seemed to have for their experience and then their decision-making and so at the way a market institutionalised with intermediaries actually works.

In the last chapter we have just seen how my respondents had significant experiences of uncertainty and information asymmetry. Trying to search out and hold on to stories which were exceptional and safe presented ongoing emotional conflicts – ones which, however, were also likely to be experienced by their clients. Indeed, what might be called the 'sales' scripts with which asset management companies seek both to tempt and to reassure their clients, anticipate just such dilemmas.

> Equity markets offer frequent opportunities for contrarian investors. However, we recognise the importance of not becoming emotionally attached to individual shares. We constantly check and recheck the quality of our analysis, and look out for new events that may lead us to reconsider our opinion on an investment.
>
> If prices fall, our process requires us to revisit our shares to determine if we are still convinced of our original view. At this point we have the opportunity to buy more shares, sell some or leave our position unchanged.

The statement, taken at random from the website of a leading asset management company, is rather typical and puts into words the structured role conflict my respondents then experience with their clients. It is clear that clients (principals) are being presented with the opportunity to work with managers (their agents) who, it is promised, will run against the crowd and so implicitly have the chance to make above-average returns. At the same time clients are being reassured that their managers will be constrained in various ways so that their investments will be safe. Specific sources of potential error such as that managers might get 'emotionally attached', not do enough checking, not watch the news properly, and not monitor the reasons for their commitment, are all raised as matters of potential deviance it is necessary to control. Something called the 'process' is reassuringly offered to manage that feat. Statements about mission and process have been examined briefly in Chapter 2 and intermittently thereafter. Those used in the sample usually included promises about trying to attain superior benchmark and peer performance targets as well as reassurances about how much risk managers would be allowed to take – again illustrating the underlying conflicts because they are usually expressed in terms of constraints as to how far managers may actually be contrarian, that is, hold different portfolios of stocks compared to their peers and benchmarks.

The effects of such efforts to define and constrain the agency relationship between the portfolio managers I interviewed and their clients will be the theme of this chapter. I will present further data on what my respondents told me to draw out features of the institutional role relationship they inhabited and its influence on their subjective perspective on the risks they ran and how they tried to manage them. In addition to the risks they had to contend with holding to theses while processing the news, they also suffered from having to experience and anticipate the consequences of uncertainty among their clients. They worried both about the possible outcome if they were 'seen' investing in stocks that fell in value or made losses and also about the possible penalties from missing out on winners.

Fear of loss

I have mentioned many times that the price of financial assets is volatile. Both the portfolio holdings and the daily performance of the fund managers I interviewed were also often transparent and public. Clients could move funds in or out quite quickly. In managing the experience of falling prices discussed in the last chapter, therefore, my interviewees had to manage not only their own feelings but also anticipate those of their clients and their advisers. Their evident worry was that even if at difficult times they could hold their nerve this might not be true of their clients, who might then move funds away. Should adversity arrive, mandates and mission statements, therefore, were to be taken with a pinch of salt.

Duncan Smith, one of the four managers introduced in Chapter 2, had a variety of anxieties about underperforming and its consequences. He told me that even after 30 years he really could lose his job if performance dropped off, but at the same time he thought his clients did not really understand the mandate or mission statement he had contracted to fulfil for them. In theory, he thought, they had said 'right, I've got a long-term horizon and I want you to take more risk' so I give you 'a chance of outperforming by 5 per cent'. But did they truly realise that gave him just as good a chance of underperforming by 5 per cent? He wasn't sure; 'The risk is, if I underperform by 5 per cent you take your money away'. Clients, he elaborated, might not 'think of the downside, whereas we, as fund managers, have to be aware of the downside, and the business risk of underperforming'. The emotional conflict was evident in his next spontaneous comment: 'That's not to say that you don't do the things that are going to produce the outperformance, but you just have to be aware that the more risk you're taking the bigger the business risk, if you like.' Smith's house built portfolios which advertised they would control the risk of underperformance using statistical measures of Value at Risk calculated (for each stock in the portfolio and the portfolio itself) using a series of assumptions about what had happened historically and might happen. He understood such measures created 'a 95 per cent chance of being plus or minus 2 per cent, or 3 per cent' but couldn't tell you whether you're actually 'going to be up or down'. At the same time he rather obviously tried not to worry. 'We have a team of people who sit down and work out how you can achieve it, and they will put restraints down there, but it's to meet the client's objective, and as long as people remember that, then they shouldn't get too hung up about it.'

Another respondent, Gordon Hamilton, made a number of interesting comments about the issue of what he called managing 'relative risk', worrying about what others were doing and covertly matching them. For him it was 'an incorrect part of our investment philosophy'. He thought they should compare themselves to benchmarks but not use them to decide what to hold. 'Because you're starting at the wrong end.' He thought that if they 'truly believed in the sort of three- to five-year intrinsic value approach' that was part of his mandate they would simply hold a reasonable number of good stocks which they had worked out had a good chance of making superior returns after assessing the risk and returns for each company. The trouble was that this created the possibility of diverging from the peer group and he 'didn't know' of a 'large investment company that can really get their arms around that' because of the fear that if things did not go well short term it would be 'such a conflicting thing'.

Many respondents in the sample mentioned spontaneously how they feared being caught by client anxiety if things were not going well. As discussed when I looked at screen-watching and short-term performance pressures in Chapter 4, they were aware that this created short-term pressure potentially derailing their theses. To illustrate I have sampled four respondents talking about this at random.

Mark Devreaux was described in Chapter 2 as struggling with the falling price of his *Computer* holdings, which fell after purchase before eventually making the expected rise. In the end he had got sufficiently worried to make what was a bad sale; the stock coming up well in line with his thesis but only after he sold and so could not benefit. While discussing that scenario he quite spontaneously mentioned the fact that he operates 'in public': 'It's bad enough if the stock goes from 27 down to 20'. But it's really 'not good because we are compared to the benchmark every day'. 'We are judged on a daily, weekly, quarterly, monthly and yearly basis and if you buy a 27 stock and sell at 20 you made a mistake.' By selling at 20 he creates 'a permanent loss of capital' with 'no chance to recover'.

Morris Lawn's comment on this point came as an aside. He told me that one month the portfolio was 'down about 7 per cent'. He added that he was fortunate because he 'went off to get married' leaving his colleague to deal with 'sitting in on the calls' and taking 'the flak'. Apparently clients had been very anxious although they knew 'our process well'. They 'tried to coerce us to change our process and change stock.'

Alastair Topp said a great deal around this topic. For him 'official mandates' and 'what clients expect' were two potentially very different things. As a fund manager he said he 'needs to be very alert' to that when making decisions and communicating them. Officially 'the risk for the fund', he said, 'is that we do a bad job and underperform the index'. But it wasn't so simple. Although 'I should really care about whether we do badly relative to the benchmark and so should our clients', in reality 'our clients have another issue' they're not so well aware of. A number of clients 'don't fundamentally understand the risk'. 'They think they are giving us money, to beat a benchmark, sure, but also to make money in an absolute sense, and they don't realise that's not what they've asked us to do,' he said. In other words, if the market is down and he is down much less, he has done well. But he has still lost money and his clients may not feel happy. 'I think there's a lot of confusion there' and he thought it was a major driver at some periods for money to flow to certain kinds of hedge funds which promised absolute return rather than relative performance. He said it worried him.

Finally, Dominique Lyon, describing what he called the 'soft guide' he used to make decisions managing his client's funds, said all the same things in a different way. 'As a soft guide in the back of our heads when we talk about these portfolios', he said, 'we always kind of repeat the mantra – the clients are going to be more pissed off if we lose them money outright than if they don't get all the upside.' He felt there was nothing worse than facing criticism when things were going down and that 'even if they don't gain all the upside' it's much better to be safe than sorry.

Fear of missing out

It did not surprise me that neither managers nor their clients liked the idea of losing money and that managers coped against this eventuality by being cautious. Nor was I surprised by the feelings managers conveyed when they had missed out on some hot stock. Some degree of conflict between the fear of loss and the fear of losing out on gains seems inevitable. What did surprise me, however, was another source of error. Towards the end of the study, when I had begun to ask some slightly different questions about my respondents' performance, George Monroe began spontaneously to talk with regret about 'missing Enron'. Perhaps because I realised I had made a wrong assumption and became more attuned to the issue, three of the next four managers (all in the United States) then talked in the same way about missing out, but this time on 'dotcoms'. I had (I suppose naively) expected those who had not got caught up in 'bubbles' to congratulate themselves. But far from it! The losses from not having done what others did still irritated them.

Monroe actually got rather emotional. 'You know, I missed World Com, I missed Enron,' he said. 'I never owned a share of either of those because I ploughed through the numbers' and decided they were not 'good investments'. Instead of being pleased at this accurate foresight, he was depressed. 'They hurt me forever!' His pain was not only historical. In the year before interview one of his two main reasons for dissatisfaction in the past 12 months was that he had missed the initial public offerings of several US power companies. They had not been 'big in our benchmark' but because they had been inefficient and near bankrupt companies he had rejected them as stocks he wanted to own. But fuel shortages meant the quality of the company didn't matter. They had been 'monstrous performers' and he hadn't 'owned them'. In fact his carefully researched good companies had increased in value by 30 per cent whereas these environment destroyers and polluters were up 70 or 80. 'I wasn't so comfortable. I gave up upside to my detriment.' In short, careful, painstaking, fundamental analysis and independence of mind is not necessarily rewarded; going with the crowd and being able to resonate with the 'mind of the market' often is. This introduces a further layer of emotional conflict.

What I was discovering was that managers faced the possibility not only that their clients might be inconsistent over the issue of falling values and potential absolute loss but also that they feared they would be harsh if they felt their fund manager had a portfolio with 'dopey' or 'dead' stocks or was missing the more exciting current opportunities from which others in the market were benefitting – a finding with obvious implications as to why managers might 'join' in asset price inflations.

Daren Cooke's early sale of Tec10 is an example of how the conflicting pressures to keep gains and avoid losses can influence managers to do what they called 'capping profits' and so miss out on further gains – which only really has a meaning in terms of relative performance figures. 'I think the ones that I'm sometimes left kicking myself about a little bit are ones where I've bought something and the shares have gone up, and then I've taken a profit too early and it's run on. ... Granted, I was still enjoying the run from the ones that I'd kept but it wasn't quite as glorious as it might have been if I'd kept all of the ones that I'd originally bought.' When asked for an explanation he said it was probably driven by a conservative focus upon immediate short-term reward: 'I think there's an inherent conservatism. It's always easier to take a profit. You're not going to introduce any downsides in your decisions; you're just capping your upside by taking a profit.'

The theme of 'missing' things (particularly if this was because the investor felt that he was being especially attentive to the risk of loss) recurred many times in the comments made in interviews and was particularly a feature when I was talking to the 'quant' managers, some of whom had found their asset management firms performing very badly at times when everyone else in the market seemed to want to purchase highly risky investments – such as during the dotcom bubble. Such managers have responded to their past experience by seeking to incorporate what they consider 'momentum' into their computer models, precisely so as not to lose out from the tendency of markets to herd.

Daren Cooke, Alan Thomas, and Noel Sheraton were three randomly selected instances among ten stock-picking managers who had very similar accounts of the same kind of predicament. They all offered examples of missing what turned out to be very good opportunities because, although they liked the situations involved, they feared being caught out by market exuberance and their anxiety and caution about fundamentals then held them back from investing. So Cooke missed mining companies because while the business model was a solid one that appealed to him, the share price had never been fundamentally attractive enough to invest: 'although the analyst always said these were great businesses and we ought to own them, he could never convince us that the upside in the share price was great enough to warrant buying them at the time.' 'The valuation element of it was never formulated in an attractive way to make us get exposed,' he said.[1]

The balance between sensibly based caution on the one hand and optimism on the other is fundamentally conflicting. As we have seen in the last chapter, managers worried whether they should trust enterprise management or about what importance to attach to market fads and rumours and it was in that context that their prejudices towards caution came into play mediated by their recent performance experience as well and so their level of confidence. For example, Charlie Fraser talked about two causes for dissatisfaction which had resulted, in his view, from being overcautious. He had felt the price of *BigTools* was too exuberant to be sustainable and regretted that he had not pursued an opportunity to invest 'aggressively enough'. 'It was a capital goods producer and he 'had identified the whole investment cycle as a theme to play' but 'didn't back our view aggressively'. He explained how 'we were cautious of the market as a whole, and we expected a downturn'. He expected 'a lot of the growth sectors would get hit'. So he waited to time his purchases to when there was a downturn. But what happened each time prices fell was that 'there were other buyers, maybe more nimble than us, who came in and maybe had the same view'.

Asmir Singh worked for a house whose mission statement involved getting to know companies in depth and over time. But this then led him to miss out on shorter-term stories and to be unhappy. He told me a story about deciding against taking up shares in *CreditCard* because he had been unable to convince himself that things would work out. He thought it sounded like 'a decent business' but he 'was struggling with some litigation issues they were having'. The prospectus document must have been 'a good inch and a half thick' and there was a lot of litigation referring to anticompetitive behaviour about which they had been accused. He looked at what 'a sell side analyst was forecasting' about the potential outcome of litigation and, using his numbers, 'came out with' a valuation that was 'pretty low'. But the share price then tripled. He was 'kicking himself' because he also knew that 'when companies come to market' they often have 'artificially lower earnings' and then 'just completely smash them in the first year'.

Singh's story illustrates the problem of the emotional conflict caused by the need to resolve fundamental analysis and prediction about market sentiment in a situation of fundamental uncertainty. Tristan Cooper (a hedge fund manager) tried to use his conviction, based on fundamental analysis suggesting the price of a hotel chain was far too high, to make money by shorting it and waiting for the fall. However, it turned out that, although the hotels didn't do that well, a property bubble inflated their valuations and went on doing so long after Cooper imagined possible. 'A lot of the time, when I see a situation like that, I think, it's crazy, it's not going to last' but the assumption 'I should make' is what happens if it lasts? 'What happens if they do find guys ready to pay 4.5 per cent yield with no guarantee?' It turned out that was exactly what happened. 'I was too rational', he complained, 'pricing the reversal of the bubble or the situation before it happens.' This situation and its emotionally experienced correlates explain why those who do avoid some of the more spectacular bubbles do not see their action as particularly valuable – a factor apparently tilting the market towards risk-taking rather than prudence and contributing to the pressure to give in to *groupfeel*.

Pressures and problems managing conflicts

So far in this chapter I have explored the inherent conflicts managers faced from their clients' likely reactions when they tried to take a long-term view or wished to err on the side of caution. As discussed in Chapter 1, in standard finance theory the mind of the market is created by omniscient foresighted demons whose collective decisions represent the best available assessment of the fundamentals facing each company. Competitive discipline then ensures a close equation between the levels of risk associated with a given level of reward. Such competitive discipline was less obvious to the managers I interviewed. When they felt reasonably certain about long term fundamentals they were very conscious that the market might not, at least for a long time. As we saw in earlier chapters this was a factor that made it difficult for them to hold to long-term decisions based on fundamentals. This was especially true if they had to manage not only their own doubts but also those of their clients. The anxiety and uncertainty induced by daily volatility constantly threatened the possibility of the short-term underperformance of their portfolios which might then lose them assets and fees even if their thesis was right in the long term. Being prudent was not easy. In this context it is interesting to look at those who found it easier to stick to their decisions than others.[2]

Chen Chang, interviewed in June 2007, led the team in which Asmir Singh also worked. The aim was to invest long-term in the United States with low turnover; aiming at average holding periods of around five years. The mission statement was that there should be no attempt to seek safety by matching the composition of the portfolio to the composition of the benchmark index. Rather, the idea was that careful in-depth research and constant attention by a team of individuals to gaining detailed insight into companies over the long term would provide an information advantage, a structure for long-term holding and a protection against maverick or myopic decision-making. Chang told me that therefore the stocks they held were not the 'momentum-type high beta stocks' which flashed up and down, but ones that were 'boring and stodgy' and with long-term potential. He thought of himself as 'trying securely to position us for difficulties ahead'.

To find these stocks Chang and his team specialised in a programme of detailed research into individual companies and intensive discussions with their management to whom they would regularly return. Companies were tracked over long periods and the shares bought when at 'the right' price, using their superior information advantage, and then held long. But when Chang was asked to speak about decisions that had disappointed him the conflict in doing this emerged; he spoke about three stocks which the team had liked but which they had ultimately decided *not* to purchase because they felt current market valuations were too high and exuberant.[3] He spoke with regret and the sense of 'lost opportunity' was palpable, as was his fear that at a time of rising exuberance his approach would be penalised by clients for underperformance. In fact when he answered a question about his benchmark, he rather unusually answered by talking about what had gone up in value recently that he did *not* own. Like other managers he then explained the anxiety. 'If the market's up 15 per cent and we're up 12 per cent, you know, in absolute terms, 12 per cent is a good return. But they [clients] would say, well, you're useless because you're 300 basis points short of the index.' He elaborated this view at some length explaining that to do better he thought he would have to take more risk but that this was dangerous. Supporting that view he told me a story that weighed on his mind but no one else had mentioned to me. It concerned a 'big court case about five years ago where one of the pension funds had underperformed the index' and the fund manager had said 'I was just investing as I saw fit' and the client was saying 'we didn't give you a mandate to take that much risk'. 'You know in this industry', he said, 'you have to be sort of careful on how you define risk, and also how it compares to client expectations.' So although Chang worked in very favourable institutional conditions in one way – he could hold 50 stocks long term in his portfolio and none of them needed to be in index – he could not forget what he called 'business risk'; that is to say the conflict between the fear of losing money and the fear of achieving less gain for his clients and the consequent risk of losing assets to manage.

One reason why Chang may have felt particularly pressured might have been because his funds had not established a clear track record over the long term. The firm had been reorganised within the past five years after a period of poor performance. Consequently confidence may have been more brittle and more pressure may have been felt from clients and superiors. In this sense Chang can be contrasted with another manager, Len Williams. Williams was one of the first managers interviewed – in March 2007 – and was responsible for investing $30 billion in the largest 350 companies in the UK market. He had built up this very large fund and a formidable reputation by using a strategy which aimed to eliminate companies whose prospects of long-term profit growth were judged at risk from his portfolio. He then held companies long term and aimed to be inactive. His decisions to buy and sell were not based on any form of trying to control his performance risk by benchmark tracking. For Williams tracking error was 'not an indication of risk' and he paid no attention to it.

Considered from the viewpoint of the potential for managers to be worried about information asymmetry, uncertainty, and client ambivalence Williams seemed one of the most relaxed in my sample. He appeared to find prudence rather easy and considered short-term price variations as 'noise'. He did little buying and selling. 'You can see' from the turnover that 'as long as the analysis is right' all 'we have to do is sit and bide our time to acquire those stocks that we want to acquire.' His strategy demonstrated a particular mindset which appeared to accept that in adopting caution he would very likely miss out on some exciting short-term developments from which a more active manager might or might not benefit. Consistent with this he said the decisions that most satisfied him in the past year were when he had done nothing. 'I like to sleep easy at night...I have a tendency just not to buy, if there's something we find that we don't like, we just stop buying that.' This approach was strongly risk averse and very firmly backed by a set of consistent highly sceptical and conservative procedures that seemed to protect him against the issues of information asymmetry and uncertainty that threatened to overwhelm others. Although Williams's preferred companies would be vulnerable to macroeconomic uncertainties, they were selected to be much less volatile than others.[4] Moreover, because his fund was marketed as cautious and he had increased funds under management with this strategy, he seemed well placed to resist the pressure to adjust to short-term performance troughs by adjusting his strategy.

I found it interesting that although Len Williams had a similar long-term strategy to Chen Chang and Asmir Singh, he did not have their worries about falling behind and so did not seem to feel their pressures. It seems likely that Williams's many years of good performance stood him in good stead with his clients and his employers and gave him protection from the conflicts Chang and Singh experienced. I understand their company had had some rather serious difficulties about five years earlier and had then changed their approach so perhaps they were not able to make it clear to clients that underperformance for a time was part of the price of security.[5] It is interesting in this regard to compare Williams's and Chang's comments at their interview with those of Fraser Hobbs.

Hobbs did not manage portfolios himself but was interviewed because he was the CEO of Andrew Smith, Fiona Wellington, and David Allen – the first three respondents in the study, interviewed in January 2007. The team had many performance anxieties and these were apparent in some of the interview material mentioned earlier. Such anxieties seem to have been implicated in several instances of 'capitulation' – loss of nerve. The context for their difficulties provided by Hobbs was less auspicious than that experienced by Williams or Chang. Hobbs told me he had quite recently been put in charge of the team. The institution had been shifting its goals and its policies following, first, a period when they had had unparalleled success and growth in asset management and, second, a subsequent period when they had underperformed and so lost assets to manage. His team was having patchy performance when interviewed. He knew what that had done to his managers' morale and was trying to change the culture in that situation. The approach he was trying to instil was essentially the same as the Williams/Chang approach. He wanted to identify good companies that could be held long term because of their superior profitability.[6] The problem was holding long term when performance and share prices were volatile – and when Hobbs and his team had no past record to help them and their clients to feel secure and sustained enough so they could all put it into practice. To hold the good companies for long enough for the theses to play out, when uncertainty meant the thesis might be wrong in the first place, created anxiety and short-term pressure conflicted with the long-term idea.

What needs to be stressed here is that managers operate within an institutional context which in turn operates within the wider context of expectations and pressures from clients and client advisers. It turned out that Hobbs did not have what another manager, Donald Crumb, told me were 'grown-up clients' able to look five years ahead and evaluate accordingly. Hobbs told me that the clients and investment consultants who bought his fund, which had a mission strategy to invest long term, nonetheless put pressure on him whenever there were poor short-term results. Our clients are 'like that', he said. It's 'staggering' that they actually want 'a report weekly'. They are 'very large investors working for government institutions' mostly in Asia and 'seriously smart guys'.[7] 'Why do they do this?' he asked himself. 'I don't know. I don't know', he said. 'Can I tell them it's silly? No!' They comprised 30 per cent of his assets under management and so his revenue.

Feeling the pressures they do, some managers had become very cynical about clients. But the problem is more fundamental. Although Donald Crumb's 'grown-up clients' 'positively prohibited' him from investing in a passive index-tracking way, or from holding cash, and were not standing over him breathing down his neck causing the conflicts others faced, the relief was not great. Given all the problems of fundamental uncertainty, interpreting information, and share price volatility we have been discussing, anxiety about performance and emotional conflict is ever-present. The only issue is how it is managed. Although Crumb did not have to look over his shoulder every day he still had to decide when companies with news that might indicate long-term issues needed to be 'let go' and when companies or sectors that might just be benefitting from 'frothy' market conditions should be ignored, or not. In other words, the problems that other managers put down to clients are in fact simply intrinsic. Crumb still had to worry about how to reduce the danger that his information was inaccurate, or whether he had incorrectly taken into account some factors, or that his decisions would become derailed by unknown unknowns.

Beyond this, my impression was that the institutional circumstances Crumb benefitted from could not change the underlying problem. Financial assets have the three characteristics mentioned. Although share prices do relate in some way to fundamentals much of the time, they also relate to market sentiment. Changes in share price and news, therefore, cannot simply be dismissed as 'noise'. Crumb said he had the opportunity to ignore the 'noise, and lots of trading, lots of headlines' and 'all this stuff on the TV' – 'bubble vision'. But he also knew it was not too easy. 'You can wait a long time for these sort of theses to play out and the problem is in the long run you're all dead and that the market can stay irrational longer than you can stay solvent and keep your clients. I'm lucky with these clients that they're all grown up. But at what point would you say that the good idea actually is a bad idea?' Among the examples Crumb described that were successful were decisions to underweight US stocks in the portfolio, and he was also very pleased and optimistic about investing heavily in European retail banks. But his decisions to invest in Japanese banks had hurt performance as had a focus on technology (flat-screen television providers). Like George Monroe above, he had also missed out on utilities – which his team had been sure was a bubble and so had sold very early on and been penalised.

The question as to how to respond to what others are doing in markets is a difficult one. Using the term 'irrational' in the way he did, Crumb draws attention to what one can do about a judgement when the market has succumbed to *groupfeel*. In the last chapter I mentioned the interviews with three managers who stood out as different. They were all financial services experts and prided themselves on being able to ignore what was going on in the market and stick to their judgements and their analysis. In the context of this chapter the interesting thing about what they said is that they appear to have dealt with the inherent conflicts simply by dismissing them. They felt 'above' others in the market.

Mike Brown, Brad Johnston, and Sol Abram all gave reasons to suggest they looked down on many in the market and the way they were gripped by emotions and, at interview, had got away with it. I talked to them in the summer of 2007 after the first concerted central bank action on interest rates but they were still all rather definite that they were not going to be caught up in the market's panic over subprime. In fact, they were going to hold their nerve and benefit from it, something most of the managers told me was their response to what they called 'corrections' in May 2006 and February 2007.

Mike Brown worked on a very prestigious team with total investments of $50 billion. Four of the six institutions which we discussed and in which he was investing were later bailed out by the US government.[8] Still more interestingly, when asked if he had any particularly special investment on at the time, he told me he had just invested his own funds in a US insurance company specialising in arbitraging the difference between its capacity to borrow funds using securitised instruments based on its AAA rating and its capacity to issue debt to local authorities with lower credit ratings. It had significant subprime exposure. He had bought into the company in a significant way because he thought the stock's low price due to subprime and related worries was the product of investor irrationality and emotions. He described how he overrode anxieties and was not easily panicked by short-term events. 'My colleagues marvel at how I keep my emotions in check. I try to have a clear eye view of what the value of the company is as opposed to react to the short-term volatility. I tend to think of a lot of the daily news as being noise and I really try to tune out most of it. Most of the day-to-day information that crosses my desk is not relevant.' Interestingly, he spoke very clearly about the risk of 'loss of capital'. 'People' get 'lulled into' thinking that the only risk is 'the tracking error risk against the benchmark', he said. But the 'bigger risk' is the risk of 'loss' of capital. So, although he had a clear idea about the danger that his investments could produce capital losses and had all kinds of very careful ways to assess the underlying situations in his companies,[9] at the same time he was taking some of the most 'confident' decisions to be found in the sample.

Brad Johnston, also interviewed at the very end of August 2007, worked in a relatively benchmark-free institutional framework, seeking to pick seriously undervalued financial stocks to hold for very long-term investment. His company did achieve low turnover in their holdings. Talking about his own decisions during the interview, Johnston was one of the few fund managers who did not find it easy to think of things that had gone wrong or dissatisfied him. One decision he did talk about involved experiencing doubt. It concerned the falling price of the shares of a major bank (*VeryWellKnownBank*) which he believed was being treated unfairly by the market. He thought the market was unable to get some of the problems the bank might have had with subprime into perspective. As the share price continued to fall his dissatisfaction was with the market, which he described as being 'unfair' on the bank. He had not changed his position on the stock, saw its price fall as an opportunity, and had no intention to 'capitulate'. He was adamant that if the situation was considered calmly and even if the bank share price went on losing ground and underperforming for a further 12 months, he would still want to hold shares in it. Obviously, the danger here was that the market would not come round to his viewpoint – which, as the bank concerned is now in public ownership, was real. But what Johnston had emphasised at his interview was that his institutional situation allowed him to analyse fundamentals and to develop and hold convictions. He would not expect a lot of pressure to rethink his decision at coming team meetings and in his view his company was 'almost unique in the industry'. 'What would limit your life expectancy around here', he said, 'would actually be to run counter to what we stand for' and not look out long term.

Agency issues and inherent conflicts

Looking at those (many) managers who wished to take a long-term view, we have seen how some of those who worked in team situations were able to cope with pressure with a degree of success because there was a degree of firm alignment between the time frameworks they were expected to use and the career risks they experienced. In these circumstances the long-term holding strategies their firms were trying to achieve seemed possible – along the lines often credited to Warren Buffet.

But we have also seen that the success of such institutional approaches is neither straightforward nor guaranteed. The underlying dilemma as to how to know when short-term news is of long-term significance is intrinsic to human life. The ability to take a long-term view in the sample of managers interviewed seemed to depend on whether managers believed their past track record would really be believed enough to support them and their clients in holding their nerve – in other words, whether clients would give them time and how they used it. In some cases discussed above investors seem to have felt they had time but in others it was not so clear. Thus, how long Sol Abram, Brad Johnston, and Mike Brown, who felt confident when interviewed, will go on being so and will be backed by their firms and investors if their performance suffers is an interesting question.

What I am stressing here as elsewhere is that the interviews make clear the significance of experience lived out in time. A central issue for any theory of financial markets (apparent both from this chapter and the last) is that a core belief among all the respondents with whom the topic was mentioned was that when clients ask a manager to try to do exceptionally well they are not actually taken to mean they are willing to risk doing exceptionally badly. In other words, the state of mind in which clients sign mandates seeking reward is not taken to be the same state they will be in if they suffer loss.

In this context it is possible to think that the attraction in financial markets of some economic theory and modelling (as well as some of their statistical derivatives) is not perhaps for their 'truth' value but for their aid in appearing to map the future, in making a very uncertain future 'feel' more controllable. The attraction a statistical concept like 'tracking error' or 'value at risk' may have is that it can perhaps create the impression fund managers are managing. Rating agency attributions may perform a similar function, allowing asset managers to leave their thinking to them. 'Our institutional clients sometimes define risk as tracking error,' said Roger Sampson. 'They're looking to maximise their information ratio, yet you can maximise your information ratio and minimise your tracking error and drive your portfolio right off a 40 per cent cliff.... In that case risk is about career risk, right?'

Evidence suggests that a strong trend in the finance industry has been to use mathematical modelling to manage anxiety rather than to sharpen enquiry. Similar processes can be observed, potentially, in the industry devoted to the production of hourly, daily, weekly, and quarterly information dissemination within the financial market, much of which, it can be argued, develops the appearance of information creating relevant to knowledge, but which actually functions to manage anxieties about what is going to happen.

Talking with the sample of fund managers, the direct pressure they felt to demonstrate exceptional performance at any and all times was related to direct recent experiences with clients. 'We have to measure ourselves against a benchmark, because that's what the clients use to measure us,' as Mel Angel put it. 'We were down about 7 per cent in one month and I went off to get married and [my colleagues] had to sit in on the calls and take the flak. Clients were very anxious. ... They know our process well and they tried to coerce us to change our process and change stocks...,' said Morris Lawn.

In this way managers 'felt' the contradictions of the situation in which they were placed. They then tried to deal with it as best they could. Essentially, although they usually accepted the formal propositions of efficient market theory (namely that to achieve ongoing exceptional returns at a certain level can only be done by taking a similar amount of exceptional risk), they did not feel this was always the case with clients or indeed investment consultants. Against their peers managers could do well but still fare badly in absolute terms – doing better than others but losing money. 'I should really care about whether we do badly relative to the benchmark, and so should our clients, but, in reality, our clients have another issue, I think, that they're not so well aware of. Some are and some aren't ... a number of clients don't fundamentally understand the risk. They think they are giving us money to beat a benchmark, sure, but also to make money in an absolute sense, and they don't realise that's not what they've asked us to do,' said Alistair Topp. He had to cope with this situation. 'And so I think we spend a lot of time trying to make absolutely crystal clear what we've been asked to do, and what we're doing about it, and what we haven't been asked to do, which is what ought to be their responsibility, but I think there's a lot of confusion there. And you saw that, and it's been one of the drivers of the hedge fund industry, clearly, that when markets went down, in an absolute sense, a lot of people didn't really care that we'd done less badly, you know, they really didn't care, and you can understand why, but that's not what they asked us to do. And so this is driven to a greater extent, the flow of funds, towards hedge funds, because by and large they didn't go down,' he added.

Julian Edwards experienced a similar ambiguity between what he was formally expected to do and how he thought his clients would react. 'On the mutual fund side, you know, you always have to wonder if your typical mutual fund investor doesn't understand. They need to see absolute returns and they don't really understand benchmarks so much, so you hope that the market will do okay so that they're relatively happy, but, yeah, it's a funny thing. I mean, my father will call me and tell me how great a fund he has and then I'll ask him what fund it is and I check the benchmark and it's underperformed. Two thousand three was a great example of that. In 2003 the small cap markets were up something along the lines of 40 per cent that year. The average manager is down 600 to a 1,000 basis points relative to benchmark. We were up, fortunately, 600 basis points above the 40 per cent, so we did particularly well; it was a very good year for us. But my father would call me up and tell me how he was up, you know, 32 per cent, it was a great year, and I'd say that's a terrible year; your manager added no value for you, he just detracted value. But that's framing. ...'

Summary

In this chapter I have looked at the way institutional situations in which respondents worked influenced their decision-making. We saw that one of the conflicts they faced was that between their fears they would lose their clients' money by particular investments or miss out on profitable scenarios by not taking part. The conflict causes them to be very watchful of what others are doing and facilitates the developing of *groupfeel*. The conflict is inherent in what asset managers must do and made it difficult to take a long-term view even in the most promising institutional circumstances. It was considerably worsened by the anxieties and pressures that evolve from price volatility and the uncertainty accompanying what it was signalling – price moves always led to questions about whether short-term moves were trivial or fundamental. The inherent conflict promotes defensive behaviours. A further push in the direction of *groupfeel* comes from the efforts asset management companies have developed to constrain the tripartite agency relationship between companies, clients (and consulting advisers), and asset managers and the anxieties dependency on an agent creates for a principal. Metrics like tracking error and benchmarking, together with league tables of performance, all exert homogenous influences on managers and seem mainly to function to try to deal with anticipated client anxieties. But by stimulating *groupfeel* they may make markets more dangerous and unstable.

8
Experiencing Success and Failure

My respondents had survived at least ten years in the industry and among them controlled a great deal of money. To have remained in the business and often to have achieved very senior positions they needed to have achieved success more often than not and also to have found ways of coping with failure.

In this chapter I want to compare the stories they told about the investments that had satisfied and dissatisfied them in the year before being interviewed and to focus on the explanations they offered for their success and failure. The crucial point is that I could find no difference between the stories they told me to support their actions when recounting the decisions that satisfied them and those they told me to support those that later dissatisfied them. The only difference was the outcome. The findings will illustrate how human minds have an enormous capacity for producing explanations. They contribute feedback effects from which we draw conclusions but which then create an ideological framework for appropriate behaviour in future.

I began to look briefly at the differences between satisfied and dissatisfied narratives when considering Duncan Smith's stories in Chapter 6. In this chapter I will continue that comparison by looking at the stories a second manager told me about his successes and failures and then I will test the developing conclusions by summarising what four randomly selected others said. Finally, I will compare the stories managers told that satisfied them and those that did not and draw conclusions from the lack of the difference.

Leonard Frost

I described one of Leonard Frost's stories, his satisfaction in purchasing *CarEngineering*, in Chapter 5. The main example he gave me about a decision with which he was not satisfied (and in fact very anxious) serves as a useful introduction to the fundamental difficulties all fund managers faced. Frost was interviewed two weeks after the first onset of the credit crunch in late August

2007 but before the dramatic events that were to engulf markets in 2008. His story was about doubts he was having that day but managing so far to stave off.

He had bought *Housebank* on the basis it was very 'well positioned' in the 'value chain' and had an exciting new business model. It was the 'lowest-cost producer of mortgages' in the UK market place. Going back five years, he said, 'these people' had doubled and redoubled their market share 'because they've got a very low-cost production model'. They used the 'originate and distribute' model and so didn't keep mortgages 'on their own book'. 'They generally securitize them', selling them on 'to someone else'. All this meant they were a bank historically giving 'an over-return on equity'[1] and Frost had bought a significant holding.

Frost said that *Housebank*'s loans were not, by and large, of the sub-prime kind but that as the news had come in over the last few months about subprime securitised mortgages in the United States, he had got worried and had been having to maintain his conviction as the share price had been dropping. He explained it by management error. Apparently for a while they had not allowed for the possibility that interest rates could vary between the instant a customer signed a contract and the moment they hedged the loan in the market. But they had learned their lesson on that and he said it had now been corrected.[2]

What about subprime worries and the credit crunch? Frost told me how he and his team had just recently completed a 'full investigation' to explore the substance for market anxiety, to re-evaluate and to 'take a view on the mortgage market'. The result, he said, was that he had concluded he had grounds to remain 'quite relaxed'. 'Unless house prices were going to fall' there was 'a stable and growing market in the UK' and *Housebank* were 'winners within that field'. Rather than panic, he maintained clear analysis of events against the original case was needed. 'Has its position in the value chain moved? No, it's still the lowest-cost producer. What's happening to that value chain? Well actually it's quite interesting because a lot of people are pulling out of the mortgage market. Investment banks are pulling out; some of the subprime lenders have pulled out. So the mortgage market in the next 12 months is far healthier.'

In summary Frost was convinced *Housebank* still looked appealing and so 'we've kept holding. We've bought more'. Saying that he was unhappy that the share prices had dropped on the day of the interview, he then volunteered remarks that go to the heart of the conflict I have been identifying. 'I have a view that you only really make money in this industry if you don't sleep at night. If I buy a portfolio of stocks where I can sleep well at night then I will under-perform.' He argued that 'you get return from taking risk' and it was 'when people don't want to invest' that an opportunity existed to 'make your most money'. It was 'when people say to me, oh, I wouldn't touch that or I wouldn't go near that' that he became interested in buying. He was at least in some senses quite aware of the risk. 'The downside risk is that in the current market, securitisation markets don't open up again, so they can't fund any more mortgages, so they don't write any more mortgages, so you get no growth.' Did he really think that possible? His next comment probably lay at the heart of the thinking of many professional investors leading up to 2008 and to the subtle and unnoticed risk-shifting that was taking place in an exuberant atmosphere governed by *groupfeel*.[3] He pointed out that in the worst case *Housebank* wouldn't be able to fund any mortgages because 'Nobody would be able to lend any money to mortgages'. But if that was the case 'we might all be out of work anyway, so would it matter?'[4] Other respondents referred to this as the 'end of the world' and clearly felt it was not a risk they could do anything about so that, in effect, it didn't matter.

Frost told me other stories about decisions he made which did not satisfy him. They involved situations where the kind of reasons that had worked to identify an exceptional opportunity in one instance did not in another. Great management teams brought value or he could be let down by management.[5] The analysis of the 'dissatisfied' stories from four other randomly selected managers supports this point. The kind of story that worked well in one situation didn't in another.

Testing

Andrew Smythe, Gordon Hamilton, Morris Lawn, and Brad Johnston were the four managers randomly selected to test whether the finding just mentioned could be generalised. It could. All four managers had both successes and failures and what was again remarkable was how a strategy that worked in one instance did not in another. Hamilton for instance had success being highly contrarian with *Engineering*, pitting his views supported by strong narratives against negative market consensus, but miserable failure when he tried to repeat the trick with *Resprop*, *Photos*, and *News*, all discussed briefly in Chapter 6.

The thing about the stories all four managers told to support their actions when recounting the decisions that satisfied them was that they were very much the same as those with which they supported the ones that did not satisfy. The same kind of story worked in one situation but not in another. Johnston, for instance, believed he successfully saw through the smog to be successful with *Worldbank* but found the market didn't agree with him in the case of *VeryWellKnownBank*. Leonard Frost argued that *Housebank* was well positioned in the value chain, had an innovative approach and were taking market share from other mortgage lenders aggressively. It was a chance to get an over-return on equity. Similarly with *Advertise* and *Gadgets*. But in all three cases management then 'let him down'. They had failed to protect themselves

Table 8.1   Ten satisfied decisions

Basis of buy case	Brief description of outcome
Company whose share price was very low due to negative analyst reports. In-house analysis suggested company had fundamentally strong business plan and that share price was an opportunity. Bought large holding on confidence in own analysis. *(GreatBuild)*	Share price came up strongly as others (including other large buyer) agreed.
Market-leading company which was identified as likely to benefit substantially from regulatory change – gases in many refrigeration units being phased out and new ones required. *(Refrigeration)*	Company did well as expected. 'It's not rocket science, it's just ears, eyes and nose and using it in the right way. That's pleasing.'
Low-valued company due to market perception this sector does badly with high interest rates. Carefully identified, this one had very strong market situation in certain regions and so was undervalued. *(Lawsons)*	Expectations proved correct.
Archetype of sound investment ticking all the boxes: 'It was a new listing, quite a big company but as a fund manager if you buy a stock there's a sort of list of ticks in the box; barriers to entry, good margins, free cash flow, good management, etc. ...' *(Wafer)*	It worked very well, continues to work and we had good value. If I have any regrets about that it's just we didn't have more, we could have backed it more heavily.
House analyst had identified the potential of the sector, based upon the region's growing inability to meet its own high level of energy demands, need for gas in power station issue, things much worse than people anticipated. Region had to drill more, build pipeline or import. Anticipated would do the first two but not third if could avoid. Bought companies involved in drilling and pipelines. *(Gas)*	Drilling like crazy. So, you've had this fantastic environment for exploration and production companies, all the oil service companies, the rig companies, all these people. Shares have gone up a lot.
Engineering was a growth industry fuelled by the 'building boom' and government funding partnerships. The profitability of the sector further strengthened by the dearth of suitably qualified entrants to the industry: huge price power in engineering. They were huge. It would be huge in PFI. We've got big, big stakes in that area. We were into PFI really early. In the doors, right before anyone else because we just realised that it's off balance sheet funding for governments. It's a bit like heroin – once you've tried it once, I'm sure it's pretty addictive. *(BigBuilders)*	BigBuilders – that's the beneficiary – fuelled by a building boom – the shares have doubled.
Shares hit by rumours of litigation and big compensation pay outs. Investor considered them very cheap as management was sitting on a pile of cash and would find a way to give it to shareholders not victims. *(Greatsmoke)*	They did. Spun off profitable companies leaving liabilities in other companies left behind.

Continued

Table 8.1 Continued

Basis of buy case	Brief description of outcome
Complex new company others in the market did not appreciate because too lazy to look at documents and prejudiced against by past performance. Fantastic but undiscovered story. *(Goodfoods)*	Success came through and still coming through.
He liked the management team and their acquisitions. 'The reason we've ended up running quite a large position is because the market has always underestimated their ability to find value adding acquisitions, and it has also consistently undervalued the quality of their assets, and the demand growth for metals. The market had 'irrational negatives'. *(Bigmines)*	Shares ran up well.

from happenings in the market and as a result the story was not playing out. We could say that Frost first identified managements and plans which looked promising – as he did when he was satisfied – only to find that in these instances they were not. This was the case for Andrew Smythe, Gordon Hamilton, and Morris Lawn. Lawn's two successes, for instance, came about because he did not buy into companies which subsequently did badly but his two failures came about when the same caution caused him to desist and thus to miss out.

Stories and their outcomes

A more formal analysis of the stories told by all my respondents supports the conclusion just reached. Altogether, 43 stock-picking managers among them told me 165 stories to support the decisions they made to buy stocks. One hundred and three of these stories led to what they felt were satisfying outcomes while 62 did not.[6] Every story was then analysed together with its outcome. Table 8.1 summarises, highly schematically, key features of the 'buy' scripts for ten randomly selected stories in which the manager felt there was a 'satisfactory' outcome and Table 8.2 summarises the same features for ten more randomly selected stories in which she or he did not.

Looking down the left hand column of both lists, it is apparent that the stories my respondents developed to give them the confidence to buy and hold are pretty similar in type whatever the outcome. The stories enshrine the five core script features discussed in Chapter 5. The sole difference between those stories that led to a satisfactory outcome and those that did not is derived from the right hand column – whether in fact the story worked out or not. In one way this is encouraging. Managers had a consistent strategy in selecting stocks with the types of stories they liked.

Table 8.2   Ten dissatisfied decisions

Basis of buy case	Brief description of outcome
Underpriced company and we thought could see a good future. (*JBank*)	Market didn't have insight. Was a too clever thesis.
Company with an expanding and interesting business model. (*CleverEnerg*)	Turned out to be too reliant on external finance. Normally would have noticed (as one of the boxes to tick) but did not. Also price flattered to deceive for a while.
Company with great business model that works elsewhere and with proven record of high profitability and market power. (*Outfits*)	Market unable to interpret temporary sales blip because too impressed with maverick behaviour of CEO/Owner and doesn't see strengths of this high value but non-sexy business.
Good product based on interesting technical ideas. (*Digi*)	Very large company came in and undercut margins nearly driving it out of business.
Felt could see through to the real value of this company despite the 'Q' model managers used to test ideas suggesting otherwise. Therefore, overrode the model because thought it must be wrong. (*Enerco*).	The model was right.
Thought the company management was on top of the business and the business cycle was turning in their favour so that low share prices made a good bargain. Shares beginning to go up. (*Insure*)	Lost confidence in management because company had more problems than realised and the initial share price rise was caused by a '9/11 bounce' and not underlying improvement; so it was actually flattering to deceive.
Management with great new ideas for taking handpicked stores forward with likely consequence for very large jump in profits. (*Goodfoods*)	Profits and share prices performed as expected. But couldn't persuade team that doubts about this management from past record were not important and so did not buy.
New business model with strong place in value chain. (*Housebank*)	Business model turned out flawed and management made mistakes.
Good business with good management team with business model in underrated sector whose potential not yet recognised in the market. (*Leave It to Us*)	Lost faith in management team after profit warning. Then shares did well (as predicted) after we sold.
Identified that flat screen televisions would be sold worldwide and have hugely expanded sales providing opportunity for expanding profits for companies with pricing power. (*Flatscreens*)	Underestimated the power of the end user in getting prices down so that the expansion of sales did not increase profits.

But there is more to it than that. Fred Bingham's comment about his success with *Refrigeration* is pertinent. 'It's not rocket science, it's just ears, eyes and nose and using it in the right way', he said. But Bingham's other stories involved the same ears, eyes and nose. He identified other very plausible themes in those other instances – as with *Leave It to Us* where success proved elusive, in fact because share prices dipped and created unmanageable doubt before the thesis played out. Table 8.2 shows he was not alone.

The conclusion so far, therefore, is that the very features that made a good story for a satisfied investment were also those features associated with the reverse. This was true when the causes of satisfaction or dissatisfaction hinged around the reason *to* buy stock as well as the reasons *not* to do so. Cautious managers (e.g., Lawn) told stories about satisfactorily identifying companies citing various aspects of the secure features of stories. But then they would also talk about missing out on other opportunities because they could not feel sufficiently confident. Respondents who identified amazing situations and were successful in one instance also found that for one reason or another they were not in another. Respondents who identified enterprise managers with interesting and unusual business models they thought they would execute had success in some instances but also discovered in other cases either that those managers could not deliver or that the story was mistaken.

Explaining misfortune

The management and explanation of misfortune is an important issue which has classically been discussed in social anthropology and related to theories about the social function of religion and magic (Durkheim 1915; Evans-Pritchard 1937). It has also been discussed in medical sociology and organisational sociology and organisational theory and in the wide-ranging literature on accidents and errors (Tuckett 1976). Misfortune provides an opportunity for feedback but also tends to threaten social cohesion and morale. In psychology there is an extensive discussion of how individuals respond to inconsistency (Laird-Johnson 2010) and in psychoanalysis theories about the differences between learning from experience and expiating it via blame and pseudoguilt (Bion 1962; Riesenberg-Malcolm 1999). An overwhelming finding from all these perspectives is that human beings have an almost endless capacity to fit patterns and explanations to events – often to advantage but sometimes at the cost of the truth (e.g., Laird-Johnson 2010).

When things worked out my respondents almost always thought of their searching and calculating activity as the cause of their success. But how do they explain misfortune? To look at this we examined what they had volunteered by way of explanation in some detail. Although not every manager offered comments that were useful for this analysis (and so conclusions are particularly tentative), it emerged that we could divide what they said broadly into five main classes of reason and then determine how many managers supplied which class – with the possibility their chosen explanation fitted more than one:

1. Failures and errors on their part. (Mentioned by 51%)
2. Happenings one just could not expect or predict. (Mentioned by 14%)
3. Unexpected developments in the market. (Mentioned by 14%)
4. Incompetent or misleading enterprise managements. (Mentioned by 12%)
5. Mistakes by others advising them or in-house process. (Mentioned by 12%)

Looking at the brief descriptions to be found in the randomly selected examples given above in Table 8.2 the accounts of the outcome of buying *Jbank*, *Outfits*, and *Digi* are typical instances of those citing unexpected developments in market sentiment; the accounts of *Outfits*, *Housebank*, and *Leave It to Us* are instances of where they felt undermined by managements. The *CleverEng* story and its outcome was one where respondents thought they had relied too much on others and the *Goodfoods* thesis had been prevented from paying off by team process. Developments with *Digi* and *Flatscreens* are illustrations of how sometimes misfortune was blamed on the inherently 'unpredictable'.

An important and perhaps counterintuitive finding is that overall by far the most common explanation offered for lack of satisfaction was not to blame others, the market or the unpredictable. Rather, nearly half of my respondents said that their misfortune was in some way their own fault. So this was the explanation given for many failed theses and specifically those pertaining to *Jbank*, *Clevereng*, *Enerco*, *Insure*, *Leave It to Us*, and *Flatscreens*, above. In these and similar cases what seemed to be happening was that managers were trying to take some kind of control over their situation and to do this had developed an explanation which made them responsible; in this way they could, so to speak, live to fight another day. So, they said they had been taken over by irrationality, or they had ignored advice, or they had acted prematurely, or they had been prejudiced, frustrated or stubborn, and so on. Such reasons were offered three times more commonly than the others.

Psychoanalysts have long observed that taking blame (even inventing stories to make one responsible) is one way to feel in control when one is in fact helpless; the need to retain such a feeling and its negative impact on performance have also been discussed in the psychology literature (e.g., Langer 1975). For instance, it played a significant part in the findings of a mixed interview and experimental study of UK traders, which found that measures of 'illusion of control' were somewhat negatively correlated with performance. 'You need a positive view of yourself', and 'you need to believe in your ability when things go wrong', two traders were reported to have said (Fenton-Creevey et al. 2005, p105 et seq.).

It is important that the way my respondents 'took control' seems to have been more by making an emotional claim than by engaging in any useful forensic examination. In many cases what could be observed was 'effort after meaning' (Bartlett 1932). In other words, the story they told was designed to make retrospective sense in a way that enabled them to feel responsible, but was not based on sufficient introspection to guarantee that it would lead to preventive changes in behaviour. Brian Anderson, for instance, described his investment in *HardDisk* as 'shockingly bad'. According to him its profits and share price began to fall because it appeared to be being 'obliterated' by competition from larger industry rivals who had decided to sell their products at prices well below those of others in the industry and perhaps even below the costs of production. Anderson said he had been 'caught out' because he simply didn't think a large company would act 'so irrationally'. As a specialist company *HardDisk* just couldn't compete with this 'cross-subsidising' because with a single product they had nothing with which to cross-subsidise. When he was asked directly if he had learned anything useful from the experience Anderson's reply was interesting. He said he would now 'always' know to remember to be 'very aware of anyone that can compete with you irrationally'. He made this statement very confidently. But when I asked him how he might anticipate such situations in future he found himself saying 'he could not' and 'it can always happen'. He then became eloquent: 'If you and I had $1 billion we could go and make life very tough for Tesco in Cambridge', he elaborated. 'If we wanted to we could go and build some stores and stock them with bananas for free. But Tesco would look at us and wonder how much cash we've got or stop supplying us with the bananas and put us out of business.' Apparently a little disturbed by my question, he then suggested that perhaps 'when you see irrational competition it's understanding why and understanding how long it can last for'. 'And if the answer's it can last for quite a while, no matter what the answer to why is, you probably don't want to be there.'

My impression was that answers of the kind just mentioned seemed to matter to Anderson and others because they needed to have *some* explanation. What it was or how tractable it would be in future didn't really matter. So, among those already discussed above in this chapter, Smythe said of several of his 'mistakes' that he was going to learn how to avoid further capitulation by 'reviewing the trades'. Crawford implied that the *JBank* example would teach him to avoid being too clever with his theses. Talbot suggested the lesson from *Enerco* would be to trust his model. Brown implied that the message from *Insure* was that he would need perfect foresight. From *Goodfoods* Singh would have to learn how to persuade his team and from *Digi* Crumb would have to be able to distinguish better when the end-users would have more market power than producers. It seemed far from likely that these 'lessons' would be useful.

The essential problem is that the 'unimaginable' as a source of risk for things going wrong is just that. Fund managers, like the rest of us, simply found some eventualities beyond their thoughts at that moment. Whether the claim is made that the various events not predicted are intrinsically beyond imagination, so that nothing can be done, or alternatively, that they are matters that fund managers can and should work to take into account through 'their process', is equally interesting. The question is how they dealt with uncertainty. In part asset management firms compete with each other by making claims that their fund managers can take steps to be on top of events – whether this is by what they call managing risk or by being so careful and so well informed that they are able to surprise the market rather than being surprised by it.

Unimaginable or unimagined?

Among my respondents it was an open question whether falls in share price were due to unimaginable and unanticipated news, which was inherently uncontrollable, or failures 'in process', which might be correctable. Duncan Smith spoke as if he thought the sudden revelation of negative research results in the case of *Pharma* was unforeseeable and Chuck Bronsky seemed to feel entirely surprised about what happened to *Lap Wireless*. Peter Ross went so far as to state there was 'no way' he could have foreseen the fraudulent accounting at *Construct*. Other reasoning of this kind applied to macroeconomic issues. For instance, David Allen explained things that went wrong for him because he could not have predicted the Japanese market would reverse in 2006 after doing so well the year before. Similarly Fiona Wellington said she could not have expected hurricanes to affect shares in *Cruise* and Alastair Topp felt he could not have expected that *Premier* would lose their TV football rights. Leonard Frost had not anticipated that *Yachts* would suddenly be unable to sell their navigation systems for luxury yachts due to a global turndown and Ed Morse had not been expecting avian flu, higher inflation and a prime-ministerial coup in Thailand to create such an impact for *Airways*.

But the kind of thing they thought 'unimaginable', is what another might say they had failed to imagine. So in contrast to Ed Morse, Nick South reported that one of his most satisfying decisions had been his ability to predict and act on his expectations of future events in Thailand and their negative effects on share prices.[7] At first sight Fred Bingham's account of the fall in value in his investment in *Burgers for Schools* might be another example citing the unimaginable. But in fact he didn't think so. 'Well, there is always an excuse, isn't there? There were other issues, obviously, and the debt was the main one, in fact, and we got it wrong. We did our analysis, trusted the management to deliver it and unfortunately they didn't, and we didn't get out.'

The main point is that whether things went wrong because they were unimaginable or because the manager did not on this occasion manage to imagine enough of the future sequence, what was always at stake were conflicting feelings. The explanations offered were ambiguous perhaps because they were designed to cope: they were an effort to try to control managers' doubt, doubt engendered by their failures. By talking simultaneously as though they both believed in totally unexpected events on the one hand, and as though they prided themselves on being able to do the work or to have developed protective systems on the other, they could go back to the 'front line'.

'Flexible' explanations of this kind, which could function as covering stories (like the generalised beliefs that support asset price bubbles), were a feature of many interviews. The explanations offered made sense if they were not too sceptically examined. This disconnect was particularly obvious when managers spoke about their time horizons, or if one stopped for a moment to compare what was said about mission statements with the detailed decisions actually taken.

Brian Anderson, for example, outlined a general approach in which he said he had access to an enormous amount of information starting with his firm's 'unparalleled global research base' with people 'in every sector in every region around the world' and on top of that 'quant' screens, and a variety of impressive sounding rules of thumb concerning valuation.[8] He summarised his belief that this equipped him and his team to be very good at 'understanding companies' and that 'globally' 'lots of different things' 'get flagged'. But then he said that he often went away and looked for companies himself which weren't particularly 'well covered' or had been forgotten by his regional teams. Again the time frame he had in mind was 'two to three years' but 'yet again, for this one in particular we're very pragmatic'. He elaborated that it's not actually about 'owning it for three years'; 'it's about owning it until we think it's fair value.' And so on. The approach seems likely to prepare Anderson for many eventualities and such 'flexibility' can help to cope with the underlying conflicts of having not only to perform long-term but to be seen to be doing so even short-term.

One way to deal with contradictory ideas causing conflicting emotions is not to be fully aware one has them, to treat them serially or in other words to 'split' them apart as I described in Chapter 3. When this happens in a regular way it makes sense to talk of a *divided state* of mind. In effect individuals invest emotionally in only one part of a story which would otherwise produce a conflicting experience. Or they tell such flexible stories to themselves that contradictions are glossed over. Reflecting more fully on how Anderson and others managed their situations it seems they adopted several contradictory coping strategies to such an extent that they can be considered in this respect to think in a *divided state.* Such a state is supported specifically by various features of ambiguity I observed. They seem to have found ways to rationalise their situations by selectively interpreting them, by taking protective measures in the way they present their activities to themselves, and by reinventions of themselves when things got really tough. In consequence, whatever the past had been and so long as they stayed at their posts, they found ways to feel good about the future.

Selective interpretation, multiple objectives and reinvention

I have quoted extensively from Fred Bingham in Chapter 2. The way he spoke about his time horizon is a good example of ambiguity. He defined his holding period as 'over the length of a business cycle' but when asked how long that was replied 'over three years'; invoking a rule of thumb commonly applied by financial intermediaries but with no conceivable justification in macroeconomics. With equal ambiguity, he also mentioned that some of his funds may go up and others down and told me how he drew comfort from this 'hedging' of his performance 'bets'. He clearly and understandably felt better that he did not have all his (emotional) eggs in one (client) basket. By selectively framing his performance across several portfolios he promoted his chances of at least some doing well at any given moment and thus causing himself to feel satisfied at least somewhere, even if his overall performance was poor. He was actually quite clear about it. 'We run a group of funds...we haven't got just one fund' and so he is not 'under pressure because that one fund is performing badly'. This approach, which appeared to create the impression that one was doing well somewhere, seemed to be very common across the sample – nearly all managers had several funds and even benchmarks to choose from, just as the firms they work for have many fund managers from among which to choose some exceptional performers to advertise. Funds and managers can be dropped off selectively to preserve this impression.

Such selective perception also works for asset allocation and relative performance. In both cases managers could find ways to make themselves look better and feel better (or at least less bad) by framing their perception positively. Samuel Swindon was explicit. 'Our job is to deliver relative performance, so in that sense, it's another way that I suppose in my role I'm insulated from emotions to some degree, because in truth, a couple of years of the market falling 20%, I don't really care because I am trying to deliver relative performance.'

Statements such as Swindon's make sense in many ways but they have what we might think of as an asymmetrical emotional effect. Emotionally speaking, the bad feelings that go with underperformance in absolute terms (and which might prompt real consideration about the underlying situation) can be shifted away from the manager or his firm, by not fully absorbing the situation emotionally or even by divorcing it from consciousness. But this is selective, because it did not seem to hold when managers outperformed; here credit was claimed and bonuses paid. Talking about his performance, Brian Anderson again brought his flexibility to bear, saying that 'I don't really want everything to work at the same time anyway. I want different things to work at different times. And so my patience can actually be quite long; as long as I'm still on the roadmap that I've set out; as long as my plan at the start is the plan that is actually being delivered on I actually can wait quite a long time. When we have no tolerance is when we deviate from the plan.' It is easy to see that with such flexible theories Brian Anderson and those like him should be able to find a silver lining to any cloud he encounters.

When investments failed and managers underperformed they knew they were at risk. Many volunteered to me that at such times confidence declines and taking decisions becomes difficult: whereas they felt that success breeds success, failure is thought to breed failure. One way they coped and tried to stay confident and optimistic was by trying to tell themselves and others stories which reinvented their strategies, while at the same time maintaining that they were really staying true to their philosophy; further evidence it would seem of a *divided state* relationship to reality. Effectively most managers thought it tantamount to suicide to admit their philosophy wasn't working.

Andrew Smythe, who we met above in this chapter, was in a team which had been struggling. He had been working for the house for two and a half years and during that time their investment approach had been 'out of style'. They had responded by reorganising the way they used their in-house financial analysts and were also in the process of moving from what they called risk constrained tracking error type managed portfolios towards concentrated ones while maintaining, he insisted, their basic approach. 'Our approach' has been 'out of favour for four of the last five years'. But 'we have an investment philosophy and if we're true to ourselves, we have to stick with our investment philosophy'. What he said they tried to do was 'to make changes' in terms of the way they organised analyst portfolios which 'I spoke about'. Because their analysts now had to make precise predictions about stocks and were being made accountable by being remunerated against results, they were hoping the advice they got about what to put into portfolios would be better. With better advice the portfolio managers were switching to concentrated or high conviction 'best ideas' portfolios. So 'accountability, communication and transparency' will be much better', Smythe declared. He said that they had tried to 'tweak the process a little bit' but 'we haven't changed our philosophy'. Selective attention was then being deployed to make things better. Last year had been poor, he said, but this year would be better – they were meeting in the third week of the year. 'It feels like it's coming our way', he said. 'We get the same questions from our clients' but 'if you change your philosophy then you've got nothing'.

In a different direction Mike Brown told me how his team had been completely reorganised four years previously, following very poor performance results during the Internet bubble and then again in 2003. But in their case they had moved away from concentrated portfolios to a strict policy of not being able to deviate from the benchmark proportions – something he called 'risk control'. They now had to stay with the crowd. 'You couldn't change your whole mindset', he said, but 'we were running very concentrated portfolios then and that was with a different CIO'. Now that they had more risk controls in place 'we couldn't underperform by as much we did'. Alan Thomas had another kind of story based on selective perception to explain a performance hiatus. He worked in more emerging markets and his stocks, having run up, were this year 'taking a break'. He felt they were all too expensive and he could not at that time find bargains. Things would improve later.

Helping others to cope

My respondents were on average more successful than the average portfolio manager and a significant number held high-level managerial responsibility. The remarks of three I spoke to in August 2007 as the financial crisis began to break are interesting if we think of them as coming from a group of people who had been selected by success in their world in the period leading up to it. One way of understanding how they thought is by noting the comments they made about the ways they helped younger colleagues. These comments reinforce the picture of ambiguity, selective attention, and suppressed ambivalence that I have been noting. It further emphasises the pressure to take up a *divided state* attitude to reality.

Novak Jones was interviewed in mid-August 2007 a few days after the first day of what we now know were to be many days when the world's stock markets panicked on hitherto unknown scales. His comments are those of someone not yet gripped by what was to happen and able to maintain a confident narrative in times of crisis. Jones said that on that day he had sent his team home. He feared that they would panic and he wanted to keep them inactive. It was the end of 'what had been quite a tough week'. 'The markets will be here for you on Monday', he had said, 'just go and enjoy yourself and put the markets behind you.' His decision was based on the idea that markets get taken over by irrational fears and it was 'all too easy to get sucked in and become entranced by the numbers on the screen'. You can 'over-analyse things', he added, and 'at the bottom a properly managed portfolio should represent their medium to long-term conviction'. The more he had managed money, he said 'the more you come to appreciate that keeping the level of turnover in a portfolio down is positive; and every time you transact you incur a cost and it's effectively a drag on performance. It's all too easy to get sucked into the short-term noise in the market place.'

Leonard Frost was also a team head and also made some interesting remarks about confidence. His remarks made consistent sense at one level but at another level were quite ambiguous. Like others in the sample he thought 'the behaviour of someone with three up years is going to be far superior to the behaviour of someone with two down years'. This was because, he said, the latter have to do something either to bail themselves out or to take the risk off, for fear of the third bad year. In his view the biggest risk with an underperforming fund manager is that 'they stop doing things and stop backing their judgement'. With his younger staff his view was 'back them or sack them' because 'if you have someone who's underperforming and you're on their back, they will make all the wrong decisions'. I asked if he fired anyone and how he decided to do that. If someone has underperformed over one month, three months, twelve months and three years, he said, 'then I think you've got a real issue on your hands'. He would then begin 'by trying to understand where underperformance had come from' and look for 'some systematic reason'. He said patience was needed. 'All fund managers know that they will go through periods of underperformance and what they look for from their peers is help and tolerance.'

Frost had come in a year ago to manage the team which had been having a very bad track record. 'And the first thing I said to people was, when you're in a hole, stop digging.' He thought 'there was no conviction and there was no rigid process' really being employed so that his approach was 'to strip that team back down and say, you'll run a concentrated portfolio'. There was 'a lot of resistance to that' but 'ultimately it's starting to show through, and people, I think, are beginning to realise, one, their actual job's easier because they're more focussed; and, two, they know what they should be doing and how they're supposed to go about it.' The 'horrendous underperformance' had stopped and 'confidence was coming back. I remembered that Frost had said it was really difficult to measure performance (see above), and so, to correlate skill and outcome, I asked him directly if it really was useful to sack people. It was here that his replies revealed the ambiguous rules of thumb that feature throughout this chapter and all fund managers' work as they try to deal with the very complex question of what good performance actually is and how it comes about. 'It probably is rational to sack people but it's who you sack and when you sack them. We measure their performance in terms of buys less sells. It's simplistic. We measure how everyone else does in their sector.' 'I always say to the guys you've got three years. And I'm quite honest when I recruit people, I'm not short-term, you're going to get three years. Now we could easily argue I should give them all ten years, but we're in the real world and basically in three years you should know if someone's any good or not. If someone isn't delivering on one of those years but is on the others, you can live with it. So if this person was not delivering for the first two years, you take the assets away from them, that's the first thing you do, because it's back them or sack them, but the process of getting rid of someone actually takes 12 months.'

Throughout this chapter and elsewhere we have seen that asset managers can sometimes get so anxious that they panic. One way to survive in the situation I think they all feared is to find a narrative. Sol Abram's interview also took place in late August 2007 but revealed him as a man with a great deal of self-belief. Because he thought he had both a superior information advantage and was more objective than the rest of the market, he considered the crisis an opportunity. 'I'm a big big believer in what I call emotional control', he said. He meant being aware of what the market was worrying about and what was driving the market, but being detached, and dispassionate about it. 'So, you've got to be very cold at the point of decision-making. You've got to be above it, not in it.' As head of his team he tried to instil the same confident approach. 'I try and keep people in perspective.' 'You're in an environment where you're looking at these things, and suddenly everyone is a world authority on the housing market in the US, which nobody cared about before, and the market knows what the house sales were last month in Texas.' Confidence and disdain go together, and his were reminiscent of the dismissal of opposing theses during bubble years.

In fact Abram was another respondent to volunteer the example of *Housebank*. 'It's a mortgage lender, is funded from the wholesale market and doesn't have much by way of deposits. It's getting squeezed as a consequence of this funding crisis. Now, it's quite a good company, in terms of having quite a low cost base...they focus on mortgages, that's all they do, and they've quite a good track record. They tripped up very marginally over something, but the shares were about £11.80 or £12. I started to look at it when the share went through to £7, because they had wholesale funding problems, and they are quite exposed.' 'But the market[9] really was saying, this company is going bust, really negative...funding cost issues, they will get downgraded.' Abram's approach was to meet the company, get detailed information and think 'rationally'. 'We know what the securitisation position is, so we've quite a lot of information...Forget fear but rationalise the logic.' He took his team through the issues to get them 'to behave logically with risk-reward ratios'. In the end he bought some stock but no one else did. 'You re-emphasise an objective analysis of the data. Because at the moment if the market is negative, all you'll get is negative news reinforced by the small bearish houses. The positive news is there but isn't there. So you've got to force yourself to keep looking at both sides of the equation, which can be quite difficult ...'

He rehearsed the arguments that might cause panic. 'The credit crunch could last for ages. We don't know what it's going to cost. People could lose millions. The hedge funds are all going to derail. So that will pull the market down...Interest rate costs are going to go up, the US is going into recession...the end of the world ...'

He then looked 'calmly' and rationally. 'But what's actually happened, the subprime is 1% of residential mortgage loans. In a really bad scenario, 10% of those debts are foreclosed, this is probably very bad, so a total risk...you can argue why so many people bought these things, and that's the flip, but you say that means it's probably about $100 billion loss here, if that's really bad, but that's spread through quite a lot of people. But the market is down by $2500 billion on the back of that $100 billion, and some of them were going to lose these anyway...there were pockets where they really took a large bit of that and blew themselves up. Now, you can then say, what does that mean, what actually happens? That means you get a high cost of credit. You might bring forward the fact that the interest rate cycle, which was going up, goes in the other direction, which is a positive. The people that are good credits there are not affected. In fact, they'll get better credit, because the interest rate is going to come down earlier as a consequence. China, India, who are the growth drivers economically anyway, and Asia, have they got any problems? No. So even if you might have a weaker U.S. consumer, but you've got interest rates offsetting. What is the valuation in the market? Was it particularly high? No...Rather than just go, oh my God, subprime is a disaster, what do I sell? Which is how it is portrayed if you read the weekend press, very few people say, actually, the bullish view is...because it's not so exciting, so it's just trying to stay calm and logical.'

Summary

In this chapter I showed how when fund managers looked out for exceptional stories and then 'bet' on them some worked and some didn't. As far as I could see the only difference between the stories that did and did not work was that sometimes the story proved a correct thesis and sometime it did not. The decision-making which led to buy decisions with which managers were later not satisfied was not different from that when the outcome was as desired.

When things went wrong and stories did not work out they tended to blame themselves for failures of anticipation or foresight and claimed that they would be able to learn from the experience. But I came to the view that such explanations of misfortune were actually coping devices which did not really constitute taking responsibility to investigate what had happened. They were like covering stories aimed at managing ambiguities and conflicts and attempting to maintain morale; this allowed my respondents to continue to take the spontaneous actions that were necessary so long as they stayed at their posts.

As the last few quotations have indicated the result is a strange selection. Those who succeeded believe in their capacity to find exceptional stories and are supported by their success. Those who have much more bad luck than good in finding such stories don't survive. Their places will be taken by new entrants who will try to be exceptional too. The process creates a psychological and social context, a form of strange selection, enhanced by the institutional performance context reviewed in Chapter 4, which maintains what we might call a mythology. As I shall argue in the next chapter it creates the conditions for financial markets to become wild markets at any time.

9
Emotional Finance and New Economic Thinking

I discussed in Chapter 1 how standard economic theory sets out to demonstrate how markets can work. The basic thrust of the argument is that unfettered self-seeking competitive behaviour coordinates an economy and achieves optimal wealth creation and welfare. Markets are self-equilibrating so that inhibiting the behaviour of those in them or interfering with them in any other way than to encourage competition can only produce suboptimal outcomes.

The standard economics story is a very old and specific one. It played a key ideological role in the development of English and American capitalism and emerged from philosophical debate following Hobbes and Locke as to the origin of social order and the divine right of kings. Its roots are in a developing opposition to the monopolies and tariffs imposed by Stuart kings during the English revolution and then by later English governments on their American colonists and then still later in the English nineteenth-century struggle between the landed and manufacturing classes over tariffs. The efficient market hypothesis invokes reason to argue 'freedom' from political control. To justify this political position it aims to demonstrate that far from helping a society to achieve wealth, cooperation, and coordination, monarchies and governments inhibit the working of the 'invisible hand'.

We could say that the classical theory wobbled a bit during the Great Depression. Keynes and the economics of uncertainty had its day for a while. But quite quickly thereafter, in the second half of the twentieth century, its essence was forgotten. A modernised and sophisticated mathematical version of the classical approach re-emerged in the United States which paid no real attention to uncertainty or instability and, drawing on doubts about Keynesian macroeconomic policy due to growing problems with price inflation, returned to discussing how markets should work. A major consequence of this neoclassical theory, accelerated in the last 30 years, is that it legitimated deregulation, free market ideology, and globalisation without trade barriers just as two and three centuries earlier its ideological manifestation had legitimated an end to royal monopolies and barriers to free trade.

A central question that might be used to judge any theory is to ask what it is for. Theories designed to show how markets produce an efficient equilibrium must struggle when asked why they sometimes do not. The only answer available from within the paradigm is that governments and institutions have interfered – markets aren't being allowed to work as they could. Although different at first sight, both information economics and behavioural economics can be kept within the same paradigm. In essence what they both do is show up potential interferences that need attention if things are to work – they can then be used to support measures such as transparent contracting to resolve agency issues, derivative or virtual market creation to complete markets, or behavioural finance investment strategies to 'clean up' the anomalies caused by investor biases. The last proposal is particularly popular among some finance professionals because it gives them a role, which efficient market theories do not. In any case none of these theories from within the central paradigm really has any rigorous explanation for financial instability.

This chapter aims to set out a framework to understand the minimum requirements for a new economic theory of financial markets directly aimed at understanding their empirical reality and how it can lead to persistent instability – as is now much more widely accepted to be a risk than it was five years ago. As I showed in Chapter 1 severe bouts of instability are nearly always associated with the arrival of new, exciting products and then subsequent dislocations in risk-reward relationships.

My ideas about phantastic objects, narratives, and states of mind were built up as I struggled to understand empirical reality while in a to-and-fro process of collecting data and thinking about it. They emerged as I did the interviews and thought about them as what sociologists call 'grounded theory' (Glaser and Strauss 1967; Brown 1973). I have mentioned, for example, how in my very first pilot interview it became evident that the simplified model of rational decision-making used in standard theory just didn't seem to apply to what my respondent was trying to do. He could calculate as much as he liked but he was still left with uncertainty and several equally attractive alternatives from which he selected by touch and feel. The world of the four asset managers described in Chapter 2 elaborated this first impression about uncertainty and revealed three further emerging themes. My respondents seemed to be talking about making and breaking emotional attachments to stock. They seemed to be strongly influenced by, and oriented towards, their feelings within a social and institutional context. And they dealt with all this by telling stories. These first four interviews had made clear the decision context (what Talcott Parsons (1937) called the conditions for social action) and in doing so demonstrated the very limited utility of economic rationality as a significant guide to behaviour.

However much rational logic and probabilistic reasoning my respondents tried to deploy to interpret the new information available, they were not facing simple unambiguous choices which they could get right by logic alone. They had constantly to engage in subjective interpretation. As the labour economist, Bewley, put it in the apparently very different context of explaining his decision to do interviews to try to resolve key questions about what happens to wages in a depression, 'the implications of rationality depend on the conditions constraining decision-makers' (Bewley 1999 p7). He found just what I have reported, namely that it is often knowledge as to what the constraints on behaviour are that 'is precisely what' agents are 'lacking'.

The findings I have presented more formally in the last five chapters support and elaborate the impressions emerging from the four respondents discussed in Chapter 2. They paint a picture of economic reality dominated by the need decision-makers had to cope with uncertainty. I will now summarise these core findings before using them to reflect further on the causes of the 2008 crisis and how normal markets of the kind I observed can turn into the wild ones that lead to serious crises. In the last part of the chapter I will try to specify what it is that is different about an 'emotional' finance approach and how and why we might try to integrate uncertainty and emotion into economics in a way that retains their essence.

Markets in stories

I have described how I enquired into the context in which asset managers made decisions by talking to them using standardised nonschedule interviews. The first conclusion I drew was that to understand the way financial assets are valued we must realise that, in essence, what is being traded are stories – competing imaginative accounts about the news and its impact on an uncertain future.

In chapters two and five I described how my respondents set about devising and advertising their strategies to buy, sell, and hold assets for their clients and particularly the buying decisions they made. I showed how they did it by offering general narrative accounts which were rationales, making their decision-making sensible and coherent and apparently forming a basis which allowed them conviction about what they did. When they were asked to elaborate on specific examples they recounted what happened in detail in such a way that they seemed to live out what happened. So from the first descriptions offered by Fred Bingham in Chapter 2 to the last ones offered by Sol Abram in the previous chapter, it was clear that understanding financial markets meant subjectively interpreting the latest news in the overwhelming information context in which my respondents found themselves. In every interview they told me how they had to make interpretive choices in a situation where they were overloaded with information, comment, and assessment. They also emphasised, because they were lacking in omnipotent foresight, that they never knew enough to be sure. From the start, therefore, it was also clear that reasoned calculation had limits. What mattered was how they could come to *feel* they knew enough to commit to act. They needed to find ways to rationalise the claim which went with their role – that they really could search out and take opportunities that (most) others could not find and so could not take.

To do their work all respondents started from a belief in a formal mission strategy, which had to be coherent enough to give guidance to themselves and those others they had to communicate with and yet still be flexible enough to allow for a wide range of interpretations. Such mission statements were also stories – 'covering stories' providing loose envelopes of coherence and support.

Asset prices respond to news and actions taken on the basis of news. So managers generally had to be able to select and interpret new information very quickly. To make each specific decision it was essential to feel conviction about what information mattered and what didn't – including being able to conclude in some instances (but not too many) that there was simply too much uncertainty to act. In every instance that they described of making a decision, the rational course of action to take (if, for example, determined by a fully Bayesian-framed analysis of each and every possibility) was by no means simple or obvious. If options were obvious, then there was nothing to be done as everyone else would be doing it too. The role of the stories they told, therefore, was to produce frameworks and rationales to support action.

I have described how respondents narrated to me in the interviews. As they did so, it became progressively clear that telling stories was in fact also how they managed the task of interpreting the daily information to which they were subjected and the opportunities and uncertainties it potentially created. To be convinced enough to take a decision, a feeling of commitment to it had to be created. Already in Chapter 2 Fred Bingham was narrating how he and his team gained conviction about what they did by narrowing down the mass of potential information they had to fit into themes (stories) that they considered promising. These themes engaged their emotions. In narrating them he must surely have engaged those of his listeners, as he did mine. Whether he was describing success or failure, his emotion was a palpable feature of what I conceived of as a story of a dependent relationship with a beginning, continuation, and ending. He mentioned, it will be recalled, a 'lovely company', a 'money-making machine', an 'order book stretching years'; talking about the management of the company he mentioned about those who gave 'comfort'. 'It's about trust', he said. 'She doesn't say anything she shouldn't.'

We have seen how the stories I was told contained repeated features. As analysed in detail in Chapter 5 they were narratives in which certain cognitive and emotional elements could be deconstructed into scripts with one of two types of consistent 'attractor'. First, respondents seemed to like to identify something to convince them there was some cap on uncertainty – some offload of risk, or some guarantee of visible and substantial future income streams. Such factors as market power (for example, a degree of monopoly allowing pricing power), evidence of long-run future demand, and 'visible' or reassuring management records, were all examples of features that served to underpin and render my respondents' conviction secure. Stories with these features appeared to be able to contain and make manageable at least some of the anxiety which was otherwise consequent on making a commitment to a dependent relationship with an uncertain future.

I have also shown how stories only became compelling when coupled with a second feature identified by my respondents. They had to have some reason to believe they, more or less alone, had access to a story in which returns would be exceptional and usually one not seen by others. In other words it wasn't just safety that mattered. There also had to be reasons for an exclusive attachment or 'true love'. Altogether 75 per cent of the 'buy' narratives respondents told me *either* contained the belief the stock was exceptional (because of their way of analysing it) and/or that what they had found was special (in the sense that the company or sector held out unusual prospects).

In different guises, therefore, the stories fund managers constructed were scripts that first *pulled* them towards feeling they had personally and exceptionally captured something with exceptional returns, and also helped them to *push* away doubt or uncertainty – any potential feeling of anxiety that accompanies entering a long-term dependent relationship. One of the essential properties of narrative is that it allows diverse elements of fact and interpretation to be woven together in scripts so that they coalesce meaningfully and feel right. Narrative provides a sense of conviction and truth. Their stories thus made managers' decision-making sensible and coherent, underpinning their conviction about their choices.

The importance of finding the two attractors just mentioned is underlined in that I later discovered that just these two features can also be discerned in the advertising material produced by the industry. One of many examples I found from mutual fund advertisements on the Internet was presented in Chapter 7. Another, arriving by e-mail advertisement as I was finishing this chapter, advertised 'a surprising asset class with strong historical returns' and had these banner headlines:

Do you want *100%* capital security?

Would you like the potential to earn ***unlimited returns***

– historically 10% per annum?[1]

To judge by the analysis of Harvard economists, Mullainathan and Shleifer (2005), this type of approach is rather typical. Analysing a sample of advertisements between 1994 and 2003 they found two very similar components were repeatedly present (labelled by them as 'growth' and 'protection') and also noted how the emphasis on one or the other shifted during different periods of the business cycle.

In summary, when deconstructed, the stories my respondents told me suggest that to rationalise their acts, to make decisions that they imagined could achieve the exceptional performance their clients demanded, managers were attracted to stocks with stories. These stories allowed them to develop an exciting thesis while at the same time allowing them to overcome any initial anxiety that there might be something wrong with it. To do the job and commit to action on a daily basis it seems to have been necessary to find ways *both* to be excited *and* to set aside anxiety – so avoiding emotional conflict. The finding is significant, bearing in mind that in traditional finance literature risks and rewards are treated as contradictory elements to be traded off. Through the stories outlined in Chapter 5 my respondents effectively claimed they could avoid that conflict. They could find ways to get exceptional rewards without too much risk.

Markets in emotional experience and emotional conflict

My interviews also revealed financial markets to be places where relationships are made and broken and emotional conflicts experienced and managed through time on a daily basis.

As just mentioned, the asset managers I spoke to processed a great deal of information, checked and double-checked the basis for their stories, and undertook extensive calculations to back them up. In meetings they put forward their theses and then defended them against the counterarguments made against them by colleagues. Finally, they bought the stocks. At this point the relationship pictured in a hitherto imagined story began to be an experienced reality.

In discussing what they told me about their relationships to stocks I have suggested (in fact picking up how managers themselves actually did talk) that we can use courtship and marriage as an analogy to understand what is involved in buying and then holding financial assets. For my respondents, owning stocks was rather like having a long distance inherently uncertain and anxiety-provoking romantic attachment with someone who is the subject of gossip and speculation but who remains a long way away and cannot be touched or talked to directly – only reached through successive intermediaries or a very bad telephone line.

Traditional economic and finance analysis focuses, at least implicitly, on initial decision-making. But my findings suggest that the fact positions have to be held through time makes all the difference. It creates a relationship. But unlike in a marriage the investor does not live with the stock. It is, so to speak, only news of stocks and possible implications of reports about their doings that reaches the investor, not their actuality. The news comes 'imperfectly' by all kinds of indirect inferential routes, including by observing the thinking and behaviour of 'rivals' around them and then imagining their motives. The consequence is obvious and in the interviews was striking: the holders of financial assets are taking part in what as a psychoanalyst I characterise as an uncertain and dependent object relationship. They are reliant on that relationship and affected by imagined gains or losses day by day, month by month, and year by year. In consequence they tend both to love and hate it for its potential to satisfy or frustrate.

In the interviews my respondents described how they had first to anticipate what it would be like if they bought stock and then afterwards had to experience owning it as time passed and news arrived. It was striking that when they bought stock they did so because they believed they were at an informational advantage. But as they held it and time passed (and particularly if things did not happen as expected very quickly) they feared very much that they had come to be at a disadvantage. Uncertainty created a very challenging experience. The data presented in Chapter 6 illustrate that to understand financial markets we not only need to envisage them as markets in stories but also markets in managing emotional experience and emotional conflict.

In fact, my respondents told me 23 stories about their experience of holding assets while the price was falling. The fall always created suspicion and anxiety that their investment theses might be going wrong. It was a time of particular anxiety because, although respondents were contradictory on the point, most believed that asset prices are ultimately set somewhat efficiently in the market, so that if the market did not behave as they hoped they could quickly lose confidence in what they had (at the buying stage) appeared to know; they became anxious about what others might know that they did not know, and began to distrust their judgement or those of others.

Falling prices create an experience of uncertainty and then discomfort. This feeling is not easily managed by cognition and calculation. Doubts often came to focus around a loss of the previously confident belief in enterprise management or other aspects of the safety component of 'buy' scripts mentioned above. I have reported how in their interviews respondents were particularly likely to become sceptical and critical of such managements – even showing signs of hate. In this situation the exciting element of the buy script could not survive and some then sold. They then might discover that things went well and their original thesis had been correct.

One interesting group of respondents I have described, mostly investing in financial services, tended to dismiss bad news more easily than others, hanging on to their confidence. In each case they were able to draw on features of their personality and their investment case. These specialists had ridden the wave of rising stock prices in the financial sector so that when it came to 2008 their confidence was shown to have been seriously misplaced. The finding shows how dealing with short-term doubts by having the confidence to ride them out is no more effective a solution than dealing with them by quickly panicking.

Overall, the main finding is that those investing in financial assets necessarily face an emotional predicament. The job creates ongoing and unavoidable emotional conflict. It is pretty much defined by it. It seems possible that the twin elements of the 'buy' scripts I mentioned earlier were based on learning this aspect of experience. Telling their stories, my respondents had found a way both to be excited about prospects and secure about doubts. In this way they could manage the conflicts they anticipated sufficiently to create that 'spontaneous urge to action' that Keynes (1936) described as a necessary ingredient for making long-term investments. They had anticipated that once they purchased the assets they would then have to hold on to them in an ongoing emotional relationship, experiencing uncertainty while at a potential information disadvantage and taking part in a dependent *ambivalent* object relationship in which the potential hope of gain alternates with anxiety about loss.

Conflicting feelings are a fact of ambivalent relationships. Insofar as relationships to stocks are characterised by this relationship, the crucial question for the functioning of any market is whether thinking about it takes place in what I have called a *divided* or *integrated* state. In an integrated state of mind agents can retain awareness of hope and doubt and try to reflect on both. In a divided state they cut off awareness of one or the other.

I have introduced above how following Bion (1962) we can characterise a dependent relationship to a partner in love or work (and so a relationship to a financial asset) as potentially dominated by *both* love (L) and hate (H). Dependency, because it creates potential anxiety and uncertainty as well as the prospect of fulfilment, can be hated. This formulation focuses attention on whether one or both of these relationships are 'known'. One possibility is a state of mind characterised by curiosity and so awareness (K), and the other is state of mind characterised by a desire not to be aware of or troubled by feelings of doubt, suspicion, and fears that things might go wrong (–K).

A state governed by thinking in K is an *integrated* one. In this state any frustration or anxiety are tolerated and investigated so that underlying causes can be 'worked through'. There is motivation and even pleasure gained from investigation, and optimism and pessimism can be explored equally.

A *divided* state of mind is governed by –K. In it any thoughts which create bad feelings are literally hated, and so because they create mental pain somehow turned away from consciousness. Stories about leaders holed up in bunkers and ordering servants to 'shoot the messenger' capture this state. So does what is popularly known as being 'in denial' – it is how nearly everyone deals with bad news at least for a short while.

At the moment my respondents bought stocks they had created a mental picture or phantasy as to how things would be – essentially of reward without much risk. This judgement could be reached in an *integrated* state (that is after enthusiastic enquiry into reasons for and against) or in a *divided* state (unconsciously attending mainly to only the 'upside'). My impression was that respondents tried quite hard to think both about risk and reward but that the underlying institutional context required them to behave as though they could be exceptional, which made that difficult. To act at all they had to be excited by a story. To get excited they had to remove dampening anxiety. The test of the state in which they made the decision would happen later, as reality unfolded and good and bad news came in. How did they react to opportunities to love or hate the stocks they had bought later? The evidence is suggestive.

I described in Chapter 6 how, when they had to experience and then explain adverse price fluctuations for the stocks they held, the attitudes my respondents had towards the assets they owned could often quickly shift from love (idealisation) to hate (denigration, suspicion, and criticism). This was particularly true of their attitudes to enterprise managements. They seemed to be the target for the outlet of a great deal of feeling. Idealisation is a primitive mechanism present in *divided* states which helps to ameliorate distrust when we are dependent and don't want to be troubled by anxiety (–K). We might contrast it with evaluation made in an *integrated* state characterised by real enquiry (K) leading to actual *trust*. In a divided state uncertainty easily revives distrust; human subjects can become uneasy, frustrated, jumpy, and negative without really knowing why. Furthermore, I have described the general suspiciousness my interviewees had about company managements. The fact that idealisation oscillated with suspicion also suggests a divided state – first love then hate. It also happens between lovers, patients and doctors, or, indeed, investment clients with their fund managers – particularly if the underlying situation and its consequences are not well understood.

The point is that my respondents had to buy and hold stocks in a situation of quality uncertainty and information asymmetry, made particularly powerful by the fact they were often making claims to have seen things that others had not. It is not surprising that this created a conflicting emotional experience. While it could be faced within an *integrated* state of mind, it is easy to see how it might be quickly and 'dirtily' dealt with in the short run by denial and a *divided* state of mind – in which case we would say that the dependent ambivalent relationship necessarily formed with assets is governed by –K rather than K. In –K decision-making anxiety about uncertainty is set aside. There is no longer an emotional incentive to desist from risky decisions. It creates the possibility that the attitudes and behaviour of many asset managers (particularly in a rising market and when there is pressure on them to perform exceptionally) will be excessively risky and that those who are successful will be rewarded so that it is people in a divided state who dominate the market. Those who make decisions in a divided state, if their gamble comes off, will perform better both than those who gamble and lose and those who are cautious. Market prices are only influenced by those who trade. The process may disproportionately select excessive risk-takers and predispose markets to gambling, based on –K thinking, rather than balancing risk and reward, based on K.

Markets in managing emotional inflation in groups

My interviews also made clear that financial decision-making takes place in social or institutional settings dominated by group processes in which the thinking that underlies financial agents' behaviour is very easily dominated by their subjective experiences and expectations and feelings about each other. These group processes reflect both the inherently uncertain situation they are in and the pressure put on social structures by financial assets – because they stimulate emotional conflicts for those asking asset managers to manage their assets. There is a chain of emotional conflict and emotional dependency.

One way I began to look at this social-emotional situation was by asking how respondents rationalised outcomes to me and presumably to themselves. I listened altogether to 165 stories in which they told me how they had bought stock because they were attracted by the qualities of excitement and security I have mentioned. In the previous chapter I then described how 62 of these stories did not work out. As far as I could see when things did not work out it was not because there was anything particularly different about the way my respondents had selected these stocks, nor did it have much to do with the companies in which they chose to invest. The 'buy' stories all had the the same qualities. It was just that in 62 instances the stories just didn't work out. Further analysis showed this was true whether the stories about their satisfaction or dissatisfaction hinged around decisions *to* buy stock or *not* to do so.

Cautious managers told stories about satisfactorily identifying companies, citing various aspects of the secure features of stories. But then they would also talk about missing out on other opportunities because they could not feel confident enough to commit to action. Respondents who identified exciting situations and were successful in one instance also found that for one reason or another they were not in another. Respondents who identified enterprise managers with interesting and unusual business models they thought they would execute had success in some instances but also discovered in other cases either that those managers could not deliver or that the story was mistaken.

In the previous chapter I described five classes of reason respondents gave to try to explain what had led to their unsatisfying decisions. Although some blamed developments outside their control, very interestingly more than half of them suggested it was their own fault. I argued that in fact nearly all the reasons given were mainly designed to help them cope with the emotions of failure. Managers did not seem to approach failure in an *integrated* state of mind using their capacity for enquiry (K) to work through and learn from their mistakes. They did not mourn failure, so to speak, rather they sought to move on and fortify themselves for the next battle. This is what *divided* states enable human beings to do and it is understandable. In a battle for survival of the species it is probably very useful. On the other hand, after the battle, unless steps are taken to ensure reflection, learning cannot take place.

By and large the explanations my respondents gave for failures were not ones it would be easy to translate into successful decisions next time. They were things they had not imagined at the time of the decision because one cannot think of everything. Given lack of omniscience, either one decides never to invest in anything ever again (the decision Isaac Newton is supposed to have made after losing in the South Sea Bubble) or one proceeds as before. In fact I could think of virtually no explanation my respondents gave me that they would actually have found a useful guide to future action. For this reason I came to the conclusion that their explanations for failures, like their mission strategies, were flexible covering stories, designed to preserve what psychologists call an 'illusion of control'. Explanations of this kind helped respondents to maintain the *divided* state they tended to need in order to act. They protected them from feeling the job was impossible.

To learn from mistakes you must first acknowledge you have made them. But this is no simple process. One approach used by social psychologists to describe the issues draws on the idea of what is called 'cognitive dissonance' (Festinger 1957). It was a rather radical theory at the time it was invented because it challenged the then prevailing notion in psychology that human learning could only usefully be understood in terms of offers of rewards and punishments, that is, through behaviourism (Tavis and Anderson 2007). The psychoanalytic account starts from a similar point, namely the observation that exposure to conflicting ideas in which the subject is invested creates painful feelings which cause them to be avoided. But it goes beyond the idea that the problem is just a logical cognitive conflict. It locates learning and its disturbances inside a developmental theory of thinking in which the act of learning is always emotional as well as cognitive. Learning requires the mind to engage with accurate or 'truthful' feedback and this may create feelings that are not easily tolerated. Learning from experience, therefore, occurs through a process analogous to that Freud (1914) called 'working through' which was subsequently elaborated by Melanie Klein (1940) to describe the process of mourning and grieving. Because the individual must sometimes face painful feelings associated with painful truths, such learning requires considerable effort. But – given the advantages learning can confer – it is also potentially rewarding.

Working through is necessary because many truths about life are not easily or quickly accepted in one go. But they can gradually become bearable if they are taken on bits at a time. It takes time because old ideas associated with infantile omnipotence must be given up. This can be resented or resisted, especially if it makes the individual feel weak and frightened. Mourning and learning require a willingness to be curious to find out new things and to tolerate the emotional consequences of doing so – particularly when enquiring into the source of loss and the presumed causes. In this way, insofar as what has gone wrong with actions is investigated and recognised as the product of some personal decision, then feelings of personal responsibility, bringing on a sense of guilty remorse, are involved. But because remorse is immediately painful and managed by defences such as idealisation which make it difficult to give up a phantastic object and accept that the underlying entity is ordinary, this type of depressive acceptance of loss and guilt is often resisted.

Based on this way of thinking, psychoanalysts make rather well validated distinctions between loss or grief reactions of denial, blame, and guilt (Murray Parkes 1996). My respondents mainly used the first two. In denial a problem is made unconscious so it does not exist and nothing can be learned at all. The kind of flexibility in explanation just mentioned, where the reason to claim responsibility seemed not to result from any real investigation, but rather from a wish to repair a feeling of damaged omnipotence and so to enhance a sense of control, would be an example of denial. An explanation based on blame places responsibility elsewhere (someone else needs to change), with the consequence that a system of belief can be left intact. This solution is also emotionally cheap in the short term and useful if the cause of the problem really is elsewhere, but is potentially nonadaptive in the long term. It is the kind of solution offered if losses in an asset price bubble are blamed on criminals and scapegoats. In the 2008 crisis the Chinese (for failing to revalue their currency) or regulators (who failed to prevent the bubble) or dishonest mortgage salesmen might all fit the bill. In the accounts of some of my respondents it seemed to be the failure of enterprise management or third parties who were indicted, rather than the respondents' own misjudgement.

The third alternative is 'depressive' guilt, which opens the way to remorse, learning, and repair. Depressive guilt is felt consciously in an integrated state of mind leading to a feeling of responsibility and concern. It is an alternative to paranoid guilt, which is unconscious guilt in a divided state in which the feeling of conscious guilt is replaced by the feeling of being consciously and unfairly persecuted. Precisely because it is painful and causes real doubt about what one has been doing, 'depressive' guilt is difficult to feel while at the same time maintaining action. It makes one pause for thought. Consequently, it is usually tolerated only gradually and with difficulty, but if it does continue to be 'felt' it can be 'worked through' in the same way as we gradually come to terms with loss during bereavement. Taking responsibility in this way makes it possible to think about what went wrong and learn from it before new thinking leads to wider investigation, and consequential changes are proposed. Feeling guilt in this way is more emotionally costly in the short term and would be likely to disrupt the smooth functioning of an organisation. But it may lead to potential adaptation in the future.

The three approaches to managing loss I have mentioned are each likely to have survival value depending on context. Blame and denial (maintaining *divided* states of mind) can work if the systems concerned are fundamentally sound and do not require accurate feedback. Depressive guilt (and an integrated state) will be much more productive than either if the problem is caused by behaviour which requires learning. But, as I have underlined, learning from experience requires the willingness to experience the disruption and unpleasantness of feeling at least some guilt as well as some loss of omnipotence. Change requires real or felt understanding of what has gone wrong in which people believe.

The point is that the institutional arrangements within which my respondents functioned did not appear to facilitate the kind of integrated-state learning and working through that I have just mentioned. The way their roles were institutionally constructed in fact reflected the dominance of institutionally supported *divided* states, based on the belief it is possible to outperform the market repeatedly and be exceptional without taking extra risk, from which it was very difficult for any financial agents to emerge.

As I indicated earlier in this chapter, what my respondents had to do was to exchange assets valued by stories. We can see that these stories were more or less dreams which have the power to evoke and inflate the experience of the most major human emotional conflicts: desire, greed, love, hate, envy, and jealousy, on the one hand, and panic, fear, anxiety, revulsion, shame, and guilt, on the other. Both sets of feelings are powerful motivators or inhibitors at the heart of our subjective experience of life – which is why they are the stuff of drama, novels, and art generally. Financial institutions have grown up under the pressures these experiences create and in this way have created the structure of the roles my respondents had to inhabit.

The various features of the roles my respondents were given have emerged throughout earlier chapters. They work for the institutions which have come progressively to dominate capital markets – the giant funds which compete with each other to gather assets to manage in return for fees. These institutions market their various ways to achieve exciting growth and security by a combination of advertising their own or their managers' star abilities. The essence of the situation is that teams or managers are presented as individual contrarians successfully raised above the crowd, stellar groups or individuals with brilliant strategies and special abilities to search out exceptionally beneficial stories (dreams) and so to outperform their rivals in whatever quantities of exciting growth or safety fit the mood of the time. Companies making appeals along these lines have won the business, and in winning the business they have raised further funds for more advertising and promotion along the same lines. Companies also horse-trade successful managers and financial analysts – being willing to pay huge transfer fees and high salaries for those with appropriate high-performing reputations (Godechot 2008).

What it felt like to inhabit roles defined institutionally in this way came through in the descriptions provided in Chapters 4 and 7. My respondents felt under enormous pressure but were heavily rewarded so long as they could keep it up. Their role as dream-providers was at the intersection between the promises implicit in the system of marketing professional fund management and the realities of achieving consistent performance in a market governed by uncertainty and all the characteristics of financial assets mentioned. Contradictions abounded and the essence of this situation was conflict. Managers had to do things differently from other managers if they were to perform better. But by doing things differently they risked doing worse, which made them and their clients and employers anxious. To be able to increase the assets they gather and the fees earned if clients and their consultants saw that their managers performed well, institutions have responded by rewarding my respondents with high bonus payments. Although (as Leonard Frost articulated it in Chapter 4) there is considerable luck involved in good performance, everyone in fact behaved as though results are the product of the efforts made to achieve them. Success was rewarded. Failure penalised. Even respondents who had many years of success behind them considered it very likely that they would lose their jobs if they did not perform.

The inherent conflicts between doing things differently in order to get success and not doing things too differently in order to stay safe has led to a vast and growing preoccupation with control. My respondents had agency roles and as agents had to be directed to do what was required. A mixture of stick and carrot as well as direct rules about what could and could not be done were all applied. They were incentivised by bonuses, potentially penalised by the threat of the sack. They were directly controlled by rules about how far their portfolios could be different from those of their rivals and even how much they could trade. They also had to keep a raft of records to manage regulatory distrust.

Two significant developments have been taking place in the fund management industry which seem to me to reflect institutional ways to manage the inherent conflicts just mentioned. They play a significant part in structuring the role my respondents inhabited and in creating the group environment in which they work. These are the growth of formal efforts to compare manager performance and to control risk. They are associated with the development of specialist agencies and roles to conduct these activities and particularly the growth of 'external' consulting firms and 'independent' ratings agencies. They reflect, in part, academic thinking about agency problems and risk-shifting and the idea these can be controlled by clear contracting and transparent evaluation. The impact of these developments was discussed in Chapters 4 and 7. In my view they are an institutional response to the unavoidable emotional conflicts I have been discussing but they have the effect of making the underlying situation worse.

The main way manager performance is evaluated is by the development of a wide range of statistics, based on changes in values in the investments in their portfolios, purporting to rank them against each other and various benchmark indices and frameworks over time periods ranging from hourly or daily to longer periods of months or years. These measures can then be simplified into league tables so that managers or firms can be given summary ratings like 'top decile'. The common sense idea is that changes in value over one period reflect ability and skill. In fact the difficulties with drawing reliable cause-and-effect conclusions between investment decisions and investment results mean it is not really very clear what these 'measures' mean or what should really be concluded from them as a guide to the future. There are problems deciding how to apportion factors conceptually unconnected with 'skill' (such as a bull market or one or two lucky selections or bits of lucky timing) or in drawing up the time periods against which to make comparison. Success in one time period is no real predictor of success in another. In consequence, making changes based on past performance often leads to worse results than doing nothing.

But what was not uncertain was the effect of all this on managers. They had to anticipate negative client feedback if they made losses but also criticism and disaffection if they made smaller gains than those made by others. It is one thing to wish managers do well but another thing for them to achieve it. The injunctions they were under to find exceptional investments seem to have created the constant temptation to *divided*-state responses and short-term gambling. There were high rewards for exceptional performance but a limited downside for failure – loss of one's job being serious but not so bad with a large nest egg earned by past pay. They had to manage the strain of holding theses in situations of information asymmetry and quality uncertainty and to tolerate the pressure of having to demonstrate performance transparently each day, every day. It caused them to watch their screens anxiously, and in their view it made their job harder, creating increased jumpiness and increased preference for short-term approaches, making it difficult to hold to their theses and increasing *divided*-state thinking. The time-myopia identified in this way is in large part created by the anxiety my respondents faced because of the way clients and their consultants feel about any period of underperformance. In other words, the present institutional arrangements, which have been designed to manage incentive problems in principal-agent relationships, probably do not benefit clients; because they increase conflicts and anxiety they may actually have the reverse consequence.

Very similar conclusions can be drawn from the efforts to control the way managers take risk. This is done principally by introducing into investment mandates rules as to how far the composition of managers' portfolios can be different from those of their peers. Sometimes portfolios are assessed by introducing mathematically derived calculations believed to assess the 'value at risk' (VaR) at any one time. This procedure makes all kinds of ultimately doubtful assumptions about how asset values will alter for each different asset according to past fluctuations in given time periods (Rebonato 2007). Several managers, therefore, expressed serious doubt as to the real value of this approach. For instance, for Gordon Hamilton it was 'an incorrect part of our investment philosophy...because you're starting at the wrong end'. At the same time, he pointed out, the possibility of a manager or fund diverging a long way from the peer group was too worrying and too risky, so that he 'didn't know' of a 'large investment company that can really get their arms around that'.

One way of looking at risk controls of the tracking error and VaR is to view them as ways to create a story with which to manage the inherent conflicts and anxiety endemic for asset managers and their clients. They provide an appearance of offering protection against loss. But what they actually provide is an assurance against one asset manager doing much worse than everyone else, not protection from everyone making wrong decisions. From this perspective perhaps asset management companies and the consultants who advise clients are doing no more than responding to what their clients demand. Clients want high returns but are also risk-averse. I showed in Chapter 7 how my respondents feared being caught by client anger or anxiety if things were not going well for a period. Several respondents made clear they did not really believe clients had emotionally accepted the contracts they had signed – anticipating that they had understood whatever percentage tracking error offered as a potential growth figure, not a possible loss. When things were not going well my respondents tended to get nervous and feared the clients would lose confidence in them before their share prices could recover. They also reported anxiety that clients might penalise their efforts to be prudent, if this led to them missing out on fashionable situations others were joining in. One of the most remarkable moments for me in the study was when I realised that George Monroe (and then others) was still kicking himself for having 'missed Enron'.

The conclusion seems to be that institutional procedures, like specifying 'tracking error' and performance tables, are not the effective means for ensuring agent compliance envisaged in the theorems of information economics and agency theory. Rather they are social-psychological devices to manage fundamental anxieties inherent in financial markets. My impression is that this is true of many other metrics in recent years and perhaps of all short-term financial statistics – the growing avalanche of hourly, daily, weekly, and quarterly 'information' about company and asset manager performance and the many predictions and interpretations of data from experts. Similarly, the development of rating agencies (supposedly able to assess the likelihood of a large company or sovereign state defaulting so that investors themselves don't have to bother) or various statistical buzz words, Greek letters and acronyms, all of which might have a place in a balanced attempt to think about risk and reward, mainly function as fast and frugal signals to manage anxiety. They can be used to avoid real thought, in which case they may be best viewed as further signs of a market in a divided state, managing anxiety by *groupfeel*.

The theory of competitive markets is premised on heterogeneity. Creative and innovative products are dreamt up by individuals and succeed or fail according to the response of those to whom they are offered. Insofar as markets become homogenised competition can't work and outcomes are no longer optimal. Because financial assets have the qualities I have been emphasising, and so create emotional conflicts and potentially divided states of mind, they facilitate the development of *groupfeel* – the shared tendency to abandon individual decision-making and thinking and to exchange it for the warm feeling of belonging. It is powerfully at work in markets. As Keynes (1936) put it, it is often better to fail conventionally.

We might view the present organisation of financial markets as a response to the wish to fulfil dreams – a highly seductive offer – in a situation where it can only happen to a few and probably by luck, as in a lottery. Most dreams will fail. But modern financial institutions have evolved in such a way that to survive they must offer dreams while managing failure. From this viewpoint they are in effect captured by a divided state – as illustrated by the institutional requirement placed on them that my respondents be different, but not too different. Intense competition for management fees has led to the development of a strange and relative reality. Performance tables offer excitement while benchmarks and tracking error aim to assuage anxiety. But all three tie managers into a relative world, where many are constantly looking over their shoulders. To adapt what one of my respondents pointed out, this can drive portfolios up a mountain or over a cliff together. It is a context conducive to *groupfeel*. This was evident when some of my respondents spontaneously referred to the possibility that the subprime crisis, then in its infancy, might cause a catastrophic fall in share price values. I asked them what they could do. Most shrugged their shoulders. They then dismissed such 'the end of the world' scenarios as not really worth worrying about – because then we would 'all be out of a job' anyway. Recall how in the previous chapter Leonard Frost discussed the risk that the credit situation would deteriorate so badly that *Housebank* would not be able to fund its mortgages. He told me that if that was to happen then 'nobody would be able to lend any money to mortgages' and in that case (he too said) 'we might all be out of work anyway, so would it matter?' This relative attitude to the future suggests a *divided* state approach to reality created by current institutional pressure. It illustrates the state of 'conventional thinking' I found among financial agents, which is a clear psychological basis for what is called systemic risk.

In summary, the markets I heard about were ones in which stories were exchanged within structured social groups organised by conventional institutional processes, reflecting both the pressure on social structures deriving from the emotions financial assets unleash and the way those structures have become organised, which inflames and intensifies emotional inflation further. The nature of the inherent conflicts that follow from the uncertain nature of financial assets has led to a social evolution of market institutions and practices which have created a situation where participants and therefore markets as a whole are waiting to be captured by group processes and so constantly likely to be threatened by instability. I have described how my respondents looked out for exceptional stories and then 'bet' on the opportunities they implied, believing them to exist. Some worked and some didn't, but as far as I could see the only difference between the two was that sometimes they got lucky and sometimes they didn't.

From normal markets to wild markets

In the first chapter I made the point that models necessarily simplify down to essentials and then generalise. I contrasted standard economic theories with emotional finance. The former ignores uncertainty and simplifies by leaving out memory, experienced time, experienced excitement and anxiety, and experienced group life. The latter starts from uncertainty and so the idea that at least in the case of financial markets such omissions create a theory which misses the essentials of reality.

Intuitively and based on my experience when I began I thought that it was unlikely that a theory about decisions to buy, hold, or sell financial assets could successfully disregard an economic agent's experience of the past, present, and future and that it would be foolish to regard as epiphenomenal the fact human agents have a subjective experience of time, imaginative dreams about the future, and, above all, memories. The interviews set out to talk to financial agents so as to be able to describe the decision context they faced.

The three conclusions just reached about decision-making in financial markets suggest the emotional finance view of the conditions constraining decision-making in financial markets has substance. I have shown how financial assets have particular characteristics so that the market in them is best portrayed as a market trading phantasies and dreams. It is also a market managing thinking in what looks like *divided states* of mind and subject to social-psychological processes embedded in institutions creating roles potentially dominated by *groupfeel*. The conclusions suggest that such elements are fundamental to decisions taken in markets and imply that any theory that omits them has left out fundamental matters. It is hard to see how a theory that does that could succeed in understanding the causes of financial instability.

The three conclusions offer some guidance as to how the mispricing of risk that it is generally agreed was at the heart of the events leading up to the 2008 crisis came about. In Chapter 1 I mentioned how the common explanations offered seemed to me logically flawed. While cheap credit can rather easily be imagined as a facilitating cause for an asset price bubble it does not explain why people should turn a blind eye to the prudential assessment of default risk and so liquidity risk – and some institutions were in fact more careful than others.

The returns financial institutions were making prior to 2008 were extraordinary by historical standards and so should surely have prompted sceptical investigation and explanation in the light of history – such as the history of past financial crises and the Japanese property bubble. Unless default risk had ceased or been transferred away, how could human actors running financial institutions or investing in them, and with the capacity for memory and the potential for curiosity and enquiry, suddenly consider it safe to be lending way beyond their means to others way beyond theirs? One answer is that such human actors had suddenly ceased to be possessed of historical knowledge, common sense, and the power of thought. Another, growing in popularity, is that the processes were perpetrated by 'clever' and corrupt people who, due to their incentive system, had been able to transfer the default risk elsewhere (see particularly Stiglitz 2010; Johnson and Kwak 2010). But for that to be plausible as an explanation of what happened, many other financial actors, such as my respondents and all those others to whom the risk got transferred, would also have had to be without knowledge of history, memory, or curiosity or perhaps to have been in the conspiracy too – not to mention that all the same features would also need to apply to regulators and just about everyone else. Spelt out in that way this kind of explanation (although common in the aftermath of asset price bubbles) is insufficient.

In Chapter 1 I emphasised that what has to be explained about the 2008 crisis is not just a housing bubble. The real issue is that those running banks and investing in them or relating to them failed to investigate the risks of what was going on despite warnings, such as Buffet's famous one about 'weapons of mass destruction'. The deepest problems were caused by the excited trading of elaborate synthetic derivative instruments and financial engineering such as off-balance-sheet vehicles which appeared to allow very low margin requirements – permitting very high leverage. It is also relevant that synthetic versions of these products were created and traded in ever-increasing numbers *after* the credit crunch had already begun in March 2007 at a time when investment banks could not find enough real mortgages to meet the demand from buyers for more directly asset-backed securities (Lewis 2010; Cassidy 2009). At the time sales of these *phantastic objects* appeared to inflate bank profitability and few thought they were building up huge 'hidden' risk.

The theory of *phantastic objects* I put forward in Chapter 1 explains asset price bubbles by focusing on changes in the financial market's sense of reality. Markets get caught up in the intoxicating pursuit of *phantastic objects* when an exciting cover story, good enough to support the belief that 'this time' something quite different is changing the world, takes hold of them. After an initial phase in which this idea spreads sufficiently to generate its own momentum, prices or profits are pushed up. Twin factors then propel matters further. On the one hand is the genuine excitement propelling the wish to join in. On the other is the reinforcement motivating actors to go on because, once the upward movement in profits or prices has started, abstinence is felt as painful frustration. These factors begin to interfere with the capacity to say no and provoke thinking in a *divided state*. In this state critical news and critics receive no conscious attention and unconscious forces allow triumphant dismissal, gradually leading to the effective formation of a virtual 'believers' group achieving solidarity and support in *groupfeel*. Those who are not 'true believers' are now likely to be tempted to join in. They watch their profits or performance lagging. Few can stand out and watch others doing well and very few have the courage to resist the trend by short-selling. The music can't be stopped.

The findings I have reported make it reasonably easy to see how normal markets provide fertile conditions for just such a process. The concepts of the *phantastic object, divided* states of mind, and *groupfeel* have already been useful to describe less extreme versions of these events happening every day in normal markets because they are markets essentially trading stories (phantasies and dreams), managing emotions in *divided states* of mind, and subject to social-psychological processes embedded in institutions which have created roles potentially dominated by *groupfeel*. From this context it is possible to see how 'this time is different' assumptions can quite easily grow up and gain support. The idea 'this one' is different, 'I' am different, and 'we' are different is there all the time. It is what investors are looking for, whether in response to news which provoked anxiety and threatened relative performance or in response to some potential *phantastic object*. My respondents were all looking for exceptional or phantastic storylines where they could feel rewards could be had for lower than usual risks. They were all frequently uneasy about missing out and so vulnerable to *groupfeel* and unlikely to resist joining in any asset inflation process. They knew that if they did not join they could face underperformance and the loss of funds or even their jobs. The institutional structures intensify these tendencies.

Questions of validity

The reality described through my small interview study paints a picture of uncertainty, narrative, emotion, and group influence in financial markets in which the economic man of standard theory would be hard to place. Consequently standard theory has little place as a useful tool to explain what happens in financial markets. The obvious response to this picture of reality might be to argue it is invalid. Broadly speaking this might be so for two reasons: I could have been talking to the wrong people so that my results cannot be generalised to the working of a financial market (external validity), or I could have talked to them in the wrong way so that my questioning or my methods of analysis and reporting have 'created' the results (internal validity). There is a long tradition in economics that makes the point that what economic agents might say they are doing (for example, maximising revenue) does not matter, because, in fact, they are always constrained by competitive pressures to do it by maximising profits even if they don't know. Such an argument is an instance of the general proposition that people are not always in a position to explain what they do and how they do it correctly, so interviews are worthless.

The external validity of an interview or observational study in the social sciences depends on sampling. The obvious solution analogous to that used in laboratory experiments is to select respondents at random and to repeat the research on several samples. I did not do this both for practical and logical reasons. For one thing this was an exploratory study and I had started out wanting to research a variety of managers working in apparently different contexts. But also, to draw a random sample, you first have to define the universe from which to do so. It was and is far from clear how to do that in this instance in an economical way. Would it be all investors, all professional investors, registered fund managers with certain authorities, all investing funds of a certain type or size, and so on? If so, how would they be contacted and would data as to their whereabouts so they could be reached be reliable? Would it be all fund managers managing assets above certain levels? Should the institutions or types of investments be restricted? And when people were selected would they or their institutions agree? There was no obvious answer. It is an example (also noted by Bewley 1999) of the trade-off in fieldwork between the desirability for external validity of a random sample and desirability for internal validity of good response rates.

For practical reasons this had to be a rather small sample. In the end I decided to use a form of snowball sampling institutions through a variety of personal contacts and then asking them to make some of their managers available. Those selected needed to have different styles, to have worked in the business ('survived') for more than ten years, and personally controlled and made decisions about at least $1 billion of client investments.[2] The outcome was that those I spoke to together controlled very large sums of money – over $500 billion dollars of investments held in stocks or bonds in most of the world's economies and a very wide range of industries. The answer to the question of external validity is, therefore, pragmatic. They did account for a significant proportion of global investment, worked for major houses, and worked in several major centres. Their responses relevant to the conclusions I have reached about the nature of their work were quite uniform. There is, therefore, no obvious reason to suppose findings are not generalisable. Moreover the world described in my findings seems very much the world we know from the small number of other interview or observational studies examining related aspects of financial markets. Smith, for example, held a series of informal conversations with a handful of stockbrokers in New York City and described how the situation they encountered when trying to give advice or make their own investments was full of ambiguous, uncertain, and sometimes anxiety-provoking explanations from among which it was very hard to chose one in which to be confident (Smith 1999).[3] All that said, the only real way to establish if these findings can be generalised is to repeat the work.

But what about internal validity? Could the results I have presented have been 'created' by the interview methods I used? There are weaknesses to the study because it was an exploratory effort. They could be tested and remedied in further work so that if results are repeated they would produce more confidence. The weaknesses include the fact that although I had several collaborators to help analyse the data and so make some tests to see if more than one pair of eyes 'saw' the same things, it was mainly the work of a single investigator and not a team trained to draw reliably agreed conclusions. I did also modify the interview schedule as I developed my understanding and sometimes for practical time reasons was not able to ask every respondent the same questions.

The main question, however, is whether the interview method was a valid one for drawing the conclusions I have done so far – conclusions about the decision-context of financial decision-making just set out. The main reason for confidence in this regard is that I have used a very rigorous method for analysing qualitative data – namely presentation, as stated in the text above, of randomly selected examples. All the main inferences I make are supported by randomly (rather than conveniently) selected quotations from what I was told. Because to do this as extensively as I originally planned led to a text drowning in quotations I am making available online many further details.[4]

Although interviews are no more a panacea than other methods of research, in this case I consider they are the method of choice (perhaps supported by direct observation) for describing the decision-context. I was not using interviews to ferret out deep meanings in my respondents' answers nor to discover some deep secrets about why particular decisions were 'really' made. The fact that the context described was so uniformly described makes it hard to suppose it is a mirage.

Keynes was rather succinct about financial markets focusing his explanations on uncertainty, 'animal spirits', and 'the psychology of a society of individuals each of whom is endeavouring to copy the other', which are just the kind of unconscious emotional forces I have been describing as ever-present in the context of financial decision-making. 'The forces of disillusion', he wrote, 'may suddenly impose a new conventional basis of valuation.... At all times the vague panic fears and equally vague and unreasoned hopes are not really lulled, and lie but a little way below the surface' (Keynes 1937). The conclusions so far appear to provide unequivocal evidence of the fact that because the future is inherently uncertain real financial markets are strongly influenced by subjective belief and emotion. They have, after all, regularly been described with words like trust, confidence, exuberance, and panic.

To concede that subjective beliefs and emotions matter a great deal tends to make academic social scientists both anxious and sceptical. The scientific revolution of several centuries has focused on removing subjective 'bias' and this was greatly accelerated in the last half of the twentieth century. By modifying Keynes's theories to remove from relevance his distinction between risk and uncertainty, from my perspective, economists took a step backwards. They gained a great deal of mathematical tractability but lost sight of the significance of the character of financial assets I have been elaborating.

Anxiety about what happens to an academic discipline if it permits the entry of emotion and subjectivity was and is understandable. At the same time leaving out the obvious is unwise. The characteristics of financial assets mean financial decisions take place in uncertainty and so must inevitably involve emotion and belief and, given the terrible consequences that we have been experiencing, simply to turn a blind eye to the issues because they are inconvenient and threaten loved models is to adopt exactly the 'ostrichlike' ideological and anti-scientific attitude that faced Copernicus, Galileo, and Darwin.

In the remainder of this chapter, therefore, I want to return to the discussion I began about the ideological role economics has been playing mentioned at its beginning and then discuss how it might be possible to start to include emotional and subjective belief in economic thinking without losing rigour altogether.

A New kind of economics

In Chapter 3 I mentioned some of the ideas sociologists and social anthropologists have developed about the way cultural and structural forces cause theories to extract some elements from the world and not others and so create a view of truth. I mentioned that from this perspective even science is a story. That comment was meant both to place scientific methodology in a wider context and to stress that narrative is fundamental to human life. Insofar as it is agreed that it may be necessary for better theories of financial markets to be evolved, it is agreed this may require investigating 'soft' phenomena and using new methods.

Kahneman commented in his Nobel lecture about the importance of unconscious affects, and how for a long time in the second half of the twentieth century psychology seems to have found it difficult to 'hear' how intuition and feelings influenced memory and decision-making (Kahneman 2003). He does not mention exactly how and why this prejudice came about but what seems likely to have changed (as when new glass-manufacturing techniques for telescopes permitted new observations) is not the underlying phenomena, which has surely been there all the time, but both the motivation and means to become aware of it. This has involved the new methods of recognition like fMRI scanning mentioned in Chapter 3 but also a change in the willingness to accept new ideas about how these observations can be included in the 'story'. The history of science in fact can be seen as the history of changing and replacing 'stories' as notions about how to know what is true change.

Academic economics has been developed in an ideological and social context where its role was to support the argument for free markets. Clearly many academic economists and the institutions in which they work have also been fascinated by the imaginative and brilliant mathematical attempts to develop closed system, deductive models. But this has been possible only because within the culture the data of reality was ignored. Variations in confidence, trust, and sentiment in financial markets, or the obvious fact that many markets were neither fair nor efficient, did not receive attention because somehow they were outside the framework. As in any other area of life the conventional 'theoretical approach' (Dow 2010; Lawson 2010) was supported by institutional frameworks and peer review publication and grant-awarding policies.

But, as Kahneman suggested, scientific stories change and by no means only for clear reasons such as evidence that a theory is wrong. While scientific communities aspire to be less likely to be influenced by psychological bias and conflicts or the desire to 'not see' they are working in human groups and it is not easy. One way we could think about the issues is to view all formal knowledge as constructed (in groups) in an ongoing conflict between what Freud called the 'pleasure' and 'reality' principles. That conflict may be part of the neurobiological architecture of being alive – a struggle between seeing the world as a wish-fulfilling hallucination and seeing the world as how 'it is' (Freud 1911; Bion 1991). Seeing the world as it is can create more anxiety and frustration than having it how one wants so that the situation provides fertile ground for what I call divided state thinking. There is a constant tendency for human groups (discussed below) to become basic assumption groups in which the tendency to deny information from outside reality is used to mitigate threats to feeling comfortable. Such tendencies can be overcome, and often are, by successful scientific and other innovators. But that is achieved only with a struggle.

The point is that which stories are taken for truth in any human group may have as much to do with what they offer for resolving emotional conflicts as for their contribution to 'truthful' ways of viewing underlying issues. Some matters are always being taken for granted within a group and some imaginative explanations always being curtailed. Focusing on building up knowledge *solely* on *either* Bruner's narrative or logical modes of thought, for instance, may be equally restrictive.

What is very fascinating is that although many of the main developments in economic thinking in the last 30 years have focused on ways agency and information problems mean that markets will not be Pareto-efficient, the efficient market thesis was, nonetheless, essentially treated as fact and allowed to dominate both analysis and policy. The fact that 'all economists know' (Allen and Gale 2001) that the main findings of economic analysis did not support the view that outcomes would necessarily be optimal, received little attention. It was the ideal type, rather than understanding of the serious deviations from it, that was the dominant story and the one attended to by regulators (Turner 2010).

The economist, John Kay, has described how he spent a long time successfully selling decision-making models based on the most sophisticated economics to large companies but found they did not really use them. What they did was draw on them to justify their actions (Kay 2010b). Theories in such instances are rationalisations for actions taken. They are selected because they are psychologically and normatively attractive in the domain in which they are being used, just like the 'covering stories' in an asset price bubble which 'work' psychologically (justifying the phantastic object) and are normatively supported by *groupfeel*.

The story of the Efficient Markets Hypothesis being 'taken as fact' (when actually much of the work of modern economics has been to show that its assumptions don't hold so markets are unlikely to be efficient) is one example of the way a theory can become popular and powerful and then be used for purposes other than the intellectual pursuit of the truth. The way in which macroeconomics modified Keynes in the second half of the twentieth century seems to be another. After at first appearing to dominate the economic landscape after the last great economic catastrophe, his ideas were marginalised and overwritten. Indeed in the 1970s 'at research seminars, people don't take Keynesian theorising seriously anymore; the audience starts to whisper and giggle to one another,' declared Robert Lucas, then the world's most influential macroeconomist (Mankiw 1999; Krugman 2009).

Might the laughter and giggles reflect insight that at the time was pushed aside? Did it owe something to unconscious anxiety about becoming too clever and too rational at the expense of sense? Contempt is a clinical sign of internal discontent and threatened anxiety. The late twentieth century was particularly characterised by a rather male-dominated academia highly biased against emotions and subjective experience. In this context Keynes's 'animal spirits' (borrowed from the Latin word *anima* for the 'animating principle' and rather close to Freud's *Instinkt)* was perhaps a rather difficult or even embarrassing idea to which to give a central role in a discipline whose members hope they can unravel the laws of economy like the laws of physics.

Keynesian thinking is what is called an open rather than a closed (deductive) system. A closed system is one in which event regularities or correlations occur in a consistent manner as they might in a laboratory or in astronomy and can then be modelled with occasional external shocks. But Keynesian economic agents live in an open system. They are social. They do not exist in isolation from each other but 'constitute' each other through interaction (Lawson 2010) and reflexivity (Soros 2010). And they do not know or have any way of knowing for certain what will happen tomorrow.

To model economics using complex deductive mathematics required closure. So it was precisely the open aspects of Keynesian thinking – deriving from Keynesian views on uncertainty or institutional process – which were gradually removed from economics, first through the elegant neo-Keynesian reconstruction by Hicks (1937)[5] and then others in the postwar period and then finally and decisively in the rational expectations models from Lucas (1972) onwards. Macroeconomic models of the economy (like the risk models used in banks) in the last few years forgot about uncertainty and became models based on 'known unknowns' and institution-free agents. All this appeared to make the subject more rigorous and solved interesting intellectual questions about how markets *might* work and why social institutions such as trade or labour unions holding up wages might create unemployment. But they did not in fact show how markets worked or why wages were resistant to downward pressure, which had complex causes not necessarily involving unions at all (Bewley 1999). The Lucas theory was ideologically satisfying to some. It developed, of course, at a time when money inflation had become a major disease in advanced societies and there was a major political assault on the power of trade unions that needed justification.

The macroeconomic revolution just mentioned rested on the development of rational expectations modelling in microeconomics – based on the idea that households and companies make economic decisions as if they had available to them all the information about the world that might be available. But under rational expectations, insofar as it is not corrected by the insights of information economics, the starting assumption is that not only do firms and households already know as much as policymakers, but they also anticipate what the government itself will do, so the best thing government can do is to remain predictable. In this world in which institutions play no part it is a short step to the conclusion 'Most economic policy is futile' and governments should leave it to the market (Kay 2010a) – one of the ideologies that lead to the unwinding of all the regulations put in place after the Great Depression.

Attitudes to emotion, subjectivity, and intuition within the academy (and indeed to psychoanalysis which has the task of integrating all three) have partly been provoked by the absence until recently of the kind of cognitive neuroscience we can now use. But to date they also fit a defensive pattern. Lest this seem a far-fetched suggestion, consider the example even in astronomy of the changing attitudes to the heliocentric theory of the earth's movements. We now take it for granted but we also know that this is a fairly recent development. In fact the theory was first put forward by Aristarchus of Samos and attested to by Archimedes and Plutarch but then disappeared as an acceptable idea for over 2,000 years before Copernicus and Galileo. Thinking about this paradigmatic change Bion (1991) has wondered whether the geocentric view simply felt better. For a long time it may have corresponded to a solution to prevailing emotional challenges, allowing people of those dangerous times to shelter within protecting omnipotent and omniscient phantasies (as offered to a group by the leader or pair in the basic assumption group) which, perhaps, made them feel safer. Later, science was to become part of the equipment for feeling safe – although perhaps ambivalently so at the moment, which may help to explain the widespread opposition to evolutionary theory among those with fundamentalist religious beliefs. The general point is that the views a community holds on scientific questions and methods are linked to the anxieties and emotional challenges it faces, and there may be a psychological vested interest in maintaining an established cosmology or, for that matter, any scientific deductive system. This would account for very strong resistances to upsetting established systems and also, perhaps, helps to explain why some theories, like the efficient markets theory, which promote economic freedom (including freedom from feeling concerned about selfishness), or the kind of macroeconomics which promotes theorising without human actors, can be emotionally as well as ideologically attractive.

Some economists will no doubt dismiss emotional finance out of hand. But if we are to become more realistic, how can things change and in what way? The most likely direction many economists will want to take is in the direction of behavioural economics. As I have mentioned in Chapter 1, its proponents have gone to some lengths to modify standard utility functions by taking account of the possibility that economic agents can have different time, risk, and social preferences – for example, having 'inconsistent' priorities at different times in the life cycle ('nonstandard' preferences), can be 'overoptimistic' or 'overconfident' in their beliefs ('nonstandard beliefs'), or can make decisions in different ways, such as by using heuristics rather than optimisation or by being affected by 'transient' emotions ('nonstandard decision-making'). A toolbox of terminologies such as quasi-hyperbolic preferences, present-biased preferences, hyperbolic discounting, reference dependence, and projection bias, and so on, have been developed to explain findings in the field concerning many such behaviours departing from the standard norms (della Vigna 2009).

These efforts to respond to empirical findings demonstrate a willingness to try to include new variables within the normatively valued parsimonious models and have then been entered into the standard debate as to whether or not equilibrium results are influenced. However, this kind of approach, while recognising the probable importance of mood and emotion, cannot, I think, capture the essence of the situation described by my findings – because I am stressing the reality of inherent uncertainty but also because the emotional issues I have raised concerning making and breaking emotional attachments to stock, telling stories, and functioning within a social and institutional context dominated by *groupfeel,* are not just a matter of tweaking a few equations and cannot be included in thinking so easily.

The central implication of emotional finance is that, if the future is taken as inherently uncertain, conventional equilibrium modelling isn't a useful way to start and, especially as far as understanding instability, isn't helpful. Nonetheless, there may be possible ways to widen the framework of analysis to take account of my findings while still achieving a more general analytical framework. One potentially useful innovation in this area is agent-based modelling,[6] derived from attempts by physicists to predict the behaviour of very complex systems (for instance, Farmer and Foley 2009; Alfi, Cristelli et al. 2009; Pietronero 2010).

If we shift the focus from rational 'choice' to what can be called rational 'action' then because aspects of context are likely to have probabilistic causal relations to outcomes, we may be able to build models which show the impact of different choice contexts on the expected outcomes of economic decision-making. Rational action theory in sociology (Goldthorpe 2007) is an established approach that meets this requirement. It has rationality requirements of intermediate strength, allowing us to include significant elements of subjective experience and perception and then to model behaviour as consistent within the framework of more widely defined means-end relationships situated within different causal contexts. It shifts the analytic focus to that of considering 'the conditions under which actors come to act' systematically rather than idiosyncratically in a way that is 'rational from *their* point of view', even if deviating from the course of action that would follow if agents knew all possible outcomes in advance. It also implies the possibility of developing criteria by means of which actions which are open to understanding as subjectively rational can be distinguished from those that are not, and that analyses can be undertaken of the conditions under which such objectively nonrational action – when of a systematic kind – is most likely to occur. Progress depends on concentrating 'efforts on the situation of action' rather than on the idiosyncratic psychology of the acting individual (Goldthorpe 2007 p162).

As a practical manifesto, research based on understanding financial markets in terms of rational action would focus attention on the impact of the situation in which decisions are set – that is, on the characteristics of financial assets, their influence on the institutional settings in which they are exchanged, and the potential they have on the search for phantastic objects and for the development of group think (market sentiment). There is in this respect much overlap between rational action theory and the analytic approach Herbert Simon put forward with his notion of 'bounded rationality', especially as updated by Simon in his more recent reflections (Simon 1997).

Simon described the social sciences as suffering from 'acute schizophrenia' in their treatment of rationality because they are stuck between the economists' attribution to economic man of a 'preposterously omniscient rationality' with little discernible relation to the actual and possible behaviour of flesh and blood human beings, and the psychoanalysts' attempts to reduce all cognition to affect. 'To anyone who has observed organisations,' Simon wrote, 'it seems obvious enough that human behaviour in them is, if not wholly rational, at least in good part *intendedly* so' (Simon 1997 p88). His methodological insight was that in the real world human behaviour is intendedly rational, but 'only boundedly so'. The adjective is important; it points to the need to research the conditions in which different kinds of means-ends relationships are found.

Simon's psychological sophistication and immersion in real organisations and decision-making led him to emphasise what has been stressed through the research findings, namely that 'it is a common place of experience that an anticipated pleasure may be a very different sort of thing from a realised pleasure' (Simon 1997 p95). Actual experience may be considerably more or less desirable than anticipated. This is not only because consequences are not anticipated cognitively. Even when the 'consequences of a choice have been rather completely described, the anticipation of them can hardly act with the same force upon the emotions as the experiencing of them' (op. cit.).[7] In short, it makes perfectly good sense to think that in the real world human behaviour is intendedly rational but only in a bounded way. This was very much what I found. Respondents tried as hard as they could to be rational. Their stories were rationales.

The main 'trick' in economic modelling is to treat economic actions as 'revealed preferences' so that what it is rational to do with hindsight (*ex post*) is analytically indistinguishable from what seemed rational *ex ante*. Unlike in *rational choice* in a *rational action* model, as in 'bounded rationality', actions are taken 'rationally' without perfect knowledge. They are best efforts given the context at that moment in time. Such decisions do not necessarily look best later and do not necessarily succeed in achieving ends.

As a matter of fact Gennaioli (Gennaioli, Shleifer et al. 2010) have recently modelled just such a possibility to try to understand how excess risk-taking may have taken place and then lead to the recent crisis. They show how when (*ex ante*) financial intermediaries neglect (I might say 'feel') certain risks it is because they assume them 'unlikely'. They may then demand par-ticular securities with (what they think/feel are) 'safe' cash flows, to the extent their issuance of such securities (not felt as problematic by issuers who find it profitable) becomes excessive and financial markets become sys-temically fragile.

In a 'rational action' approach focusing attention on context, formal investi-gation can explore what people think as more and less risky in the risk-reward calculations they undertake. So in my study the dominant context for action in financial markets was provided by the characteristics of financial assets and the situation in which they were institutionally traded, with its tendency to facilitate *divided states* and developing narratives about the potential existence of *phantastic objects* shared in *groupfeel*. Such a context and the interactions it produces seem likely to predispose sections of the market to actions which would involve 'not seeing' and therefore mispricing risk. It is conceivable that we would start to identify features of contexts, including developments in groupfeel analysis and specific features of covering narratives supporting *phantastic objects,* which would be more likely to predict the take-off of asset price inflations. Measurement of context in such ways may predict the changes in sentiment which can produce the 'neglect' model (Gennaioli, Shleifer et al. 2010) which then generates actions which in a means-end sense make sense at every stage. It is only with hindsight, under the pressure of 'news' and the experience of anxiety and unease (when the ambivalent object relationship is reversed) that intermediaries come to suspect errors and irrationalities and then begin to want to off-load what has become perceived as risky. When they do, their actions create the very effect on price that they fear and the situation is compounded.

Although how to think further about these issues must be open to a lot more work, it seems to me that adopting a wider conception of economic agents and viewing them as economic actors rather than agents does not necessarily end our ability to make predictions and then to try to test them. The point is that, as Simon also said, when we speak of people behaving irrationally 'what we generally mean is that their goals are not our goals, or that they are act-ing on the basis of invalid or incomplete information, or they are ignoring future consequences of their actions, or that their emotions are clouding their judgments or focusing their attention on momentary objectives' (Simon 1997 p88).

Conclusion

This book set out to explore two questions: could an emotional finance hypothesis help to explain how normal markets turn into the kind of wild markets that led to the financial crisis of 2008 and in what ways could an emotional finance perspective add to a more general understanding of financial markets? It has led to the conclusion that financial markets trade stories in emotionally overwhelmed group situations and that, at present, due to the particular nature of financial assets and the ways institutions have developed to manage them, they cannot be understood or explained by theories that leave out the factors of memory, desire, and experience (animal spirits, if you will) and the ways these play out in individuals in human groups.

The psychoanalytic approach to understanding human thinking and decision-making I have introduced offers an attempt to make some sense of this type of experienced complexity, which is certainly not captured by the demonic models of mental functioning outside biological, psychological, and social context in standard economics. My respondents told stories, acted within a conflicting role situation, had to tolerate the experience of making decisions in uncertain and emotionally arousing environments, and were strongly influenced by what they imagined were the thoughts and likely actions of those around them. The core concepts of unconscious *psychic reality, phantastic objects, ambivalent object relationships, divided states,* and *groupfeel* have been offered to try to grasp these realities. The two main advantages of the psychoanalytic approach seem to me to be that it rather uniquely focuses on the relation between thinking and feeling and, by deploying the notion of the dynamic unconscious and so the notion of ambivalent mental states, can explain how it is that individuals can change their minds as situations change.

A theory of financial markets requires a focus on understanding action and the influence of ongoing experience on action. Action is the fast and frugal response of the human organism to the experience-stimulus of the environment it is in, along with the additional possibility of reflection when perceiving feedback from its actions and experience of them. I have been repeating that financial assets traded in financial markets create an ongoing and major emotional experience because outcomes are fundamentally uncertain. An experience- and action-based model has a different focus from those in which decision-making is conceived as a complex, essentially one-time-and-forever process of calculation based on the capacity infinitely to represent future possibilities and the means to achieve them. In addition to being more likely to generate meaningful research and thinking about the way financial markets work, an experience- and action-based theory of this kind, emotional finance, may have much potential to explain the changes in risk-reward assessment based on changes in confidence (trust) and sentiment that lie at the heart of the 2008 crisis but are not explained by standard approaches.

The theories we have about human activity are stories that matter. They influence activity, albeit in complex ways. This point underlies George Soros's attempt to interest economists in what he called 'reflexivity'(Soros 1987; 2008; 2010) and also the efforts of the sociologists Michael Callon and Donald Mackenzie to discuss economics as 'performative', as providing a legitimating script, so to speak, to inform social actors as to how they ought to behave in markets (see Mackenzie, Muniesa et al. 2007).

For all its fascination the story of efficient markets staffed by rational, self-serving, and isolated actors that has come to dominate economics departments for the last 50 years (with the policy implication that real markets should be made to work like those economists' model) does not work for financial markets. By focusing on individual agents without human memory, human experiences of time, excitement, and anxiety, and the experience of group life, standard theory has excluded the very core of what matters in these markets. It is then unhelpful and even grossly misleading to pretend to ask wider questions about the impact of current forms of financial market organisation on the traditional questions of how scarce resources in an economy are in fact allocated between conflicting ends. These questions will have to be considered with different models.

Financial markets have not been allocating resources in a manner that is remotely Pareto-efficient. To understand better why this is so I have suggested that standard models of rational expectations need to be broadened in the direction of rational action analysis; this will enable us to look at decision-making as consistently context-dependent and path-dependent and also reversible when contexts change. With this focus the study and understanding of context becomes an essential part of modelling. A consequence of this approach is a practical focus for policymakers – they should seek to understand, monitor and regulate the institutional decision-making context, as I will explore in the next chapter.

10
Making Markets Safer

The financial crisis of 2008 was ruinous. It has provoked many commentaries, articles and books. But will it produce change and can this change make a difference? Is there anything much can we do to make financial markets work better and be safer?

One temptation is to breathe a great sigh of relief and forget all about it. It has happened before. "There can be few fields of human endeavour in which history counts for so little as in the world of finance", wrote J.K. Galbraith in his historical study. "Past experience", he continued, "to the extent that it is part of memory at all, is dismissed as the primitive refuge of those who do not have the insight to appreciate the incredible wonders of the present" (Galbraith 1993 p13).

Another temptation is to blame a few bankers and mortgage salesmen as perpetrators of a great deception or in other ways to find other culprits. However, in the long run blame only works adaptively if it correctly identifies causes. The emotional finance argument I have been developing suggests the problem is much more fundamental than deception. To build up to the point where there was the kind of asset price bubble we had before 2008, many people in markets had at some level to have joined in the excited state and become trusting about the latest *phantastic objects,* even if they did not fully realise it. Until the panic phase most rode the wave of excitement and rising prices and very few bet against or withdrew their assets from the system. At the same time prestigious international regulatory agencies expressed satisfaction (IMF 2006; 2007). In effect, all groups embraced a 'convincing' covering story about new financial engineering and judged the validity and safety of that story positively. In this way the crisis was caused by those creating the new phantastic objects (investment banks), licensing and rating their credit-worthiness (rating agencies and regulators), buying them and holding them on client and institutional accounts (private investors and institutional pension and savings funds), authorising all the extra lending (retail and investment banks), and overseeing the system (regulators and governments). Onlookers were fascinated and warnings were not heeded.

Once crisis hits and losses happen blame is emotionally easy. But as I discussed in the previous chapter understanding and allocating responsibility when you have been involved in failure is emotionally more difficult. If we want to adapt and learn from what went wrong then rather than indict a few banks or rule-breaking individuals, it will be more useful to recognise there has been a widespread failure and to consider responsibility in more subtle ways.

The argument so far is that what happened in the recent financial crisis (like in many before) was the product of a shift in mental states. It had its origin in a failure both to understand and to organise markets in a way that adequately controls the outbreak of risky and unrealistic decision-making states that the desire to trade financial assets must inevitably unleash. If this is right future prevention must rely on better understanding – taking beliefs and emotional states seriously and allowing them a much more central place in economic models and regulatory thinking – and then using it to design and regulate the way markets are organised.

My interviews showed how markets are dangerously structured around stimulating the belief in phantastic objects, divided state thinking, and groupfeel. In fact many people working in markets believe they really are phantastic objects themselves.

I consider that the organisational failures followed from the power phantastic objects exert on mental states and the way institutions have increasingly stimulated this power for advantage and then increasingly become ruled by it. Having offered exceptionality they have at least to appear to provide it. It follows that to make markets safer we have to examine the institutional context in which financial assets are first gathered up and then traded and in that context to consider steps to reduce the potential for markets to be seriously captured by phantastic objects, divided states, and groupfeel.

Emotional finance regulation of financial markets would begin by understanding the power of financial assets to create divided states and so armed address the incentive structures and risk-taking they unleash. Haldane (2009) has borrowed from epidemiology to argue that systemic risk to a financial system may be posed at key nodes within a financial network. These nodes may function as key infectors or as firebreaks. From this perspective one priority for regulation is to identify these nodal points and then to understand the inhabitants of these key positions. The next requirement is to ensure they are trained to identify with behaviours to ensure the healthy survival of the institutions for which they work and that their incentive systems support the same ends. It is they, with regulators, who will be required to disinfect the system and say no at a future point when growing excitement and so divided state thinking might be getting out of hand.

A starting point is to train those in key positions to understand the role stories and states of mind play in financial markets and how to recognise divided states and groupfeel. This means to embrace a very different form of economic understanding than hitherto. It might start with appreciating how and why phantastic objects are so seductive and lead to being able to recognise divided states and groupfeel as well as the forces which make it is so difficult for people to give up their pursuit. I shall argue in a moment that the way to build such support and the underlying consensus that adult integrated state regulation requires is for regulators to persuade all financial institutions to look more thoroughly at what has been happening.

So far, despite the enormity of the crisis and its ongoing and long-term negative consequences for ordinary lives, there are uneven signs as to how far there is willingness to accept the need for real change in economic understanding and indeed very little appetite for real enquiry or real institutional change. Fatigue is setting in. Meanwhile the leading banks have been lobbying against restrictions on their activities – such as attempts to impose a 'Volker rule' to limit their speculative activities, to separate their clearing house and credit supply functions (Kay 2010c), or to force them to change remuneration and related practices to reduce the risks posed from what the newly created international Financial Stability Board (FSB) terms the 'moral hazard of systemically important financial institutions (SIFIs)'. There is also impasse at the international level over managing the currency and balance of trade issues that economists identified as facilitating causes.

Change creates winners and losers. The existing banking interests that might suffer from losing their government guarantees, or from structural changes in what they are permitted to do, have in fact gained from the crisis so that today they have even larger resources to find arguments against and to lobby and resist change than before (Johnson and Kwak 2010).

Nonetheless, the final stage of a crisis, while the memory and distress of what happened is fresh, is an opportunity. It is a moment when because so much suffering is being created by a crisis obviously caused in financial markets there may still be motivation to re-examine conventional ways of understanding them and ensuring any new regulatory structures really are based on learning from experience. The severity of budget cuts or sovereign debt crises may even create opportunities where it will be in the interest of politicians to insist this happens.

I have examined the need for a new economic understanding of financial markets in earlier chapters. My aim in this one is to discuss the implications for prudential regulation and to argue that, in the policy context, better emotionally informed understanding of financial markets is much more than an academic pursuit. It is a vital tool both to underpin the motivation to act now to reform markets to reduce the likelihood of further catastrophe and to equip regulators and the management of banks and asset management companies they regulate with what they need to ensure sound integrated state judgement in future.

I will start by examining the extent to which unreformed economic theories and the idealisation they produced hid the conflicts at the heart of the financial system identified in previous chapters. I will then suggest some practical ways to use an emotional finance understanding to design regulatory activity and to modify the context in which financial decisions are made – so as to address the dangers in financial markets and prevent future asset price bubbles before they get out of control. I will then suggest some of the ways the new authorities might act and how regulators need to be empowered to achieve it. Finally, I will comment on the role of the ordinary everyday investor – everyone with a pension or savings.

Understanding

The way one understands one's work influences how one does one's work. So how those working in financial markets and particularly those regulating them understand what happened to us all before 2008 will guide future action. Since *divided* state understanding produced crisis, the question is whether we can initiate a process of inquiry and *working through* to reach the *integrated* state understanding that is required to be realistic about preventing it all happening again.

Psychoanalysis marries belief in the power of reason to an equally strong belief in the power of passion. Acquiring understanding from this viewpoint is therefore an emotional as well as intellectual challenge. In the case of thinking about financial markets in an integrated way it means increasing sceptical curiosity, reducing idealisation, and being able to conceive in a realistic way both their strengths *and* weaknesses.

Looked at from clinical experience it has long struck me that a central problem of financial markets is that hitherto their regulation has been viewed by many within them in what I think of as an adolescent framework – rules put in place by stodgy parents which are there to break if you can get away with it. This is regulation in a *divided state*. It leads to what economists call gaming (and regulatory arbitrage). But gaming with consequences such as we have witnessed is no game at all. In reality it is delinquent antisocial activity which when called a game seeks to evade both worry and guilt. The consequences of what happened prior to 2008 affected nearly everyone, including the institutions which permitted employees to indulge in the behaviours that caused it. Regulators seem to have been viewed as people to play 'Tom' to the industry 'Jerry' – while everyone else watched the chase.

I mentioned in the previous chapter that the ideology of efficient markets has its origins in the struggle with the absolutist powers of English kings. Now that that power is broken the theory of the invisible hand as legitimating 'anything goes' might be considered an adolescent interpretation of the way an ideal world works – without parents. Certainly in recent times a great deal of activity has been aimed at getting round the rules and sometimes this has even been encouraged by those in government who appointed the regulators (Johnson and Kwak 2010). Either we need rules or we don't. If we do need them to have safe markets, evading them is hardly wise. It is a symptom of a divided state.

If we say we need grown-up regulation then we require it to be set up in an integrated state. The first step is to recognise it will not work by *dictat* and lots of rules. Rules invite evasion. Adult regulation, like making the most of education, requires internalising and developing norms that have moral force and receive consensual support (see Akerlof and Kranton 2010). The first step is to realise its necessity.

One way to understand and build consensus is for those in key positions to learn together from recent experience, which might lead to agreement about the necessity for regulation in the way it did in 1929. Investigation will show that in the years leading up to the 2008 collapse, financial markets were not characterised by individual independent thinking but by groupfeel. Nowhere was this truer than within the governance of banks and regulatory agencies. Perhaps some in key positions in those institutions accepted their bonuses and turned a blind eye to what was happening. But most of them were handicapped for different reasons. They had to draw on a flawed rather than useful theory.

It seems clear that so long as current standard economic theories based on how markets might work hold sway and retain their legitimacy, regulation is likely to be flawed. Well before the crisis regulators already had a great deal of power to prevent what happened but did not think there was a problem. The crucial issue then and now was not lack of powers but lack of consensus as to when to use them. At the time, based on their adherence to the market ideal, policymakers and their economic advisers were far from convinced either that financial markets create important problems that the market cannot manage itself or that their actions to create limits or to curb excess would be either acceptable or effective.

For example, in the summer of 2003, shortly after the ending of bubbles in Japan, the rest of Asia, and the dotcom bubble, the Federal Reserve Bank of Chicago and the World Bank brought together many of the world's most influential economists and central bank policymakers to discuss 'asset price bubbles' (if they even existed, which was one stream of the discussion) and what to do. Close reading of the proceedings (Hunter, Kaufman et al. 2003) make clear the extent of unresolved intellectual and ultimately political conflict at the heart of economic thinking. Instead of convinced conclusions and action, the conference report is full of parallel but conflicting positions and paralysis in the face of uncertainty. In many ways that paralysis remains.

On one side were those who (despite the lack of evidence) took economic theory to suggest that, on balance, markets were always efficient and best left to themselves. On the other side were those who pointed out that principally because information in markets was asymmetrically distributed it was far less certain that the financial markets were so efficient. The latter were worried about very recent housing bubbles, the recent dotcom bubble, and new instruments and derivatives which they saw as potentially destabilising innovations. The debate between them and the efficient market proponents produced no change and if the same conference was called today the same arguments might very well be heard.

Whatever institutions are set up now are likely to run into the same problem. At the point a bubble is suspected political interest groups will be able to exploit the central conflict identified in earlier chapters: the conflict between the exciting lure that innovative and potentially phantastic financial assets possess to change the parameters of reward and the possibility that it is a mirage as usual. The whole point is that regulators will be uncertain. They will know nothing for sure. But love of innovation is powerfully and ambivalently built into the human psyche and is very likely mood-dependent. The moment regulators act to inhibit innovation in order to reduce potential risk by requesting abstinence they take sides in the conflict and so create disappointment.

In his closing contribution to the Chicago symposium, Vincent Reinhart, a member of the Board of Governors of the Federal Reserve System, made it very clear that seasoned central bankers feel the conflict even if they have not appreciated its full significance. He listed five lessons to take from the meeting. Authorities should pay attention to asset prices, maintain capital ratios at suitable levels for times of stress, focus macro policy on macro outcomes, encourage diversified systems (because they are more resilient), and get used to increased volatility. But then he introduced what makes most of those tasks impossible. He reminded his audience of the words of the legendary British banker Alexander Baring. He had warned about the 'evil' of financial speculation in the South Sea bubble and subsequently. But, Reinhart reminded his audience, policymakers should beware that in putting a stop to one 'evil', as Baring called it, they might also put a stop to what he called the 'spirit of enterprise' (Reinhart 2003 p558).

As Keynes's (1936) idea of 'animal spirits' was intended to capture, once we accept that the situation we are in has the characteristic that its outcome is truly uncertain, no long-term financial investment decision is possible on the basis of logic alone. It requires that we can take up a state of mind and allow a 'spontaneous urge to action'. If this decision-reality is considered in a divided state it creates no problem. We do what we want and somehow push aside consequences. If it's done in an integrated state, however, it's more difficult. We must both trust our gut and really know the risk in doing so. If and when regulators want to act to inhibit financial activity they will be in that position – just like the epidemiologists who advised widespread inoculation against swine flu without knowing for sure whether all the trouble and expense would be worthwhile. Financial regulators stand to be mocked not just for wanting to impose costs by taking the punch bowl away from the party or stopping the music and dancing but actually for taking the life blood away from human enterprise and its power to create wealth and do good. Health professionals, at least, have the advantage of trying to save lives.

The conflict between innovation and abstinence was creating regulatory caution and preventing action in 2003. It is likely to go on doing so. Moreover, innovations are potential phantastic objects that create love affairs. The new financial instruments were idealised and one could say loved. They created a huge if only apparent increase in profitability – at the time little attention was paid to wondering if they were a mirage, although this is what they turned out to be (Haldane, Brennan et al. 2010).

The point is that the very moment when regulators might need to be most active and enquiring about finance and financial innovation may be the most difficult one in which to develop scepticism. Before 2008 finance was receiving publicity unparalleled since the last major bubble. It was riding high in popular culture and imagination. The City and Wall Street seemed to be glamorous and attractive places for the highly intelligent and ambitious to be – apparently even the chosen place for some bright young graduates wishing to do 'good' (Johnson and Kwak 2010).

Baring's inherent conflict between the evil of allowing speculation and the evil of dampening enterprise is a slightly disguised version of the everyday one I described in Chapter 7. Those respondents feared to make absolute losses but they also feared to miss the gains being made by their competitors. Divided states hide the underlying conflict and so easily lead to excess. Integrated states make it apparent but at the cost of restraint, which when imposed tends to cause frustration and anger.

The crucial point is that although we can be aware of the central risk-reward conflict, uncertainty about the future values of financial assets means we can never remove it. And this is the reason why standard finance theory and its sophisticated mathematical version of Adam Smith's idealised 'invisible hand' can be so dangerous. It hides the reality of the conflict created by uncertainty and the nature of financial assets. Financial markets are not an ideal welfare-optimising solution to the problem of human greed. In fact the conflicts are intrinsically irresolvable. A theory assuming the conflict away – along with its effects on human groups, collective memory, and states of mind – actively assists denial and the creation of a context which is antithought (–K). When accompanied by idealisation (the idealisation of financial markets) it not only becomes an unquestionable religion (Nelson 2001), but is part of a divided state.

To a psychoanalyst, idealisation is usually a warning. It signifies an unstable and immature solution to unrecognised unconscious conflict – an exaggeration. It has the function of removing inconvenient thoughts from awareness which would otherwise create unease and stop you doing what you want. And the evidence is that standard theory was contributing to just such thinking difficulties in regulatory circles. Adair Turner (2010), for instance, has vividly described his impression of how dominant and overconfident the simplified 'finance' version of equilibrium theory had become in regulatory circles in what we might call the Greenspan era. The simplified version played the role Kay (2003) ascribes to what he called DIY economics. In Turner's words the regulatory version of economics was bound up with an 'idealisation of the market' and with it of all the innovative efforts apparently to make markets complete by adding all kinds of insurance and mathematical sophistication. In fact to model financial markets as a closed system in the way that was done, in the face of the formal analyses from information economics and the empirical reality demonstrated by LTCM, is explicable only insofar as we understand that a group process was operating typical of the *Basic Assumption* group discussed in Chapter 3. In such groups evidence from outside the group, from reality, need not be searched out. If by some chance it does come in, it is explained away and has no influence on thought.

During the Greenspan era regulators and their advisers thought market completion via financial innovation *was* actually delivering both economic efficiency and stability. For risk managers in banks and rating agencies imported academic finance theory in the shape of 'value at risk' calculations of assets was providing security – but without much forensic examination of the underlying assumptions about uncertain realities (see Rebonato 2007). The lack of curiosity signifies both a divided state and processes of idealisation rather than thought. Again Turner points out that whether the detail of mortgage contracts or samples of recent past events truly carried strong inferences for the probability distribution of future events was not investigated. The underlying ideas were never challenged. Rather, he concludes, 'they were part of the institutional DNA, part of the belief system' (Turner 2010).

Strong evidence of this basic assumption group (–K) thinking also exists in the IMF's Global Financial Stability Reports in 2006 (IMF 2006) and 2007 (IMF 2007). Although issued only 18 months before the crisis broke, the 2006 report hailed the new financial innovations as a success. Close reading is instructive. There was 'a growing recognition', it claimed, 'that the dispersion of credit risks to a broader and more diverse group of investors... [had] helped make the banking and wider financial system more resilient. The improved reliance may be seen in fewer bank failures and more consistent credit provision' (IMF 2006). Written after the crisis had broken and based on analyses done not by staff but by Lehman Brothers, the 2007 report went so far as to declare that US house price falls were already well advanced and posed no systemic threat. It states: 'weakness has been contained to certain portions of the subprime market (and, to a lesser extent, the Alt-A market), and is not likely to pose a serious systemic threat. Stress tests conducted by investment banks show that, even under scenarios of nationwide house price declines that are historically unprecedented, most investors with exposure to subprime mortgages through securitized structures will not face losses' (IMF 2007 p7).

A basic assumption group reassures itself. Even when events began to unwind, the IMF group seemed to have 'forgotten' the serious doubts about new instruments raised by insiders just a little time before (BIS 2005 p142; Rajan 2005). Could they or agencies have investigated the situation on the ground for themselves? After the crisis evidence has emerged that this would not have been difficult. It was actually just a matter of taking a plane and car to the relevant Florida or California street mentioned in the asset-backed security small print, which a few people looking for items to short actually did (Lewis 2010).

Idealisation in a divided state is based on the human infant's desperate need to trust its environment when it feels frightened of what is happening in its body and mind. It is the glue at the heart of love affairs, identity formation, and attachment. It is supported by neurobiological processes and stimulates fast and frugal decision-making which remove the need for curiosity and investigation – potentially undermining realistic investigation and thinking. We need gut feelings of this kind and they work to create the necessary bonds and attachments in our social relations or activities and in economic decision-making, as in Keynes's 'spontaneous action' or in the important identificatory processes underpinning many economic activities described by Akerlof and Kranton (Akerlof and Kranton 2010). But identification and idealisation can mislead badly. Idealisation of markets, for example, confers magical power in a way that is entirely dubious – as with the argument the 'market is telling us something' wheeled out time and again in arguments about whether apparent bubbles are really bubbles at all.

Insofar as they are faced with a love affair with markets regulators face a very hard situation. To question becomes a sin, to act would be evil. Mervyn King, the Governor of the Bank of England, commented soon after the 2008 crisis that the Bank had been aware of a developing problem concerning the pricing of risk and had regularly published warnings about that in its Stability Reports. He and others sensed something was wrong. But warnings alone had little effect and were themselves inevitably issued knowing the future was uncertain. Concern is not the same as conviction to act. In fact King reflected that even if the Bank had then had the powers to go beyond words, it was not clear to him whether at that stage it would have been possible to use them (King 2009). To do so would have meant taking actions to create limits on financial activity which would have frustrated potential profit-making. So, like parental prohibition, it would have led to pain and anger. The point is that to be able to act in a prudent manner when the underlying situation is uncertain requires that a central bank or government must commit to a frustrating viewpoint in the face of all kinds of ideological and interest group objections even when it cannot be sure it is right. Action will restrict the spirit of 'free enterprise'. The obvious riposte to regulators (and the politicians behind them) will be the one implied by Baring – they are evil in their intent and out to tax success.

Of course the crisis has led governments and international institutions to review the regulatory framework. The Basel Committee has revised its rules about how much liquidity banks need to hold. A higher profile international Financial Stability Board has been created to issue warnings and the EU has a new board too. In the United States the Dodd-Frank 'Restoring American Financial Stability' bill has created the Financial Stability Oversight Council (FSOC). It met for the first time in October 2010 and is tasked with identifying and responding to risks to US financial stability; promoting market discipline by 'eliminating expectations' that the 'government will shield institutions and individuals from losses in the event of failure'; identifying which nonbank financial companies could create systemic risk (e.g., a GE Capital or an AIG) so they should be supervised; and recommending to the federal financial regulators new or better regulatory standards. In the United Kingdom legislation is creating a new Financial Policy Committee (FPC) in the Bank of England. Instead of the tripartite system, dividing power between the Treasury, Financial Services Authority (FSA), and the Bank and so creating competing interests, the Bank will hitherto be responsible for overseeing the whole financial system. The FPC within it will have the specific responsibility to target asset-price inflation. Like the now well-established Monetary Policy Committee (MPC) of the Bank, which targets the retail price index by altering interest rates, the FPC will have a well-defined mandate and be composed of independent voting members each of whom will reach an opinion on the current state of risk in the economy and whose deliberations will be minuted and published.

Both FSOC in the United States and the Bank in the United Kingdom are supreme oversight authorities created to overcome previous weaknesses created by division. They are also not just there to issue warnings and advice. They will have considerable explicit power to intervene in financial institutions, to require them to be wound up in an orderly manner, to change liquidity requirements, and so on. They have been created out of awareness of the danger financial institutions pose and the cost of irresponsible risk-taking implicitly backed by government guarantees. Ongoing commissions have also been established to decide if banks need to be broken up.

The structure of the new arrangements has some interesting variations. In the United Kingdom policy will be in the hands of independent technical experts, albeit appointed by the government. They will have a narrow remit to take a view of what is going on in the economy and their deliberations will be backed by research expertise in the Bank. In the United States the FSOC will also have powerful resources through support from a new Office of Financial Research. But FSOC is not comprised of independent experts and an independent chair. It is made up of the heads of the key agencies and will be chaired by the Treasury Secretary. Decisions will therefore be made by politicians, who may find it particularly difficult to resist groupfeel.

One of the great difficulties, as the 2003 Chicago conference also revealed, is that in the area of asset inflation there is as yet no agreement about the signals to which to respond, the objectives that should be pursued, or the policy levers that are available to bring matters under control. Standard economic theory offers no guidance. It therefore seems likely that such difficulties will interact with deep conflicts mentioned so that there is a great danger that when and if the new regulatory bodies want to act they will be viewed as basing their policies on political and personal prejudice rather than technical skill. This risk also lurks in the traditional area of monetary policy. But in that case economic theory is much more developed and some degree of broad consensus has been built to support the suitability of central bank independence.

For the new institutions to work a great deal of effort will be required to agree on what an asset price bubble is, to devise signals to indicate the probable need for action, and to have ideas about what steps can be taken to influence outcomes in an uncertain future. From an emotional finance view the challenge facing the new bodies is, first, whether they will be able to say 'no' in the face of uncertainty, and, second, whether, when they do, they will be supported in their efforts.

Saying no won't be easy and success will have few obvious rewards. Highly political debates about what policy would have been best at the time of the 1929 great crash still rage. The point is that, as in a successful public health campaign, a crisis prevented is never experienced.

Asset price bubbles occur because people pursue reward without fully realising the risk. They are in a divided state of mind pursuing phantastic objects in a context dominated by groupfeel. When they do realise that everyone else has also become overextended they panic and lose trust in everyone else. But by the time this happens there is no easy exit.

The first step to prevent it all happening again is to have adequate understanding and a good theory of how it can happen. Incorporating emotional states and beliefs into economic theory is necessary. The second step, which follows, is then to empower regulatory authorities to create an institutional context to support *integrated state* decision-making throughout the market. This context must include a wide recognition of the necessity for such authorities and support for them. I think six practical measures will be of use.

Taking powers to work through what has happened

Attention must first be given to creating the context for grown-up regulation. Anticipating the moment when they will want to say 'no', the newly created institutions need to use their powers now to insist that those in the key nodes in the financial network build a body of knowledge about how they got where they did and ensure that knowledge remains available for the future. How organisations acquire and manage knowledge within them is a complex and somewhat controversial matter (see Spender and Scherer 2007; Hall and Paradice 2005) but a starting point would be to set a deadline by which every financial institution (including trustees of pension and other funds) will be required to have conducted their own investigation, documented it, and shared it with regulators – possibly under Chatham House rules.[1]

The aim of such a process is to build up a formal knowledge base and to have worked it through. The situation in the finance industry in 2011 will be analogous to the situation in South Africa post-apartheid. There a 'truth and reconciliation commission' was established to help face emotionally difficult truth and work it through. Along these lines a statutory framework might be created to ensure all financial institutions complete forensic enquiries into their role in the crisis – looking particularly at what happened to curiosity and critical thinking in the ten years prior to 2008. Reports should be published, but to encourage real discovery and truth rather than blame it may be useful to exempt findings use in any subsequent litigation. Staff in key positions throughout the industry (including the FPC itself) should then be given a statutory responsibility to maintain an institutional memory of the conclusions and incorporate them into future training.

To build support for 'grown-up' regulatory intervention these enquiries require those at key nodes in the financial network to attend to ways human psychology in the shape of *phantastic objects, divided states,* and *groupfeel* interact in financial markets to affect thought. In context emotion and gut feelings are not something of which to be ashamed. They are useful signs to guide enquiry just as 'common sense' is an essential adjunct to formal mathematical risk calculation (Rebonato 2007). Like any single indicator, gut feelings are not infallible but they can be another way to reach for truth. Emotional states requiring particular curiosity are those involving shame, arrogance, or unease – particularly if people seem to want to ignore them. Gut feelings of unease tell us something requires attention. Absence of curiosity and the unthinking use of pseudo-information, often characterised by arrogance, are a sign of unwillingness to think (–K). The current situation provides a window of opportunity to insist on the kind of mandatory inquiries just mentioned to build an integrated state of mind within the market.

Making the risk climate transparent to reduce divided states

Specific measures will also be useful to reduce the effect of divided states on thinking. Information in the form of small print or warnings is always available during an asset-price bubble but never gets used. On its own and without the context of adult regulation just suggested it does little to reduce the likelihood of divided states. Nonetheless, having information available and publishing it in an authoritative fashion supports the context in which regulations must work. The new Office of Financial Research in the United States and other bodies elsewhere could play an important role in seeking to develop, oversee, and publish a full range of indicators or 'red flags' (with commentary) to make risk more transparent to the financial community. Authorities seeking to act need signals to know when to do so and indicators against which to test their actions. No doubt these will include a range of traditional measures of trading patterns, bank leverage, debt, and asset price/fundamental ratios but measures of sentiment excitement data might also be developed (using questionnaires) and backed by agent enquiries (along the lines the Bank of England and other authorities already use).

New financial products and other potentially exciting developments should routinely receive rigorous forensic attention from regulatory bodies and ratings agencies who should attempt to demystify them and promote integrated state assessment of them. (Prejudice against innovation is a divided state response as well). In particular, the regulatory body should make discussion and relevant risk calculations between themselves, rating agencies, and initiators transparent – publishing full supporting data for their assessments in accessible form – including commentary on the evidence base for their statistical assumptions and their sources of data. Ratings offered by Rating Agencies within the market should be transparently checkable and supplemented by central authority comment and evaluation in a way similar to how pharmaceutical products are licensed for safety, efficacy, and cost-benefit. Efforts should be made to develop a community of expert peer commentary and debate.

Demystifying exceptionality

Integrated thinking deflates idealisation. Earlier chapters made clear the extent to which my respondents and the financial market as a whole are dominated by a subtle pursuit of phantastic objects, by anxiety at being left behind, and by very short-term time horizons created by the fundamental risk-reward conflicts financial assets create and the excitement and anxieties they raise. The present context effectively rewards and promotes lucky short-term gamblers and myopic behaviour so that prudent managers (for example, those who did not invest in Enron) can actually be penalised. The overall effect is to turn financial markets into gambling casinos, disguised by respectability and pseudo-science.

A range of steps should be taken gradually to alter this context. It requires regulatory agencies to work with asset management companies in a realistic way to try to return the bulk of ordinary investment markets to being 'boring investment' with speculation only around the edges. The main way to do this is to do much more to create realistic anxiety about loss and to diminish idealisation by seeking to alter the basis on which asset management houses compete. They need to move from the myopic divided state pursuit of the phantastic towards long-term prudential management.

To do this requires reflection as to what has happened as well as extensive discussion to overcome 'first mover' hesitance on the part of any asset management house wishing to be different. Regulators certainly need to take much stronger steps to ensure asset management companies (and their advertisements) disclose their performance realistically. This would mean much more disclosure of fund manager performance over the long term as opposed to the short run and full disclosure of all fees and costs of all kinds.[2] Particular attention needs to be paid to ensuring advertisements about fund performance do not misrepresent the success of the group or the manager by any misleading selection of good results only. It should be impossible to select only some high-performing managers and some highly performing funds belonging to an entity or to hide 'underperformance' by amalgamating or withdrawing funds, changing names, and so forth. Other details, such as manager turnover for every fund, should be easily available, along with past track records.

Asset-gathering advertisements should be much more stringently licensed by the authorities. Fund managers do not outperform the market and do not achieve 'phantastic' performance. Therefore, it should not appear in any way in 'reality' that they do so. Finally, such measures to influence the information context should be backed by fiscal measures to tax short-term as compared to long-term profits and perhaps to attach stronger voting rights to 'patient' capital (Brown and Snower 2010).

Reducing the potential for institutionally divided states

I have mentioned that the context in which my respondents work revealed significant problems throughout financial markets, which result from the inherent but hidden conflicts trading financial assets create. Divided state solutions to these conflicts are widespread in investment mandates and incentive arrangements and almost certainly contributed to the crisis.

Fund managers (and their employers), for example, are set up institutionally to compete with each other by gambling with other people's money in a context where success and failure are asymmetrically rewarded. Investment bank activity is similar. The problem has intensified over the last 30 years since major financial institutions moved from a partnership model, where *their* own money was at risk, to incorporation with shareholders, a situation where the risk was transferred to shareholders and clients. We saw in Chapter 7 that clients' efforts to control this by demanding transparent short-term information make matters worse. Insofar as large bonuses are paid for short-term performance success but are not accompanied by equivalently large penalties for short-term loss, there is a problem. The situation is dangerous; promoting risky gambling and *divided state* thinking.

Information economics long ago modelled the likely consequences of agency problems of the kind described, and regulation and taxation should now be designed to remove this 'moral hazard'. Several methods have been proposed to meet such objectives including changes to taxing bonus and incentive structures as well as creating solvency-convertible debt – which is a way to ensure shareholders in financial institutions watch very carefully what is happening and governments do not foot the bill (Brown and Snower 2010).

Creating informed investors

The pressure that creates the search for phantastic objects and divided states comes in part from the whole community which feels the psychological effects financial assets unleash just like anyone else. Euphoria creates the conditions where it becomes difficult to stay out of the exciting development and becoming rich or receiving an apparently free gift is attractive – be it from investing in dotcoms, hedge funds, or some other latest phantastic object (Bernard Madoff's clients were a good example).

Divided states create a disconnection between actions and consequences and also breed passivity. Much of the money invested in financial markets ultimately derives from ordinary citizens – money from pension funds and savings schemes. My respondents and probably also the financial consultants and even pension fund trustees who receive fees from clients to employ them, all have to look over their shoulder to avoid being criticised and blamed for being left out. Regulators are subject to the pressure that they might inhibit initiative.

The measures suggested so far are all aimed at trying to introduce integrated state thinking and to reduce the pull of phantastic objects by increasing awareness of risk and so anxiety. This is not just a matter for financial market participants alone. Regulatory authorities need public support to maintain their legitimacy and the community as a whole needs people to save for retirement and ill fortune and to feel that their savings are secure. If capital is misapplied and not available for 'real' innovatory activity and human creativity this is also impoverishing. An important long-term aspect of prudential regulation may therefore be to step up community and investor education by introducing everyone to the fundamental conflicts introduced in this book. Gambling, and knowing one is doing it, is very different from investing for a pension. The notion the whole financial market is a 'phantastic object' is dangerous and the development of much more widespread financial literacy might be a long-term goal for an effective democracy with particular attention being paid to pension fund and other trustees.

The need for new economics

Many working in the financial sector have some kind of economics training and the general climate in which policy debates takes place is influenced by economic thinking. To mitigate future asset inflations and their inevitable consequences, therefore, it is important to ensure that the teaching of economics and finance theory – particularly in business schools and in investor and banking training programmes – becomes realistically focused on how markets actually work rather than only how they might. The days where an economics course devotes only the last lectures to anomalies and problems should be gone. The consequences of what happened in 2008, which will be experienced for many years to come, create an obligation on every major financial institution and on the relevant parts of the economics profession to engage in more curiosity and self-reflection than is currently evident – particularly as to how traditional assumptions and theoretical approaches have actual been highly misleading to public policy. Economic modelling of risk and reward in financial markets is irresponsible unless starting from the proper study of investor reality and its implications for decision-making. It now requires psychological understanding of the kind offered above (Brown and Snower 2010).

Ordinary Investors

This book is about the financial market into which the ordinary investor can join – buying stocks and bonds or various funds, or just choosing whom to manage a pension scheme. I promised also to comment on the task of such an investor.

Beyond recommending books by Kay (2009) and Taleb (2004) my basic advice is to be very clear with yourself that you separate out whether or not you want to gamble and in doing so *really* know you are taking the risk you will lose. If you want to gamble do so only with what you can afford to lose.

The main risk for the ordinary investor is the same as for the professional – the future is uncertain and stories always sound good. That is their function and potential downside is hidden whatever you do. On the whole there are actually very, very few good stories if any; only luck. In that respect standard finance theory is correct. The trouble is it's a message that is very hard to believe. A few people got rich so why not me? Meanwhile, think for yourself and hope (even support) that the main recommendations in this chapter get implemented and lead to safer and more efficient markets.

Conclusion

The financial crisis has been ruinous and will cost everyone for a long time to come. But the argument I am making is that we have an opportunity. One which if not taken will lead to a repeat perhaps sooner rather than later. There has as yet been little real reform and a significant risk that divided states and the possibility to go on regardless will prove far more attractive than what I have called integrated state thinking. Many of the main policy prescriptions now being officially discussed are based on old thinking and fail sufficiently to address how widespread and serious is the problem we face. Financial markets are dangerous and they also seriously misallocate capital, human talent, and physical resources and energies (Stiglitz 2010). They produce far from optimum results in their good times as well as their bad. Here again standard finance theory is deeply misleading. The present search for phantastic objects in a divided state is also highly unlikely to assist with the problems we face with our planet – for which we also need integrated state thinking.

While the crisis certainly had many facilitating causes, at its heart were the decisions taken by human beings subject to human psychology in the context of the organisation of financial markets. Corruption in the US housing market, trade imbalances with China and other countries, or irrational panic in markets are all factors that could distract attention. The problem was a widespread failure of human judgement and an ongoing failure of institutional development, including the lack of development of an adequate 'integrated' state theory of finance.

Human desires and emotions motivate thought and disturb it. The social-psychological perspective I have introduced sets out how a financial market creates continual opportunities to embrace delusional beliefs in *phantastic objects, divided states,* and *groupfeel*. We need to remember that there were bank directors, regulators, and rules about bank lending before 2008. Prior to 2007 regulators thought they were attending to capital requirements and 'stress testing' the system. Many were actually largely satisfied with the policies in place as were the banks themselves. Banks did not seem at that time to be at the risk they were and the arguments made to the contrary had no traction. We can be sure that human ingenuity will create innovative practices not yet imagined and that we will all want to be impressed by them. Financial markets organised in a divided state and understood by divided-state finance theory will be quite easily captured by phantastic objects and groupfeel. Unless we can develop institutions to support integrated thinking and reason and curiosity, markets will fail again. I end with another quote from Keynes: 'Speculators may do no harm as bubbles on a steady stream of enterprise. But the position is serious when enterprise becomes the bubble on a whirlpool of speculation. When the capital development of a country becomes the by-product of the activities of a casino, the job is likely to be ill done' (Keynes 1936 p159).

Notes

Preface

1. *Groupfeel* is discussed and defined in Chapter 3, along with the academic evidence supporting it. In earlier work I used the term *groupthink* to describe the same phenomenon. It has changed for this book after a discussion with Dennis Snower, to emphasise that while it does involve cognitive processes, what is at the heart of the phenomenon I am trying to capture is a built-in need to feel like everyone else, not just to think like them.

1   The Special Characteristics of Financial Assets

1. People often tend to ignore base rates (base rate neglect) or undervalue their effect. For example, if one is competing against individuals who are already winners of previous competitions, one's odds of winning should be adjusted downward considerably.
2. The first signs of potential difficulty as to subprime were detected when US house prices began to slide in the spring of 2006. Next the price of CDS contracts insuring potential losses started to rise in early 2007. Crucially, on the 15th June 2007 Moody's downgraded 131 bonds linked to subprime debt, after which, a few days later, two Bear Stearns hedge funds were bankrupt. A month later a German bank, IKB, was unable to refinance its loans on the credit markets. It was the first sign of a previously unimaginable credit crunch and the first bailout. Yet world stock markets hit an all-time high on July 20 and nearly all bank shares remained high too. Again, although the credit crunch became widespread and the first major falls in stock markets were to occur in August and September 2007 together with the Northern Rock bankruptcy, markets oscillated up and down thereafter and it was to be a further twelve months before Lehman was bankrupt and AIG was bailed out. Only then did the major crash occur.
3. For example, Kay (2003 p147) writes 'Markets trade flowers. They trade electricity. They trade risks. They also trade money itself. Money is different from these other commodities because it has no intrinsic worth.'

2   Four Fund Managers

1. Full details of the sample and many aspects of the methodology, the validity of which is discussed briefly in Chapter 9, can be found online at www.minding-the-markets. com.
2. Two of the four managers to be discussed in this chapter worked in the United States and two in the United Kingdom. I originally chose them for in-depth analysis to create grounded theory derived hypotheses (Glaser and Strauss 1967; Brown 1973) to test through analysis of all the data. They were chosen to represent somewhat different approaches and were selected at random from all those interviews about which I felt comfortable that the detailed information they

revealed could be used without prejudicing their interests or those of their firms or clients. (In their case, as in all others, I use invented names to discuss actual stock decisions.) I believe that as a group they are typical of the sample. This claim is supported by the fact that the hypotheses that emerged from this analysis are tested in later chapters by analyzing and reporting randomly selected examples from the interviews.

3 Narratives, Minds, and Groups

1. This section relies on and has greatly benefited from discussions with my colleague Rudi Vermote.
2. The correct psychoanalytic term is 'PS' (paranoid schizoid) which alternates with D (depressive). I will introduce the latter below as an 'integrated state'. The names of these terms have been altered in this book. Even in psychoanalysis they have proved unfortunate and in more general context they tend to mislead – see Tuckett and Taffler (2008) for a fuller explanation. I am grateful to Mervyn King for the suggestion.

4 Divided States

1. The Senior Banking Supervisors Group concluded that boards, senior directors and managers 'failed to establish, measure, and adhere to a level of risk acceptable to the firm', allowed compensation programs that 'conflicted with the control objectives of the firm', took no action to remedy 'inadequate and often fragmented technological infrastructures' which 'hindered effective risk identification and measurement', etc. (Senior Supervisors (2009)).
2. A question about looking at screens or other statistical representations of performance was eventually asked towards the end of the interview. However, because it was at the end it was vulnerable to being omitted when there were time pressures. I am grateful to Arman Eshraghi for the analysis relied on to support these findings.
3. Kay (2009) states that the median cumulative outperformance relative to managers' own defined benchmarks of UK retail investment funds between 1998 and 2008 was –1.2 (sterling bonds), –3.0 (UK equities), and –3.3 (global equities) – which makes this a very ambitious target.
4. Fear of getting the sack (a pink slip) was not systematically questioned. However, four of those interviewed spontaneously mentioned it as a likely prospect if they underperformed and only two explicitly stated they would not expect that.
5. Brad Johnston is discussed further below (pp). But here is a small excerpt from the performance section of his interview. Int: 'What happens if, if your performance is not very good.' Brad: 'I think what, what, what would limit your life expectancy around here is, is not that. It would actually be to run counter to what we stand for and to work outside the process. Now that's actually impossible because, you know, stocks have to get approved, ultimately the process has to be shown to have been, you know, adhered to, but if that process results in something not working out properly then you shouldn't get too hung up on that. What's most important is that people behave in accordance to what we stand for.'
6. Arman Eshraghi carried out this analysis and I am very grateful to him.

5 Finding Phantastic Objects

1. See also the account by Beinhocker (2006) p125 et seq.
2. Forty-two managers and one analyst talked about 165 specific decisions, some of which worked out as hoped and some of which did not. They have been sampled to provide the data for this chapter.
3. Robert Burton is a former trainee financial analyst and Andrew Sanchez is a social anthropologist.
4. This was a developmental study in which, because of time constraints, not all of these stories were equally probed and elaborated. Some are a bit thinner than ideal.
5. Noticing and explaining 'inconsistency' was at the heart of the strategy many managers adopted.
6. Discussed in detail below (Managing emotions).
7. All 39 stock-picking managers were assigned a number and then the first four from the 39 selected at random.
8. Frances is also judged via a benchmark but she considers it a thing of the past to judge yourself against but not to use to anticipate the future. No attempt is made, therefore, to construct a portfolio using benchmark proportions, etc.

6 Experiencing the News

1. The classic psychoanalytic description is by Melanie Klein who describes movement through the paranoid schizoid (divided) and depressive (integrated) states (Klein 1940).
2. Actual experience with trusting adults and caregivers who can tolerate children's hatred and greed rather than retaliate or behave cruelly towards them (and so do not have to be idealised to make up for the ghastly reality) is a vital component in determining how far *integrated* states are possible. See Fonagy and Target (1996).
3. Overall performance depends on the outcome of a portfolio of decisions. What is reported here is not Smith's (or any other manager's) actual overall performance which cannot be deduced from these examples. It is important to recognize that if Smith's decisions were right more than half of the time then if other things were equal he would be ahead. The equal proportions reported here are artefacts of asking for three examples.
4. Twenty-one of the 43 managers – the 39 stock pickers, the bond picker, the analyst and the two mixed quant and stock-picking managers.
5. A year later it emerged that the bank was deeply involved in securitised subprime loans; the bank ceased to be independent and its shares became worthless.

7 Divided Masters

1. This account of why he didn't do something contradicts his earlier success narrative, which posited that: 'All things being equal, we would normally say that if we've picked a company that we like, we don't care what the share price does. We'll just keep buying it.' (Darren Cook). Here, it would seem that stock price was the overriding rationale in the decision not to buy.
2. The combination of the way I selected my sample, its size and the fact that this hypothesis did not come up until later so that questions were not necessarily asked,

means that data on these questions were not collected systematically, so that conclusions should be treated with caution.

3. In fact a fourth stock discussed for different reasons also fitted this description.

4. Interestingly, in view of subsequent events, Williams said that his valuation methods didn't work with financial institutions: 'We can't do this for financial companies, banks and insurance companies. It's a bit difficult. ... We've done some work that suggests actually that within the banks you'd probably want to be a little bit underweight ... but it's a very weak data and it's only in five years. It doesn't hold up over ten.' This had caused him to underweight the sector.

5. Several of the managers using cautious long-term strategies knew they suffered at times from 'exuberance'. 'What happened during the dotcom? In 1999 our clients fired us ... we almost went out of business,' said William Booth. Some managers' response to this was to to try to work out ways to ride momentum – see the comments by George Monroe above.

6. 'We are not offering perfect outperformance always. That's not our option,' Fraser Hobbs said. 'We are simply saying we have an investment philosophy we believe in and which we think over time gets returns. We promise you we will follow our investment philosophy. If you want that for your portfolio, that is what we deliver. ... You have to clearly identify and use your investment philosophy. ... It's not just something on the front of your PowerPoint presentation to clients ... you truly have to believe it ... have to be able to say ... it will work ... you have to be rock solid. ... ' Fraser indicated that for him 'gold standard' fund management would be holding 25 names long-term – over five or more years with some moving around of smaller holdings in another 20 or so companies for diversification. As 'manager of managers' what he spent 'most of my time on' was trying to help his team to get such an approach.

7. Lewis (2010) describes similar pressures on a manager whose 'autistic' state allowed him mostly to ignore it.

8. Of course we do not know at what point he will have sold these securities or how far, if at all, he was eventually caught up in the 2008 banking crisis or not.

9. His approach to assessing the dangers facing him when he made decisions involved trying to imagine different possible situations. 'What we've found to be helpful is to develop four scenarios for each company. A case that everything goes right or maybe what the company might be worth in an acquisition scenario. A base case that we think will occur – we tend to look out about a year to develop that base case. That is the base for owning the stock. If we had a negative base case we won't be owning the stock and then [we develop] two, kind of, downside cases. One is if things go moderately wrong or ... they have reserve issues or something like that, that are unforeseen now but which might happen. Then [another is] like a draconian bear scenario where everything goes wrong. So we take those four scenarios, we try to put probabilities on that, it's an art, it's not nearly a science, but that feeds into a weighted price target and if everyone is relatively on the same page in thinking about the world and thinking about their stocks then you can make an informed decision as to which stocks should be bigger. ... ' Interestingly, given this approach and the situation which was to explode not so long after, he did not (along with nearly everyone else of course) imagine stress-testing or doing doomsday scenario explorations of the capital situation at any of the major banks in which he was invested.

8   Experiencing Success and Failure

1. Other respondents had questioned how you valued banks so because Frost's principles as explained in his mission statement were to focus on a model of discounted cash flow, I did ask Frost about that. 'You can't do that on a bank', he explained in response to a question, 'that's the trouble…banks are in the business of cash, they can't actually discount.' This is an example of the 'flexibility' discussed below.

2. 'One of the problems: they weren't then hedging that in the market place…they offered it to you but they wouldn't hedge it until you'd signed the bit of paper, which was two months later, and by that time the price in the market place had moved. So they were running an open book position, or have been doing, basically.'

3. Lewis ibid. has a fascinating description of this phenomenon based on material from various CDO and CDS product promotion conferences in 2007.

4. The answer may indicate the depth of the eventual panic in October 2008, by which time many problems dealt with in this kind of way – as unthinkable – had become no longer avoidable.

5. *Advertise* was a stock where Frost and his team had done a forecast, challenged their assumptions and reached the conclusion that the stock was cheap with little downside risk and considerable upside potential. But shortly the management had announced that forecast earnings growth was going to be reduced. With reduced earnings it was no longer a cheap stock so they sold and took a 20% loss. 'Our view of management was severely diminished, we were very dissatisfied.' *Gadgets* was a third stock that Frost was not sure about. He and his team had determined that the company's superior technology gave them a considerable edge against competing products and that demand for their products would be good; in which case returns would be stronger than the market was predicting and the shares were undervalued. This thesis has proved correct for a while but then management downgraded their forecasts of future revenues, based on their predictions of a slowing down in the growth of incomes and wealth in the United States. Frost and his team did not understand that conclusion and thought the management were being unduly careful – apparently management had actually said they didn't know whether sales of their devices would not grow but they were putting out this warning so that the market would not be disappointed. They were, so to speak, telling the truth. Frost was dissatisfied with the way they had thus created uncertainty and with the fact that there were additional rumours that the family who had established the business, and were the main shareholders, were splitting up. In short he blamed management for the resulting events.

6. To explore what sort of decisions satisfied them and did not, managers were asked to give examples of both. The resulting frequencies do not, therefore, tell us anything about proportion of successes and failures they actually had.

7. South noted that many speculators had taken the opportunity of the coup to buy cheap stock. But he thought the present regime was fundamentally more nationalistic and likely to harm the market. He was proved right when the government attempted to introduce capital controls and the market 'just completely cratered'. He had spent five years living in South East Asia and considered himself above inexperienced speculators in New York, London, etc.

8. Comparing valuations across borders is difficult and uncertain. Anderson's methods are flexible. 'That's one of the things that we do quite well. I mean PE works because it works. It's the most regularly used. It's definitely the most simple.…We also believe

in looking at cash flow return on investment...implied cash flow returns...there's quite a lot of readily available tools available....I don't think we really believe, as global investors, that any one measure works for every sector all around the world, all the time.'

9. Abram was very sarcastic at this point, as he was quite often when talking of the market – as were many other managers on this topic.

9   Emotional Finance and New Economic Thinking

1. http://www.stanleygibbons.com/investments/free-reports-summer-2010/spectator-191010.aspx
2. I have provided many background details of the study on the website accompanying this book. See www.minding-the-markets.com
3. Other sociological studies painting similar pictures include Abolafia (2005), Pixley (2004), Hardie and MacKenzie (2007), Godechot (2008), Preda (2009), and Mackenzie and Muniesa (2007).
4. See www.minding-the-markets.com
5. Hicks himself was very careful to specify that his unrealistic formulations were no more than classroom 'gadgets' (Hicks 1980–1981). See also Chick (1982).
6. The models simulate the simultaneous operations and interactions of multiple agents, in an attempt to re-create and predict the appearance of complex phenomena. The process is one of emergence from the lower (micro) level of systems to a higher (macro) level. As such, a key notion is that simple behavioral rules generate complex behavior.
7. Simon (1997) goes on to discuss the experience of loss and its effect on what would subsequently be discussed as loss aversion.

10   Making Markets Safer

1. A set of rules for discussion to encourage frankness and honesty where what is said by individuals is not reported outside the room.
2. In a conversation at the FSA in the United Kingdom in January 2009, Adair Turner and I were informed by a senior official that they had in fact had some success in forcing transparency to drive down fees. At the same time they had declined the opportunity to do more to force more disclosure of fund results. During the boom years they believed they could not rely on political support.

References

Abolafia, M. Y. (2005). 'Interpretive Politics at the Federal Reserve.' In *The Sociology of Financial Markets*. Eds K. Knorr Certina and A. Preda. Oxford: Oxford University Press.

Akerlof, G. and R. Shiller (2009). *Animal Spirits: How Human Psychology Drives the Economy, and Why It Matters for Global Capitalism*. Princeton, NJ: Princeton University Press.

Akerlof, G. A. (1970). 'The Market for "Lemons": Quality Uncertainty and the Market Mechanism.' *Quarterly Journal of Economics* 84(3): 488–500.

Akerlof, G. A. and R. E. Kranton (2010). *Identity Economics: How Our Identities Shape Our Work, Wages and Well-Being*. Princeton, NJ: Princeton University Press.

Alfi, V., M. Cristelli, L. Pietronero and A. Zaccaria (2009). 'Minimal Agent Based Model for Financial Markets I: Origin and Self-Organization of Stylized Facts.' *European Physical Journal B*: 385–97.

Allen, F. and D. Gale (2001). *Comparing Financial Systems*. Cambridge, MA: MIT Press.

——(2003). 'Asset Price Bubbles and Stock Market Interlinkages.' In *Asset Price Bubbles: The Implications for Monetary, Regulatory, and International Policies*. Eds W. C. Hunter, G. G. Kaufman and M. Pomerleano. Boston: MIT Press, 323–36.

Allen, F. and G. Gorton (1993). 'Churning Bubbles.' *Review of Economic Studies* 60(4): 813–36.

Arrow, K. (1963). 'Uncertainty and the Welfare Economics of Medical Care.' *American Economic Review* 53(5): 941–73.

Arrow, K. and G. Debreu (1954). 'Existence of a Competitive Equilibrium for a Competitive Economy.' *Econometrica* 22(3): 265–90.

Bachalier, L. (1900). *Théorie de la spéculation*. Paris : Gauthier-Villars.

Bagehot, W. (1873 (Republished 1999)). *Lombard Street : A Description of the Money Market*. London and New York: John Wiley.

Bar-Gill, O. (2008). 'The Law, Economics and Psychology of Sub-Prime Mortgage Contracts.' American Law & Economics Association Annual Meetings, Berkeley Electronic Press. Paper 47.

Bargh, J. A. (1997). 'The Automaticity of Everyday Life.' *The Automaticity of Everyday Life: Advances in Social Cognition*. Vol. 10. Mahwah, NJ: Erlbaum, 1–61.

Bargh, J. A. and E. Morsella (2008). 'The Unconscious Mind.' *Perspectives on Psychological Science* 3(1): 73–9.

——(2009). 'Unconscious Behavioral Guidance Systems.' In *Then a Miracle Occurs: Focusing on Behavior in Social Psychological Theory and Research*. Eds C. Agnew, D. Carlston, W. Graziano and J. Kelly. New York: Oxford University Press.

Baron, R. S. (2005). 'So Right It's Wrong: Groupthink and the Ubiquitous Nature of Polarized Group Decision Making.' In *Advances in Experimental Social Psychology*. Vol. 37. Ed. M. P. Zanna. San Diego, CA: Elsevier Academic Press, 219–53.

Bartlett, F. C. (1932). *Remembering: A Study in Experimental and Social Psychology*. Cambridge, UK: Cambridge University Press.

Bator, F. M. (1958). 'The Anatomy of Market Failure.' *Quarterly Journal of Economics*. LXXII: 351–79.

Bechara, A. and A. R. Damasio (2005). 'The Somatic Marker Hypothesis: A Neural Theory of Economic Decision.' *Games and Economic Behavior* 52(2): 336–72.

Beinhocker, E. (2006). *The Origin of Wealth: Evolution, Complexity and the Radical Remaking of Economics*. New York: Harvard Business School Press and Random House.

Berezin, M. (2005). Emotions and the Economy. In *Handbook of Economic Sociology*. 2d ed. Eds N. J. Smelser and R. Swedberg. New York and Princeton, NJ: Russell Sage Foundation and Princeton University Press, 109–27.

Berger, P. and T. Luckman (1966). *The Social Construction of Reality: A Treatise in the Sociology of Knowledge*. London: Allen Lane and the Penguin Press.

Berns, G. S., D. Laibson, et al. (2007). 'Intertemporal Choice – Toward an Integrative Framework.' *Trends in Cognitive Sciences* 11(11): 482–8.

Berthoz, A. and J.-L. Petit (2008). *The Physiology and Phenomenology of Action*. Oxford: Oxford University Press.

Bewley, T. (1999). *Why Wages Don't Fall During A Recession*, Harvard University Press.

Bion, W. R. (1952). 'Group Dynamics: A Re-View.' *Int. J. Psychoanal.* 33: 235–47.

——(1959). *Experiences in Groups and Other Papers*. London: Tavistock.

——(1962). *Learning from Experience*. London: Tavistock.

——(1962). 'The Psycho-Analytic Study of Thinking.' *Int. J. Psychoanal.* 43: 306–10.

——(1991). *Cogitations*. London: Karnac Books.

BIS (2005). Bank of International Settlements, 75th Annual Report.

Black, F. and M. Scholes (1973). 'The Pricing of Options and Corporate Liabilities.' *Journal of Political Economy* 81(3): 637–54.

Bogle, J. C. (2005). 'The Mutual Fund Industry 60 Years Later: For Better or Worse?' *Financial Analysts Journal* 61(1): 15–24.

Britton, R. and J. Steiner (1994). 'Interpretation: Selected Fact or Overvalued Idea?' *Int. J. Psychoanal.* 75: 1069–78.

Brown, A. J. and D. Snower (2010). *Economic Solutions 2009*. Global Economic Symposium.

Brown, G. W. (1973). 'Some Thoughts on Grounded Theory.' *Sociology* 7(1): 1–16.

Bruner, J. (1986). *Actual Minds, Possible Worlds*. Cambridge, MA: Harvard University Press.

——(1991). 'The Narrative Construction of Reality.' *Critical Inquiry* 18(1): 1–21.

——(2003). *Making Stories: Law, Literature, Life*. Cambridge, MA: Harvard University Press.

——(2004). 'Life as Narrative.' *Social Research* 71(3): 691–710.

Brunnermeier, M. K. (2001). *Asset Pricing under Asymmetric Information: Bubbles, Crashes, Technical Analysis, and Herding*. Oxford, Oxford University Press.

Buffett, W. (2003). 'Chairman's Letter to the Shareholders of Berkshire Hathaway Inc., 21 February.' In *Berkshire Hathaway Inc, 2002 Annual Report*: 3–23.

Bunday, B. (1996). *An Introduction to Queueing Theory*. Oxford: Oxford University Press.

Camerer Colin; George Loewenstein and Matthew Rabin (2004). *Advances in Behavioral Economics*, Princeton, NJ: Princeton University Press.

Cassidy, J. (2009). *How Markets Fail: The Logic of Economic Calamities*. London: Allen Lane.

Charuvastra, A. and S. R. Marder (2009). 'Unconscious Emotional Reasoning and the Therapeutic Misconception.' *J Med Ethics* 34: 193–7.

Chick, V. (1982). 'A Comment on 'IS-LM: An Explanation'.' *Journal of Post Keynesian Economics* 4(Spring): 439–44.

Dale, R. S., J. E. V. Johnson, et al. (2005). 'Financial Markets Can Go Mad: Evidence of Irrational Behaviour during the South Sea Bubble.' *Economic History Review* 58: 233–71.

Damasio, A. (2004). *The Neurobiology of Feeling*. New Orleans: International Psychoanalytic Association.

Damasio, A. and K. Meyer (2008). 'Behind the Looking-Glass.' *Nature* 454: 167–8.

Della Vigna, S. (2009). 'Psychology and Economics: Evidence from the Field.' *Journal of Economic Literature*: 315–72.

Dietrich, A. (2004). 'The Cognitive Neuroscience of Creativity.' *Psychonomic Bulletin and Review* 11(6): 1011–26.

Dow, S. (2010). *What Kind of Theory to Guide Reform and Restructuring of the Financial and Non-Financial Sectors? A Focus on Theoretical Approach.* Institute for New Economic Thinking inaugural conference.

Dresher, M., L. S. Shapley, et al. (1964). *Advances in Game Theory.* Princeton, UK: Princeton University Press.

Durkheim, E. (1915). *The Elementary Forms of the Religious Life, A Study in Religious Sociology.* Trans. Joseph Ward Swain. London: George Allen and Unwin.

Evans-Pritchard, E. (1937). *Witchcraft, Oracles and Magic Among the Azande.* Oxford: The Clarendon Press.

Fama, E. F. (1970). 'Efficient Capital Markets: A Review of Theory and Empirical Work.' *Journal of Finance* 25(2): 383–417.

Fama, E. F. and M. H. Miller (1972). *The Theory of Finance.* New York: Holt, Rinehart and Winston.

Farmer, J. and D. Foley (2009). 'The Economy Needs Agent-Based Modelling.' *Nature*: 685–6.

Fenton-Creevey Mark; Nigel Nicholson; Emma Sloane and Paul Wilman (2005). *Traders: Risks, Decisions, and Management in Financial Markets.* Oxford: Oxford University Press.

Festinger, L. (1957). *A Theory of Cognitive Dissonance.* Stanford, CA: Stanford University Press.

Finucane, M. L., A. Alhakami, P. Slovic and S. M. Johnson (2000). 'The Affect Heuristic in Judgments of Risks and Benefits.' *Journal of Behavioral Decision Making* 13(1): 1–17.

Fónagy, I. (1999). 'The Process of Remembering: Recovery and Discovery.' *Int. J. Psychoanal.* 80(5): 961–78.

Fonagy, P. (1999). 'Memory and Therapeutic Action.' *Int. J. Psychoanal.* 80(2): 215–23.

Fonagy, P. and P. Lutyens (2009). 'A Developmental, Mentalization-Based Approach to the Understanding and Treatment of Borderline Personality Disorder.' *Development and Psychopathology* 21: 1355–81.

Fonagy, P. and M. Target (1996). 'Playing With Reality: I. Theory Of Mind And The Normal Development Of Psychic Reality.' *Int. J. Psychoanal.* 77: 217–33.

Ford, J. L. (1993). 'G. L. S. Shackle: A Brief Bio-Bibliographical Portrait.' *Journal of Economic Studies* 12(1/2): 3–12.

Freud, S. (1900). 'The Interpretation of Dreams.' In *The Standard Edition of the Complete Psychological Works of Sigmund Freud.* Vol. 4: *The Interpretation of Dreams.* Ed. J. Strachey. London: Institute of Psychoanalysis and the Hogarth Press.

——(1911). 'Formulations on the Two Principles of Mental Functioning.' In *The Standard Edition of the Complete Psychological Works of Sigmund Freud.* Vol. 12 (1911–1913): *The Case of Schreber, Papers on Technique and Other Works.* London: Institute of Psychoanalysis and Hogarth Press, 213–26.

——(1914). 'Remembering, Repeating and Working-Through (Further Recommendations on the Technique of Psycho-Analysis II).' In *The Standard Edition of the Complete Psychological Works of Sigmund Freud.*, Vol.12 (1911–1913): *The Case of Schreber, Papers on Technique and Other Works.* London: Institute of Psychoanalysis and the Hogarth Press, 145–156.

FSA (2009). The Turner Review: A Regulatory Response to the Global Banking Crisis. London: Financial Services Authority.

Fuller, S. R. and R. J. Aldag (1998). 'Organizational Tonypandy: Lessons from a Quarter Century of the Groupthink Phenomenon.' *Organizational Behavior and Human Decision Processes* 73(2-3): 163–84.

Gadamer, H. (1975). *Truth and Method*. London: Sheed and Ward.

Galbraith, J. K. (1993). *A Short History of Financial Euphoria*. New York: Penguin.

Gennaioli Nicola; Andrei Shleifer and Robert W. Vishny (2010). 'Neglected Risks, Financial Innovation, and Financial Fragility.' *NBER Working Papers 16068*.

Gigerenzer, G. (2007). *Gut Feelings*. London: Allen Lane and Penguin.

——(2008). *Rationality for Mortals*. New York: Oxford University Press.

Gigerenzer, G. and R. Selten (2002). *Bounded Rationality: The Adaptive Toolbox*. Cambridge, MA, London: MIT Press.

Gigerenzer, G., P. Todd, et al. (1999). *Simple Heuristics That Make Us Smart*. The Hague: Springer Netherlands.

Glaser, B. G. and A. L. Strauss (1967). *The Discovery of Grounded Theory: Strategies for Qualitative Research*. Hawthorne, NY: Aldine de Gruyter.

Godechot, O. (2008). 'Hold-Up' in Finance: The Conditions of Possibility for High Bonuses in the Financial Industry.' *Revue Française de Sociologie*. 49 (Supplement Annual English edn): 95–123.

Goldthorpe, J. H. (2007). Rational Action in Sociology. In *On Sociology*. Vol· 1. *Critique and Program*. 2d ed. Ed. J. H. Goldthorpe. Stanford: Stanford University Press.

Gorton, G. (2008). 'The Subprime Panic.' *NBER Working Papers 14398*.

Grossman, S. J. and J. Stiglitz (1980). 'On the Impossibility of Informationally Efficient Markets.' *American Economic Review* 70(3): 123–36.

Gul, F. and W. Pensendorfer (2008). 'The Case for Mindless Economics.' In *The Foundations of Positive and Normative Economics*. Eds A. Caplin and A. Shotter. Oxford and New York: Oxford University Press.

Habermas, J. (1971). *Knowledge and Human Interest*. Boston: Beacon Press.

Haldane, A. (2009). 'Re-Thinking the Financial Network.' Speech delivered at the Financial Student Association, Amsterdam, Bank of England.

Haldane, A., S. Brennan, et al. (2010). 'The Contribution of the Financial Sector: Miracle or Mirage?' In *The Future of Finance: The LSE Report*. London: The London School of Economics.

Hall, D. and D. Paradice (2005). 'Philosophical Foundations for a Learning-Oriented Knowledge Management System for Decision Support.' *Decision Support Systems*: 445–61.

Hardie, I. and D. MacKenzie (2007). 'Assembling an Economic Actor: The *Agencement* of a Hedge Fund.' *The Sociological Review* 55: 57–80.

Hicks, J. (1937). 'Mr. Keynes and the Classics – A Suggested Interpretation.' *Econometrica* 5: 147–59.

Hicks, J. R. (1980–1981). 'IS-LM: An Explanation.' *Journal of Post Keynesian Economics* 3(2): 139–55.

Hilton, D. J. (2003). 'Psychology and Financial Markets: Applications to Understanding and Remedying Irrational Decision-Making.' In *The Psychology of Economic Decisions*. Vol. 1: *Rationality and Well-Being*. Eds I. Brocas and J. D. Carrillo. Oxford: Oxford University Press.

Hunter, W. C., G. G. Kaufman, et al. (2003). *Asset Price Bubbles: Implications for Monetary, Regulatory, and International Policies*. Cambridge, MA, London: MIT Press.

IMF (2006). Global Financial Stability Report, April 2006: Annex. Summing Up by the Chairman. April 11, 2006.

——(2007). Global Financial Stability Report.

Investment Solutions (2007). Annual Asset Manager Survey: 2007. London: Investment Solutions Group Limited.

Janis, I. (1982). *Groupthink*. 2d ed. Boston: Houghton Mifflin.

Johnson, S. and J. Kwak (2010). *13 Bankers*. New York: Random House.

Jones, E. (1908). 'Rationalization in Everyday Life.' *Papers on Psycho Analysis*. London: Balliere, Tindall and Cox.

Kahneman, D. (2003). 'A Perspective on Judgment and Choice: Mapping Bounded Rationality.' *American Psychologist* 58(9): 697–720.

Kahneman, D. and I. Ritov (1994). 'Determinants of Stated Willingness to Pay for Public Goods: A Study in the Headline Method.' *Journal of Risk and Uncertainty* 9: 5–38.

Kahneman, D., I. Ritov and D. Schkade (1999). 'Economic Preferences or Attitude Expressions? An Analysis of Dollar Responses to Public Issues.' *Journal of Risk and Uncertainty*: 220–42.

Kahneman Daniel; David Schkade and Cass Sunstein (1998). 'Shared Outrage and Erratic Awards: The Psychology of Punitive Damages.' *Journal of Risk and Uncertainty* 16: 49–86.

Kandel, E. (1999). 'Biology and the Future of Psychoanalysis: A New Intellectual Framework for Psychiatry Revisited.' *Am J Psychiatry* 156(4): 505–24.

Kay, J. (2003). *The Truth about Markets: Their Genius, Their Limits, Their Follies*. London: Allen Lane.

——(2009). *The Long and the Short of It – Finance and Investment for Normally Intelligent People Who Are Not in the Industry*. London: The Erasmus Press.

——(2010). 'Economics May Be Dismal, But It Is Not a Science.' *Financial Times*. London.

——(2010). *Obliquity: Why Our Goals Are Best Achieved Indirectly*. London: Profile Books.

——(2010). 'Why "Too Big to Fail" Is Too Much for Us to Take. *Financial Times*. London.

Keren, G. and Y. Schul (2010). 'Two Is Not Always Better Than One: A Critical Evaluation of Two-System Theories.' *Perspectives on Psychological Science* 4: 533–50.

Keynes, J. M. (1930). *A Treatise on Money*. 2 vols. New York: Harcourt, Brace and Company.

——(1936). *The General Theory of Employment, Interest and Money*. London: Macmillan.

——(1937). 'The General Theory of Employment.' *The Quarterly Journal of Economics*: 643–69.

Kindleberger, C. (2000). *Manias, Panics and Crashes*. 4th ed. New York: John Wiley & Sons.

King, M. (2009). Speech to the CBI Dinner, Nottingham, at the East Midlands Conference Centre, Bank of England.

——(2010). 'Banking: From Bagehot to Basel, and Back Again.' *The Second Bagehot Lecture, Buttonwood Gathering*. New York: Bank of England.

Klein, M. (1930). 'The Importance of Symbol-Formation in the Development of the Ego.' *Int. J. Psychoanal.* 11: 24–39.

——(1940). 'Mourning and Its Relation to Manic-Depressive States.' *Int. J. Psychoanal.* 21: 125–53.

——(1946). 'Notes on Some Schizoid Mechanisms.' *Int. J. Psychoanal.* 27: 99–110.

——(1961). *Narrative of a Child Analysis: The Conduct of the Psycho-Analysis of Children as Seen in the Treatment of a Ten Year Old Boy*. London: Hogarth Press and the Institute of Psychoanalysis.

Knight, F. H. (1921). *Risk, Uncertainty, and Profit*. Boston: Hart, Schaffner & Marx; Houghton Mifflin Co.

Knorr-Cetina, K. and A. Preda (2005). *The Sociology of Financial Markets*. Oxford: Oxford University Press.

Krugman, P. (2009). Book Review: '*Keynes: The Return of the Master* by Robert Skidelsky.' *The Observer.* London. Sunday, 30 August 2009.

Kuhn, T. (1972). *The Structure of Scientific Revolutions.* Chicago: Chicago University Press.

Laird-Johnson, P. (2010). *Inconsistency.* The Fifth Memorial A. R. Jonckheere Lecture, University College London.

Langer, E. J. (1975). 'The Illusion of Control.' *Journal of Personality and Social Psychology* 32(2): 311–28.

Laplanche, J. and J. Pontalis (1973). *The Language of Psychoanalysis.* London: Institute of Psychoanalysis and the Hogarth Press.

Lawson (2010). *Really Reorienting Modern Economics.* Institute for New Economic Thinking: Inaugural Conference.

Ledoux, J. E. (1998). *The Emotional Brain.* New York: Simon and Schuster.

Lewis, M. (2010). *The Big Short: Inside the Doomsday Machine.* New York: W. W. Norton.

Lipsky, J. (2010). *Contribution to Panel on Financial Risk Management 2.0?* World Economic Forum 2010, Davos.

Loewenstein George; Weber, E. U.; Hsee, C. K. and Welch, N. (2001). 'Risk as Feelings.' *Psychological Bulletin* 127: 267–86.

Lowenstein, L. (2008). *The Investor's Dilemma: How Mutual Funds Are Betraying Your Trust And What To Do About It.* Hoboken, NJ: John Wiley & Sons.

Lucas, R. (1972). 'Expectations and the Neutrality of Money.' *Journal of Economic Theory* 4: 103–24.

Mackay, C. (1848). *Extraordinary Popular Delusions and the Madness of Crowds.* Ware, Hertfordshire, UK: Wordsworth.

Mackenzie Donald; Fabian Muniesa and Lucia Siu (2007). *Do Economists Make Markets? On the Performativity of Economics.* Princeton, NJ: Princeton University Press.

Mankiw, N. G. (1999). 'The Reincarnation of Keynesian Economics.' *NBER Working Papers 3885.*

Matte Blanco, I. (1968). 'Comunicazione non verbale e suoi rapporti con la comunicazione verbale.' *Rivista Psicoanal* 14: 3–34.

Meltzer, A. (2003). 'Rational and Nonrational Bubbles.' In *Asset Price Bubbles: The Implications for Monetary, Regulatory and International Policies.* Eds W. C. Hunter, G. G. Kaufman and M. Pomerleano: 23–34.

Mercers and IRRC Institute (2010). 'Investment Horizons – Do Managers Do What They Say?' New York: Mercers and IRRC Institute.

Mikulincer, M. and P. Shaver, R. (2007). *Attachment in Adulthood.* New York and London: The Guilford Press.

Miller, G. A., E. Galanter and K. H. Pribram (1960). *Plans and the Structure of Behavior.* Cambridge, MA: Holt, Rinehart & Winston.

Mills, C. W. (1940). 'Situated Actions and Vocabularies of Motive.' *American Sociological Review* 5(6): 904–13.

Minsky, H. (1982). '*Can "It" Happen Again? Essays on Instability in Finance.*' New York: M. E. Sharpe.

Mirrlees, J. (1997). 'Information and Incentives: The Economics of Carrots and Sticks.' *Economic Journal* 107: 1311–29.

Mokoaleli-Mokoteli, Thabang; Richard Taffler and Vineet Agarwal (2009). 'Behavioural Bias and Conflicts of Interest in Analyst Stock Recommendations.' *Journal of Business Finance & Accounting* 36(3-4): 384–418.

Mullainathan, S. and A. Shleifer (2005). 'Persuasion in Finance.' *NBER Working Papers 11838*.

Murray Parkes, C. (1996). *Bereavement: Studies of Grief in Adult Life*. 4th ed. London: Penguin.

Mussweiler, T. (2007). 'Assimilation and Contrast as Comparison Effects: A Selective Accessibility Model.' In *Assimilation and Contrast in Social Psychology*. Eds D. A. Stapel, J. Suls New York: Psychology Press: 165–185.

Nelson, R. H. (2001). *Economics as Religion: From Samuelson to Chicago and Beyond*. University Park, PA:Penn State University Press.

Packer, D. J. (2009). 'Dissent About Collective Problems.' *Psychological Science* 20: 546.

Papadimitriou, D. B. and L. R. Wray (1998). 'The Economic Contributions of Hyman Minsky: Varieties of Capitalism and Institutional Reform.' *Review of Political Economy* 10: 199–225.

Parsons, T. (1937). *The Structure of Social Action: A Study in Social Theory with Special Reference to a Group of Recent European Writers*. New York: McGraw-Hill Book Company.

Perella, J. R. (2010). *Panel on Financial Risk Management 2.0?* World Economic Forum 2010, Davos.

Pietronero, L. (2010). 'Statistical Physics: Physicists Get Social.' *Nature Physics*: 641–2.

Pinker, S. (1997). *How the Mind Works*. New York: W. W. Norton.

Pixley, J. (2004). *Emotions in Finance: Distrust and Uncertainty in Global Markets*. Cambridge, UK: Cambridge University Press.

Preda, A. (2005). 'The Investor as a Cultural Figure of Global Capitalism.' *The Sociology of Financial Markets*. New York: Oxford University Press, 336.

Preda, A. (2009). *Information, Knowledge, and Economic Life: An Introduction to the Sociology of Markets*. Oxford: Oxford University Press.

Pástor, L., P. Veronesi, et al. (2004). *Was There a NASDAQ Bubble in the Late 1990s?* London: Centre for Economic Policy Research.

Rajan, R. G. (2005). 'Has Financial Development Made the World Riskier?' *NBER Working Papers 11728*.

Rebonato, R. (2007). *Plight of the Fortune Tellers: Why We Need to Manage Financial Risk Differently*. Princeton: Princeton University Press.

Reimann, M. and A. Bechara (2010). 'The Somatic Marker Framework as a Neurological Theory of Decision-Making: Review, Conceptual Comparisons, and Future Neuroeconomics Research.' *Journal of Economic Psychology* 31: 767–76.

Reinart, C. and K. Rogoff (2009). *This Time Is Different: Eight Centuries of Financial Folly* Princeton: Princeton University Press.

Reinhart, V. (2003). 'Planning to Protect Against Asset Bubbles.' In *Asset Price Bubbles: The Implications for Monetary, Regulatory and International Policies*. Eds W. C. Hunter, G. G. Kaufman and M. Pomerleano. Cambridge, MA: MIT Press, 553–60.

Rhodes, M. (2000). 'Past Imperfect? The Performance of UK Equity Managed Funds.' *Financial Services Authority Occasional Paper No. 9* Volume. http://www.fsa.gov.uk/pubs/occpapers/op09.pdf

Riesenberg-Malcolm, R. (1999). 'Self-Punishment as a Defence.' *On Bearing Unbearable States of Mind*. London: 93–112.

Robinson, J. (1948). *The Economics of Imperfect Competition*. London: Macmillan.

Sandler, J. J. and A. Freud (1988). 'Discussions in the Hampstead Index on "The Ego and the Mechanisms of Defence": IV. The Mechanisms of Defence, Part 1.' *Bul. Anna Freud Centre* 4: 151–99.

Schank, R., C. (1990). *Tell Me A Story: Narrative and Intelligence*. Evanston, IL: Northwestern University Press.

Schutz, A. (1967). *Collected Papers*. The Hague: M. Nijhoff.

Senior Supervisors (2009). 'Risk Management Lessons from the Global Banking Crisis of 2008.' Federal Reserve Bank of New York, New York.

Shefrin, H. (2002). *Beyond Greed and Fear: Understanding Behavioral Finance and the Psychology of Investing*. New York and Oxford: Oxford University Press.

Shiller, R. (2000). *Irrational Exuberance*. Princeton, NJ: Princeton University Press.

——(2009). *The Subprime Solution: How Today's Global Financial Crisis Happened and What to Do about It*. Princeton: Princeton University Press.

Simon, H. (1997). *Administrative Behavior: A Study of Decision-Making Processes in Administrative Organizations*. 4th ed. New York: Free Press.

Skinner, Q. (1985). *The Return of Grand Theory in the Human Sciences*. Cambridge, UK: Cambridge University Press.

Skinner, Q. (2008). 'Lectures Part Two: Is It Still Possible to Interpret Texts?' *The International Journal of Psychoanalysis* 89: 647–54.

Smelser, N. (1962). *Theory of Collective Behaviour*. New York: Free Press of Glencoe.

Smelser, N. J. (1998). 'The Rational and the Ambivalent in the Social Sciences.' *American Sociological Review*. 63: 1–16.

Smith, C. W. (1999). *Success and Survival on Wall Street: Understanding the Mind of the Market*. 2d ed. Lanham, MD: Rowman and Littlefield.

Solow, R. M. (2010) 'Hedging America. A Review of "How Markets Fail: The Logic of Economic Calamities" by John Cassidy.' *The New Republic*.

Soros, G. (1987). *The Alchemy of Finance*. New York: John Wiley & Sons.

——(2008). *The New Paradigm for Financial Markets: The Credit Crisis of 2008 and What It Means*. New York: Public Affairs.

——(2010). *The Soros Lectures at the Central European University*. New York: Public Affairs.

Spender, J. and A. Scherer (2007). 'The Philosophical Foundations of Knowledge Management: Editors' Introduction.' *Organization*: 5–28.

Spillius, E. B. (2001). 'Freud and Klein on the Concept of Phantasy.' *Int. J. Psychoanal.* 82(2): 361–73.

Steiner, J. (1996). 'Revenge and Resentment in the "Oedipus Situation".' *Int. J. Psycho-Anal.* 77: 433–43.

Stiglitz, J. (1974). 'Incentives and Risk Sharing in Sharecropping.' *Review of Economic Studies* 41(2): 219–55.

——(2010). *Freefall*. London: Allen Lane and the Penguin Press.

Sunstein, C. R. (2006). *Infotopia: How Many Minds Produce Knowledge*. New York: Oxford University Press.

Taffler, R. J. and D. Tuckett (2007). 'Emotional Finance: Understanding What Drives Investors.' *Professional Investor* Autumn: 27–8.

Taffler, R. J. and D. Tuckett (2010). 'Emotional Finance: The Role of the Unconscious in Financial Decisions.' In *Behavioral Finance: Investors, Corporations, and Markets*. Eds H. K. Baker and J. R. Nofsinge. Hoboken, NJ: John Wiley: 95–112.

Taleb, N. (2004). *Fooled by Randomness*. London: Allen Lane and Penguin Press.

Tavis, E. and C. Anderson (2007). *Mistakes Were Made (But Not by Me): Why We Justify Foolish Beliefs, Bad Decisions, and Hurtful Acts*. Orlando, FL: Harcourt.

Tett, G. (2004). *Saving the Sun: How Wall Street Mavericks Shook Up Japan's Financial World and Made Billions*. London: Random House.

——(2009). *Fool's Gold: How Unrestrained Greed Corrupted a Dream, Shattered Global Markets and Unleashed a Catastrophe*. London: Little, Brown.

Thaler, R. and C. Sunstein (2008). *Nudge: Improving Decisions About Health, Wealth, and Happiness*. New Haven: Yale University Press.

Trichet, J.-C. (2003). 'Asset Price Bubbles and Their Implications for Monetary Policy and Financial Stability.' In *Asset Price Bubbles: The Implications for Monetary, Regulatory and International Policies*. Eds. W. C. Hunter, G. G. Kaufman and M. Pomerleano. Cambridge, MA: MIT Press: 15–22.

Tuckett, D. (1976). *An Introduction to Medical Sociology*. London: Tavistock.

Tuckett, D. (2007). 'Civilisation and Its Discontents Today.' In *The Academic Face of Psychoanalysis*. Eds L. Braddock and M. Lacewing. London: Routledge.

Tuckett, D. and R. J. Taffler (2003). 'Internet Stocks as "Phantastic Objects": A Psychoanalytic Interpretation of Shareholder Valuation during Dot.Com Mania.' In *European Asset Management, Boom or Bust? The Equity Market Crisis – Lessons for Asset Managers and their Clients*. London: Asset Management Association.

——(2008). 'Phantastic Objects and the Financial Market's Sense of Reality: A Psychoanalytic Contribution to the Understanding of Stock Market Instability.' *Int. J. Psychoanal.* 89(2): 389–412.

Turner, A. (2010). *Economics, Conventional Wisdom and Public Policy*. Institute for New Economic Thinking Inaugural Conference, King's College, Cambridge.

Turner, A., A. Haldane, et al. (2010). *The Future of Finance: The LSE Report*. London: London School of Economics, Paul Woolley Centre for the Study of Capital Market Dysfunctionality.

Turner, J. H. and J. E. Stets (2005). 'Conceptualizing Emotions Sociologically.' In *The Sociology of Emotions*. Cambridge, UK: Cambridge University Press.

Turner, M. E., A. R. Pratkanis, et al. (1992). 'Threat, Cohesion, and Group Effectiveness: Testing a Social Indemnity Maintenance Perspective on Groupthink.' *Journal of Personality and Social Psychology* 63: 781–96.

Tversky, A. and D. Kahneman (1971). 'Belief in the Law of Small Numbers.' *Psychological Bulletin* 76: 105–10.

——(1974). 'Judgment under Uncertainty: Heuristics and Biases.' *Science* 185: 1124–31.

Van BavelJay J. ; Dominic J. Packer and William A. Cunningham (2008). 'The Neural Substrates of In-Group Bias: A Functional Magnetic Resonance Imaging Investigation.' *Psychological Science* 19(11): 1131–39.

Vlaev, I., P. Kusev, N. Stewart, S. Aldrovandi and N. Chater (2010). 'Domain Effects and Financial Risk Attitudes.' *Risk Analysis* 30: 1374–86.

Weber Max; Guenther Roth and Claus Wittich (1968). *Economy and Society: An Outline of Interpretive Sociology*. New York: Bedminster Press.

Widlocher, D. (1994). ' A Case Is Not a Fact.' *Int. J. Psycho-Anal.* 75: 1233–44.

Winnicott, D. (1945). 'Primitive Emotional Development.' *Int. J. Psycho-Anal.* 26: 137–43.

Wolfe, T. (1987). *Bonfire of the Vanities*. New York: Bantam Books.

Young, K. and J. Saver (2001). 'The Neurology of Narrative.' *SubStance* 30(1): 72–84.

Zajonc, R. B. (1980). 'Feeling and Thinking: Preferences Need No Inferences.' *American Psychologist* 35: 151–75.

——(1998). 'Emotions.' In *Handbook of Social Psychology* 4th ed. New York: Oxford University Press, 591–632.

Index of Respondents

Index